The Art and P
of Musical Theatre
Choreography

The Art and Practice of Musical Theatre Choreography

Cassie Abate

methuen | drama

LONDON • NEW YORK • OXFORD • NEW DELHI • SYDNEY

METHUEN DRAMA
Bloomsbury Publishing Plc
50 Bedford Square, London, WC1B 3DP, UK
1385 Broadway, New York, NY 10018, USA
29 Earlsfort Terrace, Dublin 2, Ireland

BLOOMSBURY, METHUEN DRAMA and the Methuen Drama logo are trademarks of
Bloomsbury Publishing Plc

First published in Great Britain 2022

Cover design by Ben Anslow
Cover image © Bret Brookshire

A catalogue record for this book is available from the British Library.

A catalog record for this book is available from the Library of Congress.

ISBN: HB: 978-1-3501-9334-5
       PB: 978-1-3501-9333-8
       ePDF: 978-1-3501-9335-2
       eBook: 978-1-3501-9336-9

Typeset by RefineCatch Limited, Bungay, Suffolk
Printed and bound in Great Britain

To find out more about our authors and books visit www.bloomsbury.com
and sign up for our newsletters.

Dedicated to my family,
who made space during lockdown for me to fulfill a dream

Contents

Figures and Tables

Figures

Tables

Preface

My passion for choreography began at a young age. I remember choreographing my third grade musical about fish including songs like "Guppy Love." Growing up I was presented many opportunities to watch the choreographic process, assist in developing productions, teach, and explore my own choreographic vision. This spark was cultivated while receiving my BFA in Musical Theatre at the University of Miami where I was entrusted with choreographing an entire mainstage musical. After graduation, I moved to New York and worked as a performer on tours, regional theatre, and in the city. During this time, I was also mentored by incredible choreographers and worked as a dance captain, assistant choreographer, and associate choreographer. I was awarded the SDC Observership for *Sophisticated Ladies* at Arena Stage in Washington, DC choreographed by Maurice Hines and Kenneth Roberson and directed by Charles Randolph-Wright.

I wanted to continue my studies in musical theatre choreography and reinforce my skills as an educator. However, no degrees in musical theatre choreography existed at the time. Programs in dance composition focused on creating for the world of concert dance. Performance and directing programs neglected to address the skills and issues unique to a musical theatre choreographer. I was fortunate to find a program that allowed me to tailor the experience to my personal needs and received my MFA in Theatre Arts: Musical Theatre at San Diego State University.

At each phase in my journey, I was tenacious about expressing my desires and seeking out mentors and organizations that would nurture and encourage my ambitions. As a female director/choreographer in a predominantly male field, I was fortunate to have a group of very diverse mentors who gave me opportunities to create work from my own unique perspective. I acknowledge my own privilege as a cis white female and aim to amplify voices traditionally underrepresented in the industry. After becoming the head of Musical Theatre Dance at Texas State University, I was inspired to foster young choreographers, developing a specialized undergraduate track in Musical Theatre Choreography. It is my hope that this text will start to bridge the gap between desire and a career, provide young aspiring choreographers tools to inspire their own unique artistic voices, and aid in creating a codified method of teaching and practicing musical theatre choreography.

Acknowledgments

This book was made possible by the help and support of so many people along the journey. First and foremost, thank you to Anna Brewer, Meredith Benson, Sam Nicholls, and the entire team at Bloomsbury Methuen Drama for turning this dream into a reality and for guiding this novice writer.

Thank you to Kaitlin Hopkins, for her unwavering leadership, encouragement, friendship, and for allowing me to be a part of building and shaping the vision of the program at Texas State. A special thanks to my fellow musical theatre faculty for all the roundtable discussions of what the art form and pedagogy can look like. I want to acknowledge the faculty and administration of Texas State University, for creating a culture of collaboration and shared research.

Thank you to my colleagues who took the time to review this text. They offered incredible words of wisdom and encouraged that the book reflect the world we desire to create. A special thanks to Adam Cates, Cheri DeVol, Christa Oliver, Sarah Maines, Tom Delbello, Kaitlin Hopkins, Caitlyn Herzlinger, and Greg Bolin.

A teacher is constantly learning from their students. I am humbled, inspired, and renewed by the passion, artistry, and vision of every student I have had the privilege of instructing. A special thank you to the Texas State musical theatre students and alumni. Thank you to all of the teachers who have encouraged my exploration of choreography, introduced me to new vocabulary, and created opportunities throughout my development: Scott Keys, Steven Vincent, Cheryl Carty, Cheryl Lee, the musical theatre faculty at the University of Miami, Rick Simas, and Paula Kalustian. A special thanks to Clay James for opening up the world of education to me. Thank you to my thesis chair, Paula Kalustian, and readers, D.J. Hopkins and Laurinda Nikkel, for guiding me through the thesis process, which was the germination of this text.

Thank you to my fellow MFA classmates at San Diego State University who are nine of the most progressive minds for the future of theatre and arts education. Thank you, Timothy Allen, Rafi Cedeño, Katie Donovan, Bethany Elkin, Roger Ellis, Susan Jordan-DeLeon, Mitzi Smith, Tom Vendafreddo, Korrie Yamaoka, for the thought-provoking conversations and unending support.

Thank you to the Stage Directors and Choreographers Foundation and their Observership Program. The program gave me the opportunity to be in the room and watch the brilliant work of Charles Randolph-Wright, Maurice Hines, and Kenneth Roberson. A special thanks to Kenneth for taking me under his wing and encouraging me to follow my own path. Musical theatre choreography has long been a passed down tradition. Thank you to all of the directors and choreographers who brought me onto their team and taught me the tricks of the trade, especially Peggy Hickey, Karen Azenberg, Terrence Mann, Charlotte D'Amboise, Adam Cates, and Kenneth Roberson.

Thank you to the theatres who opened up their stages and provided me with room to grow as a director and choreographer. I must acknowledge Julianne Boyd and the Barrington Stage Company, Laura Austin and the Redhouse Arts Center, Randy K. West and the Stephen Sondheim Center, Dave Steakley and the ZACH Theatre, Brian Vaughn and Frank Mack and the Utah Shakespeare Festival, and most of all, to everyone at the Connecticut Repertory Theatre.

Thank you to all of the directors, choreographers, and artists whose words and vision shaped the views of this text. A special acknowledgement to Susan Stroman, Michael Balderrama, Vincent Cardinal, T. Oliver Reid, Peggy Hickey, and Greg Uliasz with McDonald/Selznick Associates.

Thank you to photographer Bret Brookshire for creating the imagery used throughout the text. Thank you to the incredible dancers Paul Amrani, Alex Aponte, Taylor Aronson, Andrew Fleming, Joann Gilliam, Preston Perez, Cayla Christine Primous, Adriana Scalice, Hailey Thomas, and Zephaniah Wages. Thank you to Cheri DeVol for lighting design and to Scott Vandenberg, Candice Mongellow, and Sarah Maines for facilitating the photo shoot. A special thank you to Jeff Whiting for the use of Stage Write in creating diagrams and to Greg Bolin who created musical examples. Thank you to the brilliant designers Jo Winiarski and Michael Raiford for their collaboration and beautiful designs that brought the worlds to life in fresh and unexpected ways.

Thank you to David Kurs, Jeff Perri, and Deaf West Theatre for their consultation, support, and important work in setting the standard for inclusive theatre. Thank you also to Hal Leonard LLC for the use of the lyrics to "Memories of You":

Memories of You
From THE BENNY GOODMAN STORY
Lyrics by Andy Razaf
Music by Eubie Blake
Copyright C 1930 Shapiro, Bernstein & Co., Inc. and Razaf Music
Copyright Renewed
All Rights for Razaf Music Administered by BMG Rights Management (US) LLC
International Copyright Secured All Rights Reserved
Reprinted by Permission of Hal Leonard LLC

Musical theatre is the most collaborative art form. Thank you to all of the directors, choreographers, music directors, designers, stage managers, creative artists, crew members, production staff, technicians, musicians, and performers who have participated in making musicals come to life and continue to prove that theatre is vital to the health of a culture and voice of a community.

Thank you to my long-time collaborators and friends Vincent Cardinal and David N. Williams. I would not be the artist or the human I am today without the long hours of rehearsing, eating, hypothesizing, and imagining that we have all shared.

Most of all, I want to acknowledge my family. Thank you to my parents who let us move in with them during a global pandemic and provided childcare so I would have time to write. Thank you to my in-laws for offering their time and support. Thank you to Vanessa Russo,

Kaitlin Hopkins, and Jim Price for companionship during these isolated times. Thank you to my children, Beckett and Gwendolyn, who give me hope of a brighter future. And finally, thank you to my other half, Nick Lawson, for the countless hours of philosophical discussion, pep talks, critical analysis, laughter, and tears. I am honored to have you as my forever collaborator.

Introduction

A Tradition Passed Down

The role of musical theatre choreographer is complex and often misunderstood. Many people think choreographers "make up dance steps." However, successful musical choreography requires an in-depth understanding of storytelling, music theory, performance practices, and plot structure in order to achieve movement that enhances and animates the musical. Throughout history, techniques of musical theatre choreography have been learned in the field either through performance experience, assistantships, or trial and error. The aim of this text is to take an art form traditionally passed down from mentor to apprentice and make the principles, practices, and "tricks of the trade" accessible to all choreographers at every phase of their journey. This book offers choreographers information needed to create nuanced, informed, and inspired movement by demystifying and unlocking some of the secrets of musical theatre choreography. It also allows the choreographer to head into the production process with confidence. There are many paths towards a career as a musical theatre choreographer, both academically and artistically. The main objective of this book is to prepare any musical theatre choreographer for the entire process of choreographing a musical from the first script reading to the final curtain call.

How to Utilize this Text

This book is based on my research, training, and personal experience. It aims to combine the theoretical principles of choreography with the practical application during every step of the production process. These ponderings and methods represent just a few ways to approach the choreographic process—by no means the only ways. At times when I speak in absolutes, or "musts," consider the phrase "It is my belief that . . ." before each sentence and know that there can be a wide range of opinions that run parallel to or contradict my own. As with every text, readers should take what works for them and challenge ideas to arrive at their own opinions and principles. It is daunting to put in writing thoughts about an industry and art form that is constantly evolving. People will discover new avenues of creation and hopefully continue to build healthier, safer, and more inclusive working practices. It is my personal ethos that being an artist is an occupation of service to humanity and ideally this resource can be used as a foundational jumping-off point to push the boundaries of what musical theatre choreography can be.

This book is divided into two parts: the art and the practice. "Part 1: The Art" focuses on the creation of musical theatre choreography. It discusses the role of the musical theatre choreographer and delves into the first phase of choreography: research and analysis. By examining the role of dance in the musical and story structure, one will ascertain how to create a movement arc, tracking dance and movement throughout the show. Then it presents tools for how to break down a script and score from a choreographer's point of view and how to create a movement vocabulary for the musical. Next, the choreographer is introduced to theoretical principles of developing musical staging as well as large production numbers. Finally, several processes are laid out for the creation and notation of actual dance steps as well as adapting to various stage configurations.

"Part 2: The Practice" equips the choreographer with information needed to successfully navigate the production process. It addresses assembling the choreography team, pre-production, auditions, collaborating with the creative team, expectations and demands of every different type of rehearsal, staging transitions and curtain calls, and other practical elements a choreographer might encounter. Finally, the book outlines opportunities and avenues for a choreographer to find employment in the field and offers advice on developing original work.

Each chapter will conclude with an activity that will guide the reader step by step, chapter by chapter, through the process of choreographing a musical. Readers can make their way through the text in order, or jump around as the timeline of a production might necessitate a different progression. Chapters from Part 1 and Part 2 can work in tandem as a choreographer develops their own methods of creation. It is my hope that this book inspires a spark of invention and helps bring new and diverse choreographic voices to the musical theatre stage.

Part 1 The Art

The following chapters will delve into the role of a musical theatre choreographer and the functions of movement within a production. They will lay a framework for designing staging and choreography for an entire musical from the initial research phase through script and score analysis, number building, and finally the creation of steps.

1 Where to Start

A musical theatre choreographer is a role in the theatrical community that has historically eluded representation in writing and education. Despite being a key member of the creative team and essential to the development of musicals, there are very few resources available for choreographers. The road to musical theatre choreographer has mostly become an exclusive apprenticeship from mentor to student. However, the number of choreographers working in local, national, and international theatres, education, events, and other mediums demonstrates a need for accessible perspectives on the choreographic process. Maybe you just landed a musical theatre choreography job or you want to know more about how to collaborate with a choreographer. The first place to start is by asking questions.

The Musical Theatre Choreographer

What defines a musical theatre choreographer? At the most basic definition, the choreographer creates the movement for a production. But arriving at that movement is much more complicated than stringing a series of steps together. The role of musical theatre choreographer is unique in that they must be equal parts interpreter and creator. A musical theatre choreographer is tasked with interpreting the script presented from the composer, lyricist, and librettist (or working with them in the development of a new work) to discover how dance can aid in the storytelling of the piece. It is the writers' ideas channeled through the choreographer's view. The choreographer must also envision the movement through the lens of the director's vision and concept. However, the choreographer is also a creator, producing a new movement vocabulary, style, and feel along with actual steps. "A choreographer takes on the very important and challenging task of creating a movement text that complements the rest of the script and score" (Deer 2014: 157). In this way, the choreography becomes embedded in the essence of the piece. But no matter the impact of the movement on the creation of a musical, unlike the script and score, this component of the piece must be reimagined and newly created each time the show is reproduced. A choreographer walks a fine line of bringing originality to a production while honoring (or purposefully countering) the original purpose and intent of the movement.

What qualities exemplify a musical theatre choreographer? This is obviously a subjective question, but most would agree that musical theatre choreographers must play many roles. Ultimately, a choreographer is knowledgeable of human kinetics with an extensive understanding of the body and how it functions. As a historian, a choreographer researches the movement styles of the time period when the show is set as well as when the piece was originally developed. This involves having a working knowledge of the evolution of dance throughout social and musical theatre history. The choreographer serves as a movement anthropologist, mining for an authentic and culturally accurate movement vocabulary. As a translator, a choreographer communicates what is in their mind to the dancer's body. A choreographer also balances the micro level of the feel of the movement for the dancer with the macro stage picture and movement story arc. Choreographers speak a visceral language translating words, sounds, and music into a physical form.

As a puppeteer, a choreographer uses the medium of dance to manipulate an audience's focus, take them on an emotional voyage, and invite viewers to face visceral truths presented in the movement. As an organizer, a choreographer finds order in chaos. As a leader, a choreographer establishes movement while also nurturing and encouraging the individuality of each performer's authentic movement truths. A choreographer also becomes a painter or sculptor of shapes and images, depending on the vantage point of the audience. As an explorer, a choreographer forges new ground. A heavy dose of imagination and ingenuity opens up possibilities for the choreographer to move the art form forward and find new and interesting ways to physically tell a story. This requires a constant state of inquiry. A comfort of questioning rather than asserting definitive statements goes hand in hand with an acceptance of needing others on the search for answers. Questions expand the limits of what something could be and leaves room for different voices to come together synergistically.

All of this leads to the important role of a collaborator. Musical theatre as an art form requires a large number of artists to take a show from a spark of an idea to a fully realized production. Choreographers work alongside writers, producers, directors, music directors, designers, stage managers, performers, technicians, crew, personnel, and audience members to produce a performance. In great collaborations, the sum is always greater than the individual parts.

What is a choreographer's style? A choreographer's personal style encompasses steps, lines, shapes, patterns, placement, tension, tempo, dynamics, movement qualities, carriage, size, rhythms, and devices that a choreographer gravitates toward when developing movement. Many times, this style is an amalgamation of a choreographer's culture, history, lived experiences, influences, training, mentors, interests, and personal capabilities. Some choreographers lean into an idea of personal style as a means to set them apart. Bob Fosse is a prime example of a choreographer who took his abilities, insecurities, and views on the meaning of movement and developed a personal style that changed the face of movement in the United States from the Broadway stage throughout pop culture. Gregory Hines and Savion Glover were influential in shifting the lens of tap on Broadway from a nostalgic nod to the pure entertainment tap dances of the 1920s and 1930s to a highly emotive, rhythmic, and improvisational tap conversation in musicals such as *Jelly's Last Jam* and *Bring in 'Da Noise, Bring in 'Da Funk*. Even choreographers who claim not to have a personal aesthetic tend to have consistent patterns that can be traced throughout their canon of work.

Despite a natural inclination toward a quality of movement, choreographers in musical theatre are eternal seekers of knowledge. The purposes of musical theatre choreography are to tell story, develop character, express emotion, set tone, and create environment in relation to the script. Every musical story is unique in its time period, setting, culture, character experience, and vantage point. Therefore, every project demands a fresh physical vocabulary and movement context. Musical theatre choreographers are often required to be chameleons, embracing a variety of dance genres based on the needs of individual productions. As no one is an expert of all things, this involves an unending quest for information on new styles and techniques. A large portion of the job of a choreographer revolves around research. A choreographer does not want to be limited in scope by a restrictive personal style, and yet should seek work that aligns with their strengths. A big factor is identifying who is choosing the material. Is a choreographer choosing their own projects or is the choreographer in a position where a season is chosen for them and they must adapt? It becomes a balance between a choreographer being true to who they are as an artist and yet adaptable enough to tell a wide range of stories.

Where does one start? In order to create something new, we first look to the past and understand what has come before. Musical theatre and dance on Broadway were created through a convergence of ideas, cultures, customs, rituals, genres, and influences. As a choreographer, it is critical to look back and properly attribute the background of these movements and styles. One continues to educate oneself on foundational principles and techniques in order to find authenticity as well as to add personal nuance to create something new.

Musical theatre dance and dance in the United States on a broader spectrum has numerous roots, all of which have been crucial, but some of which are more acknowledged or referenced than others. Systemic racism is prevalent in the foundation of musical theatre and history is rife with examples of white male choreographers appropriating movement of other cultures and disguising it as innovation. Someone interested in musical theatre choreography should verse themselves on all the great innovators that have come before. Study the evolution of African-American dance and music. Read about and watch the pioneers of influential genres such as tap, jazz, modern, and ballet. Become familiar with Bill "Bojangles" Robinson, Jeni LeGon, and John W. Bubbles alongside Fred Astaire and Eleanor Powell. Trace the impact of George and Aida Overton Walker, Frankie Manning, Norma Miller, Pearl Primus, Pepsi Bethel, and Josephine Baker, as well as Matt Mattox and Gus Giordano on jazz dance. Study the works of Katherine Dunham alongside Jack Cole. Acquire a well-rounded, diversified knowledge of the subject matter that honors and celebrates the indelible influence of artists from all communities. Speak the names of the ancestors who paved the way to keep their legacies alive. Resources such as *Jazz Dance: A History of the Roots and Branches* (2015) by Lindsay Guarino and Wendy Oliver, *Jazz Dance: The Story of American Vernacular Dance* (1994) by Marshall and Jean Stearns, *Reframing the Musical: Race, Culture and Identity* (2019) edited by Sarah Whitfield, and the documentary film *Uprooted* by Khadifa Wong are examples of places to start.

Whether working on an established musical or a new work, having a sense of how dance incorporates into the storytelling gives a choreographer context for how dance can best be utilized. Looking back through musical theatre history, dance was not always a main part of the plot structure. Different genres of musical theatre also interact with movement in various ways. Is the show a 1920s musical comedy, or a pastiche to the genre, where dance served more as divertissements and opportunities to showcase the dance talents of the stars? A number might seem randomly placed because it was the vaudeville act of the musical's original star that was interpolated into the script. Is it a 1940s integrated musical where dance is incorporated into or advances the plot, many times through narrative dance such as a dream ballet? Is it a 1970s concept or fragmented musical that breaks apart the traditional form of narrative and infuses new functions for the movement? Is dance completely separate, fully integrated into, or the main motor driving the story? Does the musical incorporate the showmanship, virtuosity, tropes, and comedic conventions associated with vaudeville or the perfect unison and geometric patterns of the precision kickline? Is the musical escapist fun originally produced during a period of war or strife in the US, or is the musical a form of agit-prop meant to make the audience re-examine their attitudes and beliefs? Often in the Golden Age, musicals were written for an entire singing chorus and separate dancing chorus. This explains why the ensemble is singing vocally challenging notes and harmonies during a large dance section. Does the musical embrace grandeur and spectacle or is it intimate and introspective? Is it driven by the text, music, movement, or visual display? Genre and historical conventions at the time of the musical's creation can offer the choreographer a sense of how to approach the movement structure and vocabulary.

Choreographing in a New Era of Musical Theatre

As the form, function, and content of musicals continues to expand, so does the requirements of a musical theatre choreographer. In a complete reversal from the 1920s, where popular music and dance were influenced by Broadway, now the music and dance on Broadway are heavily influenced by the popular forms. In the new millennium, musical theatre began to see a large crossover of pop and musical theatre composers and dance genres. There has been a steady rise in jukebox musicals that use popular songs as their musical score. These songs are often connected by a specific recording artist, group, or genre. Musicals such as *Mamma Mia*, *All Shook Up*, *On Your Feet*, *Motown: The Musical*, *Fela!*, and *Rock of Ages* call for choreographers to tap into the dance vocabulary and feel of these artists, cultures, and time periods.

New musicals and plays with movement such as *Once, Peter and the Starcatcher*, *The Curious Incident of the Dog in the Night-Time*, *Waitress*, *Hadestown*, *Choir Boy*, and *The Band's Visit* trade in the idea of big musical dance breaks for movement that seems to simply emerge from character, setting, environment, and relationship, enhancing the story in a visceral way. Especially when working in the role of movement director, choreographer Steven Hoggett finds it important to decide how to introduce movement to an audience where it doesn't feel like they are dancing (SDCF 2014a: 28:23). His work intersperses individual personalized movement with transient unison group experiences. Many of these pieces use movement to examine the psychology of the characters.

The modern musical theatre scene is also witnessing a resurgence of choreographers crossing over from the classical and contemporary concert dance worlds. This tradition has long been a part of musical theatre history. The recent wave, sparked by modern choreographers Twyla Tharp (*Movin' Out*) and Bill T. Jones (*Spring Awakening*) has brought a rise in musicals that use dance as a driving motor as well as revivals that have completely reimagined the choreography of classics.

Despite some steps toward more diverse voices being represented on the theatrical stage, the industry has a long way still to go, especially when it comes to creative teams. The Annual Visibility Report released by the Asian American Performers Action Coalition stated that 93.8 percent of directors on Broadway during the 2018–19 season were white (AAPAC 2021: 22). Since the inception of the Tony Awards in 1947, only seven women of the global majority have ever been nominated for Best Choreography. And while directors and choreographers of color should have the freedom to tell a wide range of stories, there is a long prevailing trend of, as Tomé Cousin states, "the absence of directors and choreographers of color on projects based on stories about people of color" (Cousin 2019). Producers, artistic directors, and creatives must continue to work to amplify the voices of choreographers from traditionally under-represented groups.

Musical theatre and dance has once again found its way into mainstream popular culture. Television networks are producing musicals that are performed and broadcast live. There has been a renaissance of musical films, including movie versions of existing musicals such as *Chicago*, *The Producers*, *Hairspray*, *Jersey Boys*, *Into the Woods*, *The Last Five Years*, *Nine*, *Cats*, and *In the Heights*, as well as original movie musicals including *The Greatest Showman* and *La La Land*. Television shows featuring large musical production numbers, including *Glee*, *Crazy Ex-Girlfriend*, and *Smash* have created a new generation of musical theatre enthusiasts. In addition, shows such as *So You Think You Can Dance*, *World of Dance*, *America's Best Dance Crew*, and *Dancing with the Stars* have brought new attention and stardom to dance talent and created accessibility to a wide range of dance genres and cultures.

As musical theatre continues to expand the stories and perspectives showcased, the art form embraces a diverse mix of dance genres. A single Broadway season can feature tap, jazz, hip hop, salsa, physical theatre, contemporary, ballet, aerial, and traditional African dance, amongst others. While choreographers are hired to work on projects that fit into their main style of movement, they must also be versatile, especially when working in regional or educational theatres as a resident choreographer. This requires a mixture of continued training and seeking out consultants to ensure authenticity.

In a millennium that uses social media for communication, audiences begin to have a certain expectation of dance. Social media posts and dance competition shows tend to have a "trick-oriented" mentality. Virtuosic displays of athleticism and skill are thrilling and powerful to watch, but a short thirty-second video does not fully paint the picture of the hours and years of hard work, dedication, strength-building, and training that went into being able to execute that trick with ease. It also does not show movements in context of a story, or portray the rigor and artistry needed to develop a character arc over a two-hour evening. Choreographers in this era work to find a balance between the impressive tricks audiences have come to expect while staying devoted to the narrative and the truths of the characters. As choreographer Liz Lerman wisely wrote, "Some focus purely on the drive to define and extend what the human body can do. Others seek to extend what the human body can say" (2011: 282).

Advances in technology open doors to new ways of integrating dance and technology. Disney musicals such as *Beauty and the Beast* and *Mary Poppins* forged new frontiers in design advancements and changed the way movement and choreography interacted with technology. Some musicals have experimented with how dance and puppetry can collaborate. *The Lion King* choreographer Garth Fagan and associate choreographer Marey Griffith fused elements of African, Caribbean, modern, and ballet movement with costume and puppetry to bring the animals of the African savanna to life. Lighting and automation innovations have produced lighting and scenery that can literally dance with the performers. With more productions utilizing projections and other digital media, it makes interactions once only seen in movies possible onstage. The dance world at large continues to embrace technology such as video, thermal cameras, and motion capture as extensions for communicating through movement. Mixing mediums of dance, spoken word, video, captions, projections, and lighting can encourage the audience to discover new meanings and connections in the movement.

Process versus Product

What happens when art and commerce collide? Art is essential for a thriving society. It reflects and challenges cultural views and has the ability to affect people on a deep level, opening up avenues of compassion and understanding. However, for-profit theatre, such as Broadway, also has the goal of making money. How do the pressures of financial gain impact the creation of the art? Many times, it results in condensed timetables and less willingness on the part of producers to take a risk on an unconventional project without a proven audience or demand. While commercial theatre offers experiences that are thrilling, moving, and exciting, there is also incredibly progressive and ground-breaking work being produced in markets where commercialism is not a main focus such as academic institutions, non-profit regional theatres, and internationally. Failure and experimentation are necessary in the creation of art, but become more difficult when beholden to investors. And yet, some of the greatest and most enduring successes on the Broadway stage came from artists and producers who took the risk to buck convention and turn the art form on its head. A regional theatre renaissance is bringing attention to a more diverse range of voices and spotlights the fact that musical theatre as an art form reaches far beyond a few blocks of New York City. Although many of the examples throughout this text are from Broadway productions due to accessibility, it is also imperative to stress the inspirational work of choreographers throughout regional, academic, and international venues. Explore and celebrate the arts within your local communities.

No matter the outcome, the end never justifies detrimental means. For far too long in the theatre industry, damaging and abusive practices by directors, choreographers, and producers were ignored or even applauded based on the product created. While Jerome Robbins' work in *West Side Story* contributed to redefining the role of dance in musical theatre, it also perpetuated discriminating behaviors. He aimed to create onstage tension by segregating performers even when socializing offstage and paid the Sharks less than the Jets. Jack Cole codified a style of musical theatre jazz, but was also known for temper tantrums that resulted in dancers being abused (Loney 1984: 285–295). Some people deemed in the industry as creative "geniuses" were given passes for destructive behavior. It was the misguided and wrongful belief at the time that these methods were the best way to achieve results. However, these behaviors throughout the history of the art form led to standardized practices of abuse and a dehumanization of performers at the hands of the people in power. Acknowledging the work without deifying the person and offering a complete history can hopefully open up needed conversations about artistic ethics.

Unhealthy narratives that the show must go on at all costs, dancers have to dance through pain, performers are expendable, and standing up for oneself is an act of disrespect have led to unsafe working conditions. We must dispel the notion that artists must suffer for their art. Additionally, a person starved of time and energy cannot access the creative regions of the mind. A better product is achieved when the performance is healthy and sustainable, and its creators and executors are able to balance the work with other parts of life: a love of gardening, traveling, having a family. We are all humans first and artists second.

It is a choreographer's responsibility as one of the leaders of a production to uphold the principles of respect and collaboration in creative and performance spaces. Dancers are not blank canvases, but rather rich wells of inventive and personalized movement ideas. The best art is created when every single person in the room is empowered to have a voice in the creative process. Choreographers must also become advocates for dancers. The creative team's artistic choices can have concrete repercussions for the performers. Make sure that the choreography can safely and sustainably be executed for the entire length of the run, whether that is a limited two-week stint or eight times a week for several years. No flashy step is worth risking the career and livelihood of a performer. When any element of the production – including dance steps, lifts, stunts, costume pieces, set transitions – has the potential to cause physical harm, the choreographer has an obligation to stand up for that performer and ensure that safety is paramount.

Accessibility

As theatre artists striving to create new, exciting relevant work that engages a society and moves the art form forward, it is vital that choreographers continue to push boundaries, break preconceived biases, and widen the perception of possibilities of working with an entire range of able-bodied and disabled performers.

A dancing body utilizes principles of balance, control, weight distribution, force, timing, rhythm, and shape to express and communicate. How those principles are executed is unique to each individual. Choreographers have the opportunity to challenge culturally prescribed movement codes, especially regarding the ideas of a normative body and dancers with disabilities. Scottish choreographer Janice Parker stated, "We have to ask the question: 'Who can dance and what can dance be?' . . . Disabled people have that capacity to create extraordinary movement that has a whole other spectrum and vocabulary in there" (Gladstone 2016: 1:21). Disabled dancers innovate movement and choreographic forms. For truly inclusive spaces in all aspects, we must "see difference among dancers as cetnral and valuable, not additional" (Østern 2018: 16).

Movement in musical theatre is the physical manifestation of music. There is an inherent connection between the music and how the body expresses in response. Deaf artist and activist Christine Sun Kim describes how music transcends disability. She acknowledges that sound is a part of a Deaf person's daily life that is witnessed visually through the movement of those around, felt tactually, and experienced as an idea (Kim 2015: 1:41–5:04). Kim's art explores the deep correlations between music and American Sign Language. "A musical note cannot be fully captured and expressed on paper. And the same holds true for a concept in ASL. They are both highly spatial and highly inflected—meaning subtle changes can affect the entire meaning to both signs and sounds" (Kim 2015: 7:41). Dance shares these qualities. A change in dynamics impacts the movement's meaning. DJ Kurs, Artistic Director of Deaf West Theatre, stated, "I think sign language is a natural fit for music actually. It offers a new layer of expression similar to the way that choreography brings a new perspective to music" ("Working in the Theatre" 2016: 0:49). In musical theatre, infusing ASL into choreography, as demonstrated in Deaf West Theatre's productions, can elevate storytelling and connect the Deaf and hearing worlds.

The arts community is making a shift toward recognizing the contributions and creative power of artists with disabilities. In the 2015 Broadway revival of *Spring Awakening*, actress Ali Stroker became the first performer who uses a wheelchair for mobility to perform on a Broadway stage. She went on to win a Tony Award for her performance as Ado Annie in the 2019 Broadway revival of *Oklahoma!* Musical theatre productions are featuring a combination of Deaf and hearing performers and incorporating American Sign Language. Theatre companies such as Theatre Breaking Through Barriers, Deaf West Theatre, The Apothetae, Identity Theatre Company, Sins Invalid, Phamaly Theatre Company, Sound Theatre Company, Open Circle Theatre, and National Theatre of the Deaf, as well as dance companies including AXIS, Kinetic Light, Joint Forces Dance Company, and Full Radius Dance Company are dedicated to changing notions and misconceptions around disabled artists. These companies are breaking barriers to create opportunities for performers and dancers with disabilities.

Despite the work of companies listed above, the theatre community as a whole still has a long way to go. According to data collected by the Centers for Disease Control and Prevention in 2018, 26 percent of the population in the United States has a disability ("Disability Impacts Us All" 2020). However, most disabled characters onstage are played by non-disabled performers. For example, as of 2019, the character of Nessarose in *Wicked* as well as Crutchie in *Newsies* has never been played by a performer with a disability on Broadway (Kranking 2019). Actress Katy Sullivan, who was born a bilateral above-knee amputee, stated, "My hope is that when people start to see themselves reflected in art and in work, younger people will have something to point to and think 'I can do this'" (Clement 2017).

Equitable theatrical spaces embrace casting practices that allow disabled performers to tell their stories. In addition, disabled performers should be considered in parts that do not exploit the disability—neither as a tragic event nor an impetus of inspiration—but rather as one small piece of a fully rounded character sharing their life. Disabled performers should also have the opportunity to be cast in any part within the musical theatre canon. Saying yes to the performer with the required skillset who most embodies the character can then lead to the opportunity to discover how that informs the characters and production aspects. Part of the shift demands giving voice to creative artists with disabilities including writers, directors, choreographers, and designers. Adaptations to the physical theatres and rehearsal spaces make them accessible for all performers and personnel.

Any collaboration, including those that encompass performers of different abilities, benefits from a certain frame of mind for the choreographer. In conversation with DJ Kurs, he presented some insightful perspectives:

1 Come in with an open mind and an open heart.

2 Create a space of open communication and dialogue. Find a moment at the beginning of each rehearsal to verbalize goals and ask for any questions, ideas, or concerns. Then check back in at the end of each rehearsal.

3 Treat everyone in the space as equals.

4   Encourage workshopping. No one has all the answers but you can figure it out together as a company.

5   Do your research.

6   Ask questions.

7   Embrace that there will be a learning curve for everyone. Time and repetition are your friends.

8   Include people with experience or expertise in the process.

9   Let go of pre-conceived notions.

10 Acknowledge that everyone's experience of the movement is different. Set everyone up for success.

When choreographing for a mix of able-bodied and disabled dancers, open communication is key. Success is achieved when there is an examination of how individual bodies move rather than a goal to simply mimic the choreographer. This leaves room to investigate the meaning behind the movement and the objectives and obstacles placed before the characters. Some exercises that can begin the choreographic process include focusing on dynamic ideas rather than shape, assigning movement tasks (glide, make way to the floor, yield weight) that can be achieved with various interpretations (Cowan 2018), or giving dancers the same obstacle that can be worked through in different ways. These improvisational exercises embrace translation: "each dancer responding to and translating tasks and information to suit their own individual physicality, in order to achieve an equal outcome" (Whatley and Marsh 2018: 6). Group movement can be created through visual communication without the necessity of words through leading and following exercises. Visual cues can emphasize the rhythm. Movement can be described aurally. A choreographer can also help dancers translate group movements to other parts of the body. Ali Stroker stated, "So if they're doing something with their feet, I might translate it and do it with my shoulders or my hands, capturing the essence and the spirit of each move" (Mazzeo 2019). This creates a unified feel to the movement while retaining the individual expression of each character and performer.

Whenever approaching an endeavor that is outside of your expertise, knowledge, or culture, a choreographer should seek advice from consultants to assist in the choreographic process. It is imperative to have disability voices in the room and behind the table. In the process of Deaf West Theatre, Directors of Artistic Sign Language, or ASL Choreographers, collaborate closely with the director, choreographer, and performers "to craft translation, expression, and movement to tell the most compelling and authentic story." For Deaf West Theatre's Broadway revival of Spring Awakening, choreographer Spencer Liff spent countless hours consulting with the Directors of Artistic Sign Language not only deciding the signs to interpret the song lyrics, but also how to connect them with the music and rhythms to maintain the musicality (Fierberg 2015). Working with a mixture of hearing and Deaf performers, Liff created a system of "silent cues: hidden lights, coded gestures, timed touches, and prompting props" (Paulson 2015) to sync the performers to the music and each other. Innovative choreographic techniques open up limitless possibilities that serve the intention of the musical and create accessibility for all performers.

That accessibility must also apply to the audience experience. This leads to an examination of how theatre practitioners define and approach accessibility. Often accessibility is considered after a production has been established. Theatres offer ASL signed performances. Autism Friendly, or Sensory Adapted, Performances make modifications to the production such as keeping the houselights brighter, reducing technical aspects like bright lights and loud sounds, encouraging a more relaxed environment with noise and movement expected in the audience, designating a space to step away from the performance, and providing guides about the show and what to expect. Outside of these specialized performances, expansions in technology have allowed accommodations to occur at any performance. Galapro is an app that is compatible with audience members' personal devices that can provide closed captions, language translations, audio description, and dubbing.

As theatre artists, the question becomes: is there a way to expand the definition of accessibility? Is there a way to move beyond accommodations that are added after the production is set to fully immersive experiences incorporated from the beginning of the creative process? How can open captions be embedded in the set? How can ASL be integrated into the choreography? In these instances, it is important to approach these incorporations from a place of informed respect and authenticity rather than cultural appropriation. How can haptic technology create similar experiences for both blind and sighted audiences? The Donmar Warehouse production of *Blindness* used headphone technology combined with "immersive lighting and atmospheric design" to bring the story to life ("Blindness" 2022). Augmented reality technology has aided in the creation of caption or subtitle glasses that can imprint captions, descriptions, images, and colors onto the stage as the viewer watches through the lenses. The National Theatre in London has implemented smart caption glasses as well as touch tours, where a person can feel the sets, props, and costumes ahead of a performance ("Access" 2022). Choreography can become an integral component to these immersive theatrical experiences. How can the movement physically demonstrate the story and music? How can movement assigned to the audience start to heal haptic deprivation caused by pandemic isolation? When these elements are a part of discussions from the initial stages, the possibilities are endless.

The world of musical theatre will constantly be evolving. Dance and theatre are ephemeral arts—they happen in a moment and then are gone. It is a shared experience with every person in the room when the event transpires. It has the power to entertain, transport viewers to a different time and place, challenge assumptions and inherent biases, expand upon the cultural narrative, and speak to personal truths as well as universal realities. No matter what the current trend or new advancement, the goal remains the same: to make people think as well as feel through dance. Whether choreographing for a large-scale million-dollar Broadway spectacular or an intimate black box new work, the first step of the process is always the same: research.

2   Research

Research is an exciting process when choreographing a musical. It is a time of exploration, investigation, and imagination. Research can take on many different forms. It can happen in a library, at a computer, during a party, on a walk, or in a studio. Research helps artists develop a rich understanding of the given circumstances of the characters. Research into rules and previous practices often gives choreographers a framework to build within or the ability to break out and push boundaries to find new methods of creation. Research gives a choreographer a place to start when developing movement or to return to when they hit a roadblock. Once research is collected, artists find ways to redefine, abstract, reshape, vary, interpret, and assemble it into something new. It is important during this part of the process to sit with uncertainty and curiosity: to have questions without answers. If assumptions are prescribed at the onset, the ability to make discoveries is severed. The level of research a choreographer engages in before beginning the act of making the work might not always be consciously visible to the audience, but can be unconsciously understood in the nuance, authenticity, and specificity of the movement.

Choreographers will most likely find themselves working on one of three types of productions. The first is a revival or the licensing and mounting of an existing musical. The production stays true to the original intent of the creators and the production uses existing orchestrations and dance arrangements. The script and score are already established and remain unchanged throughout the rehearsal process. The second is a revival that is being re-imagined or modified. The pre-existing musical is refined and updated, and new orchestrations and arrangements might be developed. The third is working on a brand new musical. During the production process, the musical is constantly changing as the piece is developed and new material is continuously added or taken away. In this situation, the choreographer's concepts and movement storylines can become permanently tied to the show and even incorporated into the script. A choreographer's process, including research, will adapt depending on the type of production and the level of transience in the material.

The World of the Piece

The world of the musical contains all the elements that create the three-dimensional landscape surrounding the characters. It encompasses both conventional and unconventional methods of research. Researching the world gives choreographers a wealth of history, ancestry, and imagery from which to draw inspiration. It is important to note that when licensing an existing musical, producers, directors, and choreographers are prohibited from changing the time period, location, or setting of a show without permission.

Historical and Geographic Context

Historical and geographic context includes events, people, philosophies, social movements, customs, dress, physical environment, and political climates of a specific moment in history in a distinct location. There are three vital historical and geographic contexts to examine when beginning a production.

1 *Time period and location the piece is set*: What is the time period and location where the piece takes place? What was happening historically that impacted the lives of these characters? What were the philosophies, laws, religions, governing bodies, and power structures influencing the way people in that location thought, moved, and acted? What major events were occurring in the location of the story as well as elsewhere throughout the world? What were the customs and traditions of that country, town, or community? What is the weather and landscape of that part of the region? How does that impact the way people interacted with each other and nature? In what ways did people move? How was movement affected by dress, climate, social norms, class structures, religious beliefs, and cultures?

2 *Time period and location the piece was written*: Art does not happen in a vacuum. As musical theatre historian John Bush Jones stated, "Throughout the twentieth century musicals variously dramatized, mirrored, or challenged our deeply-held cultural attitudes and beliefs" (2003: 1). Understanding the time period and social climate in which a show was written is vital to understanding the meaning and motivation behind the piece. One must also look at the audience for which the piece was intended. *Cabaret* might be set in 1931 Berlin, but was also a message of awareness and warning to US Americans in the 1960s.

3 *Time period and location the piece is produced*: What is happening at the time that a piece is being produced? What struggles and triumphs are people experiencing? Why is the piece relevant right now? How can audiences find a personal connection to the material? How do people currently move? How similar are the movements of modern audiences with movement from the period the show is set? What principles, shapes, rhythms, methodologies, and meanings do these present and past movement ideas share? Where do they differ?

This examination of historical and geographic context through a current lens begins to give the choreographer an innovative way into movement creation. As Tony and Emmy Award winning director/choreographer Rob Ashford stated, "I don't think audiences want to see historical dance. I think people want to see something fresh and new, and I would never let historical authenticity dominate creativity and originality" (Cramer 2013: 19–20).

Culture

Author Nyama McCarthy-Brown defines culture as "a collection of social systems, customs, rituals, traditions, and ordinances that groups of people practice, share, protect, and develop" (2017: 21). A character's cultural identity can be connected to their race, nationality, ethnicity, gender identity, religion, sexuality, and any other significant community. The culture of the characters and community of a musical will affect how and when dance is incorporated into that show. Within different cultures, dance serves many purposes including but not limited to: storytelling, rituals, religious and spiritual customs, communication, celebration, historical stewardship, recreation, rebellion, competition, validation, community and social camaraderie, and theatrical presentation.

Some cultures are wary of movement while others see it as a way of life. How does the culture of the characters create, receive, and evaluate movement? Is movement separated from or interconnected to the music? Is dance a communal or a solo experience? Is dance praised for its connection to rhythm or its form? By answering these questions of cultural relationships to movement, a choreographer can begin to develop a detailed, authentic movement vocabulary and methodology of creation. In turn, audiences are exposed to different perspectives and are encouraged to take part in an open dialogue for a mutually respectful sharing of ideas and experiences.

A choreographer should also acknowledge their own cultural lens. How does my culture/history/background/lived experience align with that of the characters? How does my point of view complement or challenge the point of view of the script? Is this my story to tell? If the answer is no, the decision might be to step down from the project. It is imperative that all artists have the opportunity to tell their stories and have their truths exhibited on the stage. T. Oliver Reid, Broadway performer and co-founder/artistic director of the Black Theatre Coalition, stated: "We either have to build a bigger table, or people at the table need to push back and let marginalized artists in." Even with projects that are within a choreographer's wheelhouse, there can be components to the piece that are outside of that choreographer's expertise. This presents opportunities to bring people who specialize in a technique or represent a culture onto the choreographic team through co-choreographers, associates, and assistants or hire consultants to ensure the authenticity. Choreographers can also empower the performers in the room to speak up when something feels incongruous with the truths of the script or characters. Including voices integral to the piece can help ensure that the culture of the characters and world of the musical are approached from a place of truth and sensitivity.

Visual Landscape

The visual landscape is the pictorial descriptions displayed in art, painting, illustration, photography, statues, architecture, and print. This visual landscape does not include the literal medium of video and film. An examination of art during the three historical contexts (time period the piece is set, time period the piece is written, and time period the piece is produced) can reveal images of inspiration. A choreographer might also look at art from a different period, place, or artist that is examining the same themes as the musical to find correlations. A choreographer can survey how human figures are represented. What are the shapes and poses demonstrated? What negative space is created with the bodies? What colors dominate the art of the period? How does artwork use color, space, composition, light, shadow, shape, weight, and balance? How are these qualities translated through the body? What is the architectural design of the location and the time period the show is set?

What angles and curves are representative of that architecture? A choreographer can begin to amass a series of inspirational images that can guide creation of movement.

Words, Words, Words

Literature is a compelling way inside the minds of not just the writers, but the society at large. Choreographers might find inspiration by examining literature including books, periodicals, newspapers, poetry, song lyrics, and screenplays written at the time and place the musical is set. What are the recurring ideas? How do people see the world? What are people grappling with? How is dance viewed? A deep dive into letters, journals, and other personal, non-published writing can put a choreographer directly into the daily life of the characters of the piece. What did a typical day look like? How is movement described, if at all?

It may also be beneficial to look at literature published at the same time the musical was written. A choreographer will find writers addressing the same themes and issues presented in theatre of the time from a different angle. In reading these works, a choreographer may find language and descriptions that inspire images, movement patterns, and shapes for the stage. As a choreographer explores the way various art mediums tackle a theme, they can then start to discover the unique perspective dance can add to the conversation.

Finally, how are the themes and topics of the musical addressed in literature of today? Human trials have a tendency of repeating and re-emerging in different forms. In *Spring Awakening*, the creators found a connection between the concerns of teenagers in 1890s' Germany and frustrations voiced in contemporary rock and punk music. This mix of language styles all speaking the same truth can inform and mimic the way dance is infused into a musical.

Listening

One of the most important jobs of an artist is to listen and observe. Being present in the world can lead to moments of discovery and inquiry that can be translated into exercises, movement, and stage pictures. Inspiration can come when you least expect it. Any encounter with people, things, and nature can be research. The way a piece of fabric flows. The gestures used by a person as they talk passionately. The way wind impacts the leaves on a tree. The unintentional movement of people caused by riding a subway. The repetition and force exerted by a farmer plowing a field. Artists can seek this kind of research in many ways: a discussion with people, a nature walk, and introspection. Personal memories are one of the most fertile places to mine for revelations. As you listen internally as well as to the people and things around you, pictures and ideas will begin to materialize in your mind and appear in your dreams. Try not to judge or label them. Leave space for multiple suggestions to swirl around and crystalize in your imagination. This phase of the process is the time when everything is possible.

Style

A choreographer at this point will begin to consider what dance and movement styles most effectively tell the story of the piece. Style is a set of parameters, characteristics, and conventions. There can be styles attached to music, dance, and theatre genres, as well as associated with a time period, culture, artist, or concept. Once again, the initiation point is in questions: What style of movement does the music embody? Musical styles such as tango, waltz, or stop time evoke specific movement ideas. Are there any dance genres or steps mentioned in the script? Sometimes dance is diegetically a part of the story: the characters go out to a salsa club (*In the Heights*) or are dancers and musicians performing in a nightclub (*Jelly's Last Jam*). Other times dance is mentioned as a part of the story through stage directions: a character's only way of communicating is through dance (*Finian's Rainbow*). What were the dance styles and genres of the time period and place the show is set? A musical set in the 1940s will certainly have reference to swing dance (*Bandstand*), while a musical set in the French Antilles would explore traditional Caribbean dances (*Once on This Island*).

Every dance style and genre has its own roots, influences, and trailblazers. A choreographer looks to the past to truly understand the shapes, movement qualities, impulses, and dynamics of a dance style. While the Charleston became popularized in the 1920s production of *Runnin' Wild*, its origins can be traced much further. Juba dance, brought over from Africa, developed into "patting juba" when enslaved Africans used hands, knees, thighs, and the body to execute rhythms when they were no longer allowed to drum. Juba dance and steps of the African American communities on the coast of the Carolinas evolved into the Charleston, which was known for its wild abandon, footwork, and syncopation. It was a distinct African American creation prevalent in its native South Carolina that migrated to Harlem, the Broadway stage, and eventually to dance floors across the country. This knowledge of the essential building blocks and motivations of the movement helps a choreographer move past a simple Charleston step into a rich, charged, meaningful movement vocabulary that embodies the energy of the time. Acknowledgement of how the movement was appropriated into white social dance and theatre dance creates conversations of how to pay tribute to its roots and find authenticity in the movement. This is where knowledge of the history of musical theatre dance becomes important. For example, the procession of Dolly and the waiters in the titular number from *Hello, Dolly!*, originally choreographed by Gower Champion, is a direct descendant of the cakewalk.

Once the choreographer has ascertained movement needs present within the script, then they must look at their own voice. What conventions, concepts, or rules are being established for this production? Are there genres of dance that share similar dynamics and impulses with the characters and themes of the story? This conversation must also include the director and their vision about how dance interacts with and conveys the material.

When looking at different dance genres, each presents its own technique, or coordination, skills, and muscular development necessary to execute the movements of the style in a healthy, repeatable way. Dance styles also have varying levels of theatricality. Tap dance is inherently theatrical as it evolved through competition, challenge dances, and showmanship. It also combines the visual component of dance with the aural component of rhythm to create a visceral mode of emotional expression. Many social ballroom dances such as the waltz, foxtrot, and polka are inherently non-theatrical. They were built around simple step patterns that continuously repeat in order to make them accessible to the general public. They are also traditionally performed in a circle formation, which can exclude the audience in a proscenium configuration (Chapter 6). In these instances, modifications might be required to match the heightened energy of the musical. The styles of dance intrinsic to and chosen for a musical are assessed for their emotional, theatrical, and narrative abilities.

Movement Vocabulary

Once a choreographer has a sense of the style to be employed for a production, they can begin to amass a movement vocabulary. This can be done in several ways:

1 *Research the steps and sequences of movement associated with a specific time period or style*: These steps may or may not actually make their way onto the stage, but they will help inform the choreographer's work. Watch videos of expert dancers. See live performances. Notice the carriage and dynamics of the dancers. Research not just the movements but their roots and origins.

2 *Take class*: By fully immersing oneself into the style of a genre of dance, a choreographer gets not only a sense of the technique of the movement, but also the teaching philosophies, culture, history, and traditions of the genre. The choreographer also gets a chance to fully embody the dance.

3 *Create a new movement vocabulary*: A choreographer can begin to develop a movement language unique to the characters and world of the piece. Through various methods of improvisation, dance journaling, and movement prompts (see Chapter 7), a choreographer can begin a collection of steps and movement phrases that are appropriate to the story, environment, tone, and characters of the musical. This can be done independently as well as in collaboration with the cast.

The People of the Piece

Before creating movement for a character, it is vital that a choreographer really understands a character inside and out. What are their idiosyncrasies? Goals? Views of the world and other people? Intersections of culture, race, gender identity, sexuality, religion, nationality, and class can all impact the belief systems and practices of each character. The first place to start character analysis is identifying what is present in the script. It is crucial at this point in the research to take an objective look at the characters presented in the text without adding subjective ideas. What are essential facts and qualities of the character that are imperative to the journey of the story? The director, music director, choreographer, and performer will also have ideas about personality, vocal, movement, and emotional traits. But at the beginning stages of a project, a choreographer does not want to limit themselves to initial impressions. Questions may not yet have answers, or might have multiple answers. Analysis will continue to evolve as pre-production and rehearsals begin and the creative team and performers make discoveries together. Initial questions can be broken down into the character's outer self, inner self, lived experience, and drive. When analyzing the script, a choreographer should take note of all four elements for each character.

A character's *outer self* encompasses all aspects of the character ascertainable by others. How does the world view this character? How does this character want the world to view them? Age, height, weight, and physical traits should only be noted if they are defined in the script as being absolutely necessary for the story. A character's physicality will directly correlate to their movement. What is their posture and gait? How do they carry themselves? What part of the body do they lead with when walking? Are there any specific physical aptitudes or disabilities? Does the character have any identifiable physical habits? Specific gestures? Use of an object such as a cane or a hat? The health of the character can also dictate movement. Do they suffer from any particular ailments or addictions that impact movement quality? Vocal patterns present in the script can directly correlate to the character's physicality. Attire is also crucial to movement. How does this character dress? What is their hairstyle? What kind of shoes do they wear? Are there any cultural or period clothing or accessories (corset, petticoats, jackets, fans, handkerchiefs, etc.) that hinder or exaggerate movement?

Next, examine the character's *inner self*. Note how the character is described in the text by the author, other characters, and themself. What personality traits define the character? How are these traits masked or enhanced by movement? What is the character's gender identity? Are there any ethnic, racial, cultural, national, religious, or social groups that define the character's actions, beliefs, or values? Do they tend to function from the head, heart, or gut zone? A character's sexuality, moral compass, belief system, worldview, emotional state, and coping mechanisms can all play into their physical expression.

A character's *lived experience* consists of the history and environment surrounding them. A person can be shaped as much from a significant life event as from how they daily spend their free time. Where a character is originally from gives clues into ingrained beliefs and exposure to movement growing up. Where the character currently lives and their connection or alienation from the community can also be reflected in their movement. What is the character's social and economic status? What is the class system in the time and place the piece is set? How does this character fit into that system? What people and energy define a character's home life? A character's occupation has a monumental impact on their body. Do they have any special skillsets? Do they have repeated physical movements? Does their job require more large motor or fine motor coordination? Do they spend large amounts of time on their feet or sitting in one place? Are they confined in a cubicle or outside with room to move? What part of the body would ache after a long day of work? Does the character have any specific hobbies? Physical expression is also largely dependent on the character's relationships. How does the character view other people in their world? How are those relationships portrayed through physical attributes of distance, contact, and movement?

While the first three components speak to the character overall, the element of *drive* relates specifically to the character during the events of the musical. What are the character's goals and desires? What is their super objective, or "what they want over the course of the play" (O'Brien 2011: 10), as well as objective, or want, in each number? How do these objectives change over the course of the story? What obstacles, both physically and mentally, are in the way of the character achieving their dreams? How does the character evolve from the start of the show till the end?

With these questions, a choreographer can begin to build a unique physical language for each individual character. Dance can serve to enhance or oppose these qualities depending on how the character is revealing or masking themselves. Truthful choreography informed by the experiences, inner and outer qualities, and objectives of a character helps create a three-dimensional, complex world.

The History of the Piece

In researching the history of the piece, the goal is not to replicate work that has come before. The goal is for a choreographer to understand the original motivation of the show and the impulses of the writers in order to stay true to the meaning while finding a way to say it in their own individual voice. The source is the material on which a musical is based. While some musicals are completely original ideas, many are a new interpretation of other works or inspirations such as a book (*Ragtime*), play (*My Fair Lady*), short stories (*Fiddler on the Roof*), film (*Heathers*), cartoon (*Annie*), fairytale (*Into the Woods*), urban legend (*Sweeney Todd*), historical event (*Titanic*), historical figure (*Fiorello*), newspaper (*As Thousands Cheer*), periodical episodic (*Pal Joey*), catalogue or life story of a musical artist (*Ain't Too Proud*), or painting (*Sunday in the Park With George*). Examining the source is not only looking at the story, but the essence of the material itself. What is the tone, style, and attitude? Returning to the inspiration point helps to capture the spirit of the piece. One can also search for any language or imagery that implies movement either literally or figuratively as a jumping off point for choreography. Along with the source, look at other works by the same creator. Are there any recurring themes? What is the tone and attitude of the catalogue of work? If the author, artist, or inspiration of the original source is still living, consider contacting them for questions about intention and detail.

Then the focus can shift to the history of the musical itself. A choreographer might delve into information about the composer, lyricist, and librettist for inspiration. What kind of music were they listening to that impacted the way they wrote their own music? What dance idioms coincide with patterns of musical styles, motifs, and themes present throughout their work? How did the idea of the musical come about? Did the music or the words come first? Did the show go through any major revisions? When trying to understand the intention behind the piece itself, look for interviews with the writers about the making of the musical. If they are still living, they might also be a resource to answer questions.

While not necessary to form independent views on the material, one might also research the original choreographer. What is that choreographer's style? What other shows have they worked on? What about that choreographer's approach made them a good fit for the original production? What were their views, inspirations, and meaning behind the major dance moments in the piece? These questions might open up avenues for a choreographer to respect purpose of the movement without copying steps.

In the case of producing an existing musical, there will always be previous productions, including the original Broadway or Off-Broadway production and major revivals. Reading reviews and critical commentary of other productions can reveal information about how the musical was received by the community at the time the production was staged. *West Side Story* was not a smash hit when it opened in 1957. It lost the Tony Award that year to *The Music Man*. That speaks volumes to how the conceit and subject matter was embraced at the time. This knowledge then opens up questions of why a piece is currently relevant and how it can speak to a contemporary audience.

Watching videos of other productions is a very risky and dangerous venture. If done at all, it should happen after the choreographer has completed all of their other research and developed their own unique take on the material. Even more ideally, it should occur after they have already begun making movement in pre-production. The problem with video is that once it is seen, it cannot be unseen. Unless a choreographer has a strong vision of the piece beforehand, it is increasingly difficult to try and picture a number differently from what is viewed. It can severely limit a choreographer's creative potential, as they have to work harder to reimagine something rather than to envision it freshly from the start.

On the flipside, as long as a choreographer is firm in their approach to the material, watching video of both professional and amateur productions can be used analytically to help a choreographer identify their own impulses. Rather than watching for steps to copy or mimic, a choreographer can watch a number in its entirety and then reflect back. What did you like? Why? What didn't resonate with you? Why? By answering *why* a moment or a step spoke to you or not, you start to uncover your own opinions about the responsibilities of the movement in that number. Most of the time, this analysis reveals that moments didn't work because they stopped telling the story. By recognizing that, a choreographer is able to pinpoint what story they want to make sure they are communicating.

Revivals: Making Something Old New Again

The trickiest part of working on a revival or a production of an existing piece is finding a way to make something new. The musical must be viewed through a contemporary lens. Why is it imperative to revive this piece now? The goal should never be to reproduce the original production. Then it becomes a museum piece rather than a living, breathing, artistic work. Something that seemed new and fresh at the time the musical was first produced might seem old and dated now. Rather, the goal is to have an equivalent impact on a modern audience as the original production. Writers and creators make theatre to impact an audience: to entertain, to surprise, to challenge, to inspire, to enlighten. How are audiences today impacted? How does a creative team elicit the same response to a new demographic? What parts of the original material are problematic and how as a company will you engage with it? Creative teams must dig deep into the emotional drive and intention of a show and discover how people today express that emotion.

One way to do this is to think of the production as an entirely new musical and to return to the source. Another is to look at the original production and dissect the motivation behind the movement. Simply copying choreography will be powerless in capturing the origin point of that movement. Instead, a choreographer can identify themes, dynamics, and meaning as an impetus to craft new movement. No matter what path a choreographer takes in reinterpreting a musical, they cannot think of it as sacred, or untouchable. They must find a way to honor the script without feeling confined by older iterations. In an interview about working on revivals, Marcia Milgrom Dodge, director/choreographer of the 2009 Broadway revival of *Ragtime*, stressed the importance of not being precious with the material, especially if it is something beloved (SDCF 2014b: 23:30).

Some musicals come with very specific expectations from audiences and even producers. Musicals like *Fiddler on the Roof*, *A Chorus Line*, and *The Producers* are forever linked in people's minds to the iconic original choreography and staging. For many of these productions, the original choreography can be licensed and restaged. This allows a choreographer to expose new audiences to seminal works and for the creators or their estates to be credited and financially compensated. However, a choreographer can also choose to completely reimagine the staging in their own voice. When this happens, a choreographer might be met with polarized views, especially from purists of the musical, but they must remain confident and committed to the value of their perspective.

Problems arise when taking staging concepts from the original production that are not embedded in the script without giving proper credit. This prevalent practice is still taking another creator's intellectual property, even when no actual steps are recreated. In cases where the work of the original choreographer is being utilized, it is difficult to fit pieces of original choreography into a new concept. However, for some choreographers, their technique can be viewed as a style as much as a body of work. By utilizing a variety of movements from Bob Fosse's canon mixed with a modern interpretation of his technique, a choreographer can create movement "in the style" of Bob Fosse using his movement language without directly replicating specific sequences. Still, the choreography only becomes effective if the movement is story-driven and directly relates to the emotional state and circumstances of the character. Otherwise, it becomes an unmotivated, generalized series of movements, no matter the style.

Copyright and Licensing

Choreographers wanting to use pre-existing choreography must license that intellectual property along with the show itself. Many productions are now offering original choreography along with video tutorials, staging charts and diagrams for directors and choreographers to use. It is crucial that artists are recognized, billed, and paid for their material. It is not moral or legal to take someone else's intellectual property, even if it is posted on public forums such as video streaming services, and market it as your own.

In 1978, copyright protection was extended to choreographic works. This allowed choreographers to claim ownership of their intellectual property. A copyright holder of a choreographic work, "has the exclusive right to publicly perform a dance, to make, sell or distribute copies of the dance, to prepare adaptations or other derivative works based on the dance, and to publicly display the dance" (Haskins 2020). In order for a choreographic piece to be copyrightable, it must be original and fixed into a tangible medium such as video or film, a dance notation system, or descriptive text, photographs, and drawings.

Choreography is protected by copyright the moment it is fixed into a tangible medium (USCO 2020). As soon as a dance is videotaped or written out, it is protected. A choreographer does not necessarily have to file it with the U.S. Copyright Office. However, a dance must be registered if the choreographer wants to file a lawsuit for copyright infringement. A choreographer filing for copyright submits proof that they created the work, including the process of creation. If a choreographer decides to take legal action, the onus is on them to prove that there has been copyright infringement. Copyright lasts for the life of the creator plus 70 years after. Then, if a work is not re-registered, it becomes part of the public domain.

ACTIVITY VISUAL LOOKBOOK

Compile a lookbook of visual inspirations for your movement concept. Use images from your research including photographs and artwork. These can be literal images of bodies in motion as well as more figurative images including color, fabric, nature, and light and shadow. You can connect an image to a specific moment, number, or character in the show or to your overall approach to the choreography. The lookbook can come in many forms: a mood board hung on the wall, a physical book, or a digital collage. Several apps and websites offer virtual platforms to create and share photo galleries and compilations.

ACTIVITY MOVEMENT REEL

Edit together a short 3–5-minute movement reel that shows moments of dance and movement inspiration. These clips should not come from videos of previous productions, but rather steps, styles, and conventions that motivate you and speak to your unique take on the material. You can connect a clip to a specific moment or number in the show or to your overall movement concept. This reel is beneficial for producers, directors, and designers to understand the movement world and vocabulary you hope to create with the show. It also gives performers context of your approach to the choreography.

3   Storytelling Through Movement

Movement is universal: human beings learn to move before they are able to talk. Dance comes in many different languages as each culture, community, and individual uniquely uses motion to communicate. Dance is extremely powerful on a visceral level. When a person witnesses movement, the brain triggers muscular contractions in the viewer's body as if they were personally executing the movement (Haas 2010: 22). Our bodies house remnants of our life experiences like a moving archive. In this way, dance can equally become one of the most empowering and vulnerable methods of communication. When combined with musical elements that touch audiences on a subconscious level, dance in musical theatre has the ability to encompass the full humanity of a character, story, emotion, or event.

In musical theatre, all elements are in service to the story. Musicals are not written about the day nothing happened. Plots are based around literal or figurative life and death events in a character's journey. As the famous old adage goes, when the emotion is too high to speak, the character must sing. When the emotion is too high to sing, the character must dance. In accordance with that ideology, dance becomes an intensely heightened state of being. The narrative revealed in the movement can be outlined in the script or developed from the ideas of the creative team, as long as it stays true to the story, emotion, music, and characters. The dance should never impose a concept or theme that is not true to the intention of the show. The more truthful and specific the movement is to a character, emotion, or situation, the more viewers are able to find their own personal connection to the larger themes and ideas. One of composer/lyricist Stephen Sondheim's principles for lyric writers can be applied to choreography: "Content dictates form" (Sondheim 2010: XV). The story being told in a particular moment will help guide the choreographer on the structure of dance best suited to the content.

It is the choreographer's responsibility to get the audience accustomed to dance onstage. Musical theatre is a representational art form. While performers might strive for realism in their approach to the material, the act of breaking into song and dance at moments of emotional climax is not realistic. Audience members arrive at the theatre with a willingness to suspend disbelief. This places the onus on the writers and creative team to establish the rules and conceits of the evening. In the famous anecdote about the musical *A Funny Thing Happened on the Way to the Forum*, the show was not resonating with audiences until the addition of "Comedy Tonight" as the opening number, which laid the framework for viewers of what type of entertainment was to follow (Thelen 2000: 207). While dance can be literal, it can also be abstract and symbolic. Therefore, a choreographer can help audiences digest information by examining *how* and *when* dance is first introduced and staying consistent throughout the show in any conventions or concepts. If dance is to take on a large role in the storytelling, that vocabulary should be presented to the audience early on in the performance.

The Musical Structure

When evaluating the role of dance in a particular musical, a choreographer can gain insight and clarity by considering the larger structure of the musical as a whole. In the early part of the twentieth century, musicals tended to emulate the operettas of Europe, function as a revue of various acts serving a theme, or feature songs and dances loosely piecemealed together by a book. Famous songs by the composers and specialty numbers that showcased the stars led the show development. In the 1940s, integrated musicals became the dominant form, where dialogue, songs, and dance all worked together in service to the script. The Rodgers and Hammerstein "formula" featured character-driven stories, conversational lyrics, narrative dance, musical scenes where speech and song were seamlessly interwoven, and songs occurring during the peak of emotional intensity. In the 1960s and 1970s, "concept" musicals, where a show is built around an idea or theme, disrupted the notion of linear plot-based storytelling. Within a concept musical, the narrative and concept can work conjointly (*Fiddler on the Roof*), separately but concurrently (*Cabaret*), or the narrative can surrender fully to the concept (*Company*). "Concept musicals experimented with new relationships among a musical's constituent parts of song and dance and book scenes" (Wolf 2011: 68). Since then, musicals have experimented with form and function, constantly finding new ways to investigate themes, embody emotions, and take characters on a journey. However, there are still many standard types of songs that are often used in the structuring of a musical.

In musical theatre, songs can serve the progression of the plot, the expansion of an emotion, or the development of the character. The placement of a number helps determine its purpose. The *opening number* escorts the audience into the world of the piece. Whether a splashy production number or a simple solo ballad, the opening number sets the framework for the conventions of the evening and often establishes the normal world, or status quo, of the protagonist. The *production number* utilizes the ensemble and infuses a sense of community or unity. It can also be used to add the elements of spectacle and energy common to the art form. The *closing number* wraps up the story and leaves the audience with a final take away. This can range from a catchy, hummable tune to a prompt for personal introspection. Many musicals also feature an *eleven o'clock number*. This number, placed near the middle of the second act, is a memorable powerhouse that launches the characters careering toward the climax of the story (Kendrick 2020). It can take many forms, such as a rousing production number ("Sit Down, You're Rocking the Boat"), a hilarious comedy song ("Brush Up Your Shakespeare"), or a moving power ballad ("She Used to be Mine").

Theatre writer and historian John Kendrick claims that songs in a musical typically occur during three types of character experiences: transition, realization, and decision (Kendrick 2020). Character songs center around the emotions, experiences, and dreams of the characters. "I Am" songs give viewers information about the character. "I Want" songs glimpse into a character's hopes, dreams, desires, and objectives. An "I Want" song placed toward the beginning of the story introduces audiences to the main characters and can lead the protagonist into the inciting incident of the plot.

Frequently employed song types include solos, duets, ballads, up-tempos, small groups, production numbers, charm songs, love songs, comedy numbers, and musical scenes (song and scene interwoven). Oscar Hammerstein II often utilized the conditional love ballad. Believing it was unrealistic that two characters would fall in love so early in the musical, Hammerstein would write love duets where characters would describe what it would be like "if" they fell in love ("People Will Say We're in Love," "If I Loved You," "Make Believe").

Reprise is also a very powerful tool for the musical. By returning to a previous melody put into a new context, with altered lyrics, or sung by a different character, composers can not only familiarize the audience members with memorable tunes, but can also advance the plot, show passage of time, or demonstrate a change in the characters. Composer/lyricist Jerry Herman stated, "Very few people know its value or how to use it artfully. By changing a word here and there to switch the meaning, one can broaden the concept. To me reprise is the glue that holds the whole score together" (Citron 2004: 60). One of the most famous and successful uses of reprise occurs in *La Cage Aux Folles*, where Herman reprises the opening number, "We Are What We Are" in the moving Act 1 finale, "I Am What I Am."

Song placement is decided by the writers and creative team during the development process of a musical. Audience feedback in workshops and previews can give a valuable gauge on what is and is not working. Song and dance occur during emotional highpoints and can reveal characters' feelings, highlight the story in an exciting way, interject comedy or spectacle, or expand moments of tension. During song and dance, time slows down or comes to a complete stop in order to examine one experience or emotion more deeply. This manipulation of time creates a combination of compelling storytelling with deep dives into moments of drama, excitement, and emotion that is unique to musical theatre and contributes to the ability of the medium to be incredibly poignant.

Roles of Choreography in the Musical

Choreography in a musical can serve multiple purposes. Moments of movement can be dictated by the script or decided on by the creative team in alignment with the concepts and style of the production. The dance can occur logically within the world of the piece or create a new theatrical world where dance is part of the language used to communicate. Dance can provide aesthetic texture, explore emotion, forward the plot, or reveal information about the characters and relationships. Dance can be rhythmic, energetic, and driving, but it can also be introspective, melodic, and lyrical. Dance has the ability to manipulate time in both directions—it can speed up and slow down the action. While the movement is inextricably linked to the music or dialogue it accompanies, when viewed in silence, it should still clearly convey the story, emotion, idea, or relationship investigated.

The creative team works together to determine which musical numbers or moments in the show should dance. Choreography should always support the storytelling and progression of the event rather than distract from it. If a piece is over-choreographed, the movement, rather than the story, becomes the main focal point. Support from dance can be pragmatic, diegetic, literal, figurative, or energetic. Often choreography is serving several purposes at once.

Pragmatic choreography solves practical demands of the script or performance. Dance can cover, or divert focus away from, a set change or can actually accomplish the set

Fig. 3.1 Roles of choreography: Literal. Photo by Bret Brookshire.

change within the movement. Dance can allow time for a quick change occurring backstage. It can give performers offstage recuperation time before a particularly taxing scene or song. Choreography can also be crafted to show off a technical element such as a costume, prop, or set piece. No matter the functional responsibility of the movement, these moments must still stay true to the characters, situation, mood and style of the show.

Diegetic choreography is moments where the characters would actually be dancing within that situation in real life such as performers in a nightclub or during a ritual or ceremony. These dances are natural to the circumstances of the script. For example, many musicals feature moments or entire numbers built around social dance. Social dance is about individualist expression and community celebration. Not all social dance was built with theatricality in mind. Therefore, choreographers might make adjustments when transferring social dance to the stage to amplify its theatrical narrative capacity.

Literal choreography gives the audience information. It "communicates a story or message to the audience" that furthers the plot or reveals nuance about a character or relationship (Minton 2007: 149). Often these movement moments take everyday actions and heighten them (Figure 3.1). Through dance we can see characters fall in love, chase, have a fight, take a journey, make a decision, or struggle for their life. Literal choreography often employs linear storytelling. The audience can understand the events taking place through the movement even if the music and words were taken away.

Storytelling through movement is not always linear. *Figurative* choreography uses dance to expand an emotion, theme, or idea. Time is often manipulated speeding up, slowing down, or stopping altogether. The action pauses so a moment or an emotion can be more deeply explored. Rather than forwarding the plot, these moments tend to forward our understanding of the characters (Figure 3.2). We learn about the truths of their subconscious, see their dreams or fantasies come to life, behold the physical embodiment of their greatest fear, and witness them experience a feeling in its entirety through the body. Figurative

Fig. 3.2 Roles of choreography: Figurative. Photo by Bret Brookshire.

Fig. 3.3 Roles of choreography: Energetic. Photo by Bret Brookshire.

choreography can also become a physical manifestation of the dialogue or music, embodying the rhythmic or melodic accents and intricacies.

Energetic choreography is used to manipulate the energy of the musical event (Figure 3.3). Moments of flash and spectacle can infuse a boost of energy following a long scene or a ballad. Dance can maintain the energy from one scene into another or help transition between storylines. Dance can inject moments of comedy or humor to allow the audience time to process what has come before and prepare for what is ahead. These moments are vital as writers and the creative team craft the journey of the audience.

The Role of the Ensemble

The ensemble of a musical and the movement they inhabit can serve many purposes both as stated within the script and as developed by the director and the creative team. As the ensemble typically makes up a large majority of the cast, their onstage power is a vast resource if used intentionally and effectively (Deer 2014: 47). "A creative team's choice to have the entire cast sing together, whether standing, moving, or dancing, enforces the idea of 'the people' through the volume of voices and the volume of bodies, the aural and visual space taken up by the whole group" (Wolf 2011: 94). The role of the ensemble can shift from number to number (or even minute to minute), or follow a consistent concept established for the entire production. Joe Deer breaks down several roles of the ensemble in his book *Directing in Musical Theatre: An Essential Guide* (2014). The following approaches the role of the ensemble with a choreographic lens.

The first role of the ensemble is to manifest the environment in which the main characters live. The more detailed these characters are depicted, the more vibrant the world (Deer 2014: 44). Specificity in movement transitions a piece out of stereotypical generalizations into personalized truths. In the original production of *Sweet Charity* choreographed by Bob Fosse and Gwen Verdon, the way each taxi dancer draped over the barre in "Big Spender" painted an entire picture of that dancer's background, experiences, personality, view on the world, and frame of mind. When a musical is populated by an ensemble of individuals, unison dancing signifies a community coming together for a shared goal or experience. In referencing the opening titular number of *In the Heights*, Stacy Wolf noted, "Thomas Kail's direction and Andy Blankenbuehler's jazz and hip-hop choreography alternate phrases of unified movement with individualized steps. Musically and choreographically, the first song presents a varied community that is nonetheless a community" (Wolf 2011: 95).

Dance and movement have the potential to tell entire stories even before a word is spoken or sung. The manner in which characters dance exposes vast amounts of insight into the beliefs, attitudes, and structures of the society that the main character either fits into or is fighting against. In the musical *Guys and Dolls*, the opening sequence entitled "Runyonland" is a sequence of dance and pantomime that introduces the audiences to the hustle and bustle of the underworld of New York City. The "Carousel Waltz" which opens *Carousel* is an entire ballet that brings to life the little coastal town in Maine. The ensemble portrays millworkers, sailors, fishermen, and their families as well as the transient members of the carnival including barkers, jugglers, and dancers. The social hierarchy between the owner of the mill and its workers as well as that between the bosses of the carnival and their employees is displayed. The number creates a backdrop against which the two main characters, Billy and Julie, interact for the first time.

On the other side of the spectrum, the ensemble can come together to universally portrait an idea, emotion, or power. They can support, apply pressure, or act as an obstacle for the main characters (Deer 2014: 45). They can expand upon a feeling and give emotional cues to the audience. In *Lady in the Dark*, all of the song and movement happen in the dream world of the lead character's subconscious. In the musical *How to Succeed in Business Without Really Trying*, the ensemble of backstabbing businessmen suddenly converts into a united "Brotherhood of Man" in a rousing eleven o'clock number. Transitioning from dancers as individual characters to dancers as one thought, idea, emotion, or influence will have an impact on the type of movement employed, including a choreographer's use of unison dancing.

The ensemble can also act as a tour guide. They can provide a "previously seen on" recap, a synopsis of action not seen onstage, or foreshadowing of events to come. The ensemble can also tell the audience where to look by directing focus. This is especially important in large group numbers where the audience has to track the main story arc. In *The Music Man*, Harold Hill chases Marian through the library, turning the quiet sanctuary into a book-flying free for all. There is action happening throughout the stage, but the audience needs to follow Harold and Marian's journey. Manipulating focus is also vital and complex when working on site-specific pieces or in thrust or arena stages (see Chapter 8).

Finally, the ensemble can serve as facilitators of the musical. Sometimes this is written into the script, but oftentimes this concept is added to a production to elicit a metaphysical element (Deer 2014: 46). The ensemble works to move set pieces, establish shifts in location or time, and even become inanimate objects. In *Hamilton*, one dancer plays the role of The Bullet which ultimately brings the demise of Alexander Hamilton. "The Bullet not only interacts with characters who are about to die, but also influences others into actions that lead to another character's death" (Sandwell 2020). No matter what concept is decided for the roles of the ensemble, the rules of the concept should be presented toward the beginning of the piece, and it should aid rather than detract from the storytelling.

Script Analysis: Creating a Movement Arc

As a choreographer starts to delve into a script, they should make notes of where movement does and can occur. This might be dictated in the script but could also be ideas of where movement could serve the story. During a love duet, dancers in the background might create texture, set the mood, or embody the environment surrounding the central characters. During a solo, a dancer might be physically expressing the inner turmoil that character is experiencing. When a character is trying to make a decision, dancers could represent both sides symbolically and literally, pulling that character in two different directions. The creative team ultimately will decide the overall role of dance within the piece, any movement conceits, and what moments in the show should dance.

Once all the moments of dance have been sketched out (this can change and adapt through the rehearsal and preview process), a choreographer can begin to create a "movement arc." Any moment that employs movement, including musical numbers and transitions, should be listed. This process allows the choreographer to track the overall movement trajectory of the piece and analyze the progression of storytelling through choreography over the course of the musical. When examining each point on the movement arc, consider the following questions:

1 *What is the name of the moment?* This can be the title of a musical number or a title the choreographer assigns to the moment.

2 *What performers are needed?* Who are the main characters? How many ensemble members?

3 *What is the story being told?* This describes what is happening during the dance sequence either as stated in the script or decided on by the creative team. Where do the characters start? End up? Any imperative plot points? How does this number or moment impact, change, or reveal new information about the characters or the community?

4 *What is the main motor propelling the piece?* Why is it something that has to be expressed through dance? The motor can be an emotion, a theme, a relationship, or a plot point.

5 *What are the practical needs of the moment?* Is there a set or costume change that must occur? Do the performers need to start or end in a specific location onstage based on what happens before or after the dance sequence? Are the performers singing while they are dancing?

6 *What is the role of the choreography?* Is the choreography pragmatic, diegetic, literal, figurative, or energetic? Is the choreography playing multiple roles?

7 *What are descriptive adjectives or phrases that encapsulate the moment?* Dynamics such as stagnant, angular, flowing, and light as well as phrases that inspire ideas of motion such as whirlpool, landslide, a winding river, and caught in the breeze offer the choreographer launching points without prescribing a final product of the movement. These descriptive words can many times be pulled out of conversations with other members of the creative team.

8 *What is the music conveying?* What can the choreographer gleam based on the style, rhythms, patterns, lyrics, melodic motifs, accents, and articulations of the music?

9 *What is the movement concept?* This concept could be a constant throughout the show, or specific to a particular moment. What is the dance style or genre? Does the dance incorporate a prop? Is the dance the focal point or environmental?

10 *What is the location?* This applies both to the setting within the context of the script as well as where the dancers are physically located on the stage or throughout the performance space.

11 *What makes this dance moment different or unique from all the others throughout the show?* What makes that particular moment special? Moving? Memorable? This might be a dance style or genre, a gimmick, an integration of a prop, story point, the characters involved, or the space utilized onstage. A gimmick can be entertaining, and grab the audience's attention. But the moments of emotion and human connection will last with the audience well after the event is over.

12 *What are the writers attempting to evoke from the audience?* Is this number one that should make audiences want to jump out of their seats and join in? Is it meant to make audiences see a character or situation in a new light?

13 *What is the role of the ensemble?*

Once a movement arc encompassing the entire show has been drafted, a choreographer can start to zero in on individual movement events. One activity to brainstorm ideas about individual numbers is an adaptation of Liz Lerman's exercise entitled "Thinking Grid," which allows choreographers to envision raw inspirations and find connections in seemingly disparate notions (Lerman 2011: 288). Along the top row of the grid, choreographers can list words that describe the thoughts, ideas, or themes motivating the movement event. Along the left-hand side, the choreographer can list items that pertain to elements of dance or key innovation entry points. Some examples are shown in Table 3.1.

Choreographers can also begin to journal, allowing their stream of consciousness to reveal unearthed ideas and personal connections to the material.

ACTIVITY MOVEMENT ARC

Create an outline for the show that tracks dance or movement events including musical numbers and transitions. For each moment, consider the questions listed on pages 32–33. Not every question will be relevant to every moment, but investigating these inquiries will help define each moment as its own unique occasion as well as a stepping-stone on the greater dance journey of the musical.

Table 3.1 Adaptation of Liz Lerman's "Thinking Grid"

	Fear	Loss	Unrest
Shape	Fight or Flight	Fetal Position	Great Divide
Pattern	Retreat	Large group dwindling down to a single person	Jagged Lines
Gesture	Guarding the Body	Reaching	Pounding Fists
Image	David and Goliath	Single Tear	Teeter Totter
Item (Prop)	Mask	Locket	Sand
Color	Orange	Grey	Red
Personal memory	Standing on the edge of a cliff	Sitting in a room surrounded by people but feeling completely alone	Emotional rollercoaster of hope versus despair – action versus inaction

Source: Lerman (2011: 288).

4 Interpreting the Score

The score is critical to the creation of dance for a musical. In essence, dance is the physical manifestation of the music. The score becomes the scene partner to the dance. Sometimes they fall into perfect harmony. Other times they are purposefully at odds with each other. One of the first steps for any choreographer is familiarizing themselves with the music. Listen to it on repeat and let the fabric of the score permeate the subconscious where the body has no choice but to physically interpret every nuance. It is not enough to be able to hum the melody. The choreographer must have a deep understanding of the orchestration. What are the drums doing? What instrument is the driving beat? What does the addition of horns or strings say about the moment? As choreographers become more attune to their own creative impulses, many are able to visualize a piece of music as they listen. Images of dance or formations begin to materialize in their mind. If working on a new piece, the orchestrations and dance music might not yet exist. In these instances, the choreographer will collaborate with the dance arranger and orchestrator (see Chapter 10). Lengthy discussions center around the story being told during a dance moment and how to manifest that story in the auditory and visual experience of the audience.

While it is not critical that a choreographer be able to read music, having a basic understanding of Western European music notation—in which most musical theatre scores are written—will empower the choreographer to view a piece of music and find clues embedded within to aid in their comprehension and interpretation. The first step is to ensure the choreographer understands the various types of materials associated with a musical and their function. This helps the choreographer determine what resource, or combination of resources, will best serve their own process. Some choreographers work solely off of a libretto or piano/vocal score, while others create their own hybrid script, combining elements of each. A choreographer must be specific when asking for materials from a production manager or theatre.

1 *Libretto*: The text of a musical including all spoken words and lyrics.

2 *Vocal book*: A simple score that includes just the singer's parts with no accompaniment. Long stretches of music without lyrics, such as dance breaks, are not written out, but rather indicated by a number that represents how many measures of music there are until the next vocal entrance. This is not as helpful to a choreographer's process.

3 *Piano/vocal score*: The full score of a musical arranged to play on a piano. This score takes all the parts played by various instruments and reduces it down to one grand staff to be played on piano with the vocal parts on one or more staves above it. The

piano score is typically used in rehearsals by the music director or accompanist before the orchestra is added. This is the most common type of score used by choreographers.

4 *Piano/conductor's score*: Contains the piano grand staff plus several additional dense staves containing all the instrumental and vocal information necessary for a conductor to cue the orchestra and performers. Some choreographers may find the piano/conductor's score to be overly detailed for their purposes.

5 *Vocal selections*: Sheet music from a show that has been modified for mass production to be sung out of context of the show. Many times, the vocal selections are in a different key, have reduced accompaniment, do not contain extra measures of musical interludes, and usually do not contain the full vocal arrangements or harmonies.

The Basics

Basic score interpretation from a choreographer's perspective includes all the elements necessary to look at a piece of music and inherently identify the feel, rhythm, groove, length, and build of the song. The following are some basics of Western European music notation.

Meter and Rhythm

1 *Pulse*: Synonymous with "beat." A pulse is felt rather than heard, and divides time into regular, repeating segments.

2 *Meter*: A repeating pattern of strong and weak pulses. For example, a waltz would have a repeating pattern of strong, weak, weak. The meter is not heard. It is what is felt running underneath the music. The meter is indicated by the *time signature*.

3 *Bar/measure*: One round of the meter, or pattern.

4 *Bar line*: A vertical line on the staff that separates the measures and indicates that the pattern is starting over.

5 *Rhythm*: What is heard rather than felt. The rhythm is the timing of the notes relative to the meter. The repeating meter sets up expectations. The rhythm can then thwart or fulfill these expectations.

6 *Syncopation*: When an emphasized note is heard on a weak beat of the meter, or even between beats.

7 *Groove*: A recognizable rhythmic pattern. Grooves can comprise the signature rhythms associated with specific dance and music styles such as the tango, foxtrot, rumba, reggae, soft shoe, and hustle.

8 *Tempo*: The Italian word for "time". The tempo refers to the rate at which the pulses are passing by in time.

9 *Beats per minute (bpm)*: This is an accurate method of indicating tempo.

10 *Metronome*: An electronic or mechanical device that provides a steady tempo. These can be extremely valuable when determining speed of choreography. Many metronome apps are also available.

11 *Tempo markings*: Descriptions of tempos that typically have associated bpm tempo ranges (e.g., largo, adagio, andante, allegro, vivace).

Notes

Every note has a value that corresponds to a simple fraction indicating the length of the note relative to the other note values. For instance, a whole note will take the same amount of time to play as two half notes. The time signature assigns a note value to the main pulse. The rhythm can then sub-divide or combine these values.

A *beam* is a horizontal bar that groups multiple flagged notes together. Each note is played separately. A *tie* is a curved line that connects two notes of the same pitch, combining their note values into one long note. A *slur* looks similar to a tie, but connects two different notes. Unlike a tie that adds their value together, a slur indicates that the notes be played legato, or smoothly, as the notes change pitch. A *dot* lengthens a note by half its value. For example, if a dot is added to a whole note, the resulting note is as long as a whole note tied to a half note. *Rests* are values indicating silence. Each note value has a corresponding rest. Dots can also be used to extend rests.

Fig. 4.1 Meter, rhythm, and notes. Musical examples by Greg Bolin.

Time Signatures

A *time signature* is a simple fraction of two numbers at the beginning of a piece of music that describes the meter and assigns a note value to the pulse. Time signatures will also occur elsewhere in the piece if the metric pattern changes. The bottom number, or denominator, indicates the note value assigned to the pulse and the top number, or numerator, signifies how many pulses are in one round of the meter's pattern. For example, in the 4/4 time signature, the 1/4 or quarter note gets the beat and there are 4 beats per measure.

Most musical theatre scores will employ simple and compound meters. In a *simple meter*, each beat can be divided into two equal parts. Standard simple time signatures include:

1 4/4, or "common time," is the most common time signature in Western music. Each measure in 4/4 consists of four quarter-note beats. 4/4 is often abbreviated with the letter "c."

2 3/4 is another very common meter, often called "waltz time." Each measure in 3/4 has three quarter-note beats.

3 2/4 is a meter in which each measure contains two quarter-note beats.

4 2/2, "cut time"—also known as "alla breve" or "the Broadway 2"—has 2 half-note beats. Even though there are 4 quarter notes in a measure, it has a very different energy than common time. Cut time implies a quicker tempo and a feeling of being "in two" rather than "in four." It is often abbreviated with a "c" with a vertical line through it.

In a *compound meter*, the pulse itself can be sub-divided into three equal parts. The top number is a multiple of 3 (6, 9, 12, etc.) and each group of 3 notes is combined into 1 larger pulse. For example, in 6/8 time, there are 2 large pulses, each of which is as long as 3 eighth-notes combined, or a dotted quarter-note. Note that all pulses in a compound meter are dotted values. Standard compound time signatures include:

1 6/8 contains 6 eighth-notes per measure, but only contains 2 pulses, each consisting of 3 eighth-notes, or a dotted quarter-note. A jig is a common groove found in 6/8 time.

2 9/8 has 9 eighth-notes grouped into 3 pulses.

3 12/8 has 12 eighth-notes grouped into 4 pulses. Because of the four large beats, it relates back to 4/4 or common time if that common time were swung.

When looking at different pieces of music, or even different parts of the same song, not all measures take the same amount of time to complete. The time signature and tempo marking will have a large impact on the speed of the music. As you listen to a piece of music and follow along in the score, track the speed with which the meters occur on the sheet music in proportion to time. Sixteen bars of a slow waltz ballad in 3/4 time will go much slower than 16 bars of an uptempo song in cut time. Additionally, engraving might not be proportional. Measures containing less notes might be shorter to save space on the page, but still takes the same amount of time as other measures within that time signature.

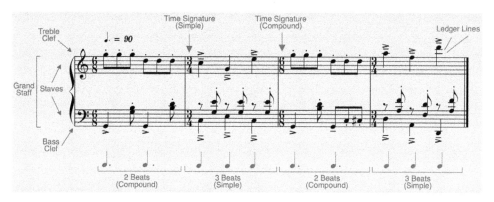

Fig. 4.2 Time signatures, staves, and clefs. Musical examples by Greg Bolin.

Staves and Clefs

The first thing to observe on sheet music is the staves. A *staff* (plural: staves) is a group of five horizontal lines and four spaces on which music is written. Each line and space represent a specific note. In Western European music notation, the staves are read left to right starting at the top staff and working your way down. A *clef* is a symbol at the beginning of a staff that indicates which notes belong to which lines and spaces. Notes range from A through G. Starting at the bottom, the notes ascend in order alternating between lines and spaces. The two most common clefs in musical theatre are the treble clef and the bass clef.

The *treble clef* is often used by higher instruments such as the flute, trumpet, violin, and voices. The *bass clef* is used by lower instruments such as the trombone, bassoon, cello, and bass. In some Golden Age scores, men's voices are also written in bass clef. A *grand staff* is a grouping of a treble clef and a bass clef staff together into one continuous staff. The treble clef staff is positioned on top of the bass clef staff. *Ledger lines* are added up or down to extend the range of the staff. Instruments with wide ranges such as the piano and harp use the grand staff. When reading a piece of sheet music, all staves connected by a single vertical line are played at the same time. There might be multiple treble clef or bass clef staves.

Key Signatures

An *accidental* is a symbol that modifies the pitch of a note. The accidental always appears to the left of the note so that when reading from left to right, the accidental occurs before the note. Two of the most common accidentals are the sharp and the flat. A *sharp* (♯) is a symbol that raises a note by a half-step. A *flat* (♭) is a symbol that lowers a note by a half-step. When an accidental appears, it remains in effect for the entire measure unless cancelled out by a *natural* symbol (♮), which reverts a note back to its natural form. An accidental only applies to the line or space that note is written on and does not apply to the same note in a lower or higher octave.

A *key signature* tells us which accidentals apply to the entire piece or until a change of key signature. As a choreographer, it is not necessary to know the details and inner workings of each key signature, but it is important to take notice of when the keys change as clues into the feel, build, and story of the song. It is also valuable to be aware of what key different sections of a dance break are in when looking for places to make cuts. If there is a large number of accidentals on the page, it can indicate that either something new is happening in the music, or that the composer changed keys without actually changing the key signature.

Understanding whether a key is major or minor has a huge impact on the mood of the music. Each key signature can represent a major or minor key. Major and minor key pairs that share the same key signature are known as *relative keys*. Sometimes a composer might shift from a major to the relative minor key, signifying an important change in the story or character, without actually changing key signatures. The *circle of fifths* is a reference that illustrates what accidentals make up each major and relative minor key.

Expressions, Articulations, and Dynamic Markings

Expressions, articulations, and dynamics all relate to how the music on the page is interpreted by the musicians. They are the qualities that make a piece of music come to life full of nuance and meaning. These markings give clues into the speed, weight, volume, attack, tone, and feel of the music. A choreographer can highlight these markings as indicators of the mood the music is establishing. Research the definition of any markings found in the score as a way to mine for inspiration. The movement can then either complement or purposely challenge these musical characteristics.

Dynamic markings indicate the volume of the passage:

1 *Piano* (p): softly.
2 *Pianissimo* (pp): very softly.
3 *Mezzo-Piano* (mp): medium soft.
4 *Forte* (f): loudly.
5 *Fortissimo* (ff): very loudly.
6 *Mezzo-Forte* (mf): medium loud.
7 *Fortepiano* (fp): indicates a loud attack that immediately gets quiet.
8 *Crescendo* (<): growing in volume, abbreviated as cresc.
9 *Decrescendo* (>): diminishing in volume, also known as diminuendo or dim.

Articulation markings describe the way the musician initiates—or attacks—the note, as well as how long the note is sustained.

1 *Staccato*: short and detached.
2 *Tenuto*: opposite of staccato—held to the full value of the note or longer with no breaks.
3 *Accent (marcato)*: emphasized with more volume and attack at front of note.
4 *Staccatissimo (martellato)*, also known as a housetop accent: the note should be accented and short, but not as short as staccato.
5 *Fermata*: note held longer than its rhythmic value—often length indicated by conductor.

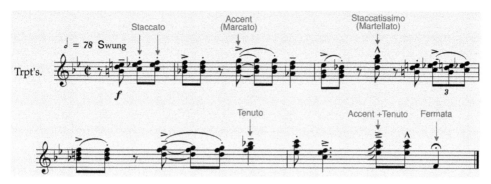

Fig. 4.3 Articulation markings. Musical examples by Greg Bolin.

Expressions indicate stylization and mood for musicians. Terms such as *agitato* (agitated), *dolce* (sweetly), *gioioso* (joyfully), and *eroico* (heroically) offer vibrant hints for choreographic intention. Expressions can also indicate a change in tempo, marking where the music speeds up or slows down. For example, *meno mosso* means less movement or slower, while *più mosso* means more movement or faster. These tempo changes pinpoint a shift in the music and the story.

Other Important Markings

There are other important markings one will encounter on the page that dictate the order in which the measures are played. These reduce the number of pages needed to notate the music. The first is the *repeat symbol*. The music in between the two repeat symbols should be repeated. If there is no beginning repeat symbol, the repeat is taken back to the start of the song. The highlighted measures should be repeated one time unless there are instructions to repeat more times (3X 8X, etc.) or instructions to vamp.

Repeated sections (or full songs) often contain multiple endings. For each ending, a bracket is drawn above the ending's bar, or bars, along with an ending number (i.e., 1, 2, etc.). On the first pass, the music is played through to the repeat sign of the first ending. Then it returns to the beginning of the repeated section, plays up to the bar before the first ending, and skips to the second ending. A *caesura*, also known as "railroad tracks," is a symbol that indicates a break or interruption in the music. The length of that break is usually determined by the conductor.

Da capo means "from the beginning" and is often abbreviated in sheet music as D.C. This tells the musician to go back and play the piece of music from the top. D.C. can also be accompanied by more instruction. For example, *D.C. al Fine* means to go back to the beginning of the music and play until the word *Fine* (meaning finish) appears in the sheet music. *D.C. al Coda* means to go from the beginning and play until the phrase To Coda appears. Then the musician skips ahead to the coda symbol.

Dal segno (abbreviated D.S.) means "from the sign." When this appears, instead of going back to the start, you return to the segno symbol. D.S. can also be accompanied by further

Fig. 4.4 Other important markings. Musical examples by Greg Bolin.

instruction such as *D.S. al Fine* (play from the segno symbol to the *Fine*, or finish) or *D.S. al Coda* (play from the segno symbol until the phrase To Coda appears and then jump to the coda symbol). Figure 4.4, composed by Greg Bolin, demonstrates the symbols and how they impact the order measures are played.

Groove and feel are vital to the expression of the music. Most grooves are written out within the score. However, often a piece that is intended to be played in a swung groove will still be notated as quarter-notes. Many times, a marking will appear at the beginning of the music stating that straight eighth-notes should be played with a swung feel.

Musical Passages and Transitions

Along with songs, scores contain several types of musical passages that each serve a unique purpose.

Fig. 4.4 Continued.

1 *Overture*: The overture is a piece of orchestral music played at the top of the show. The overture is usually a compilation of several songs showcased in the musical. Along with giving the audience an indication that the show is about to start, the overture also introduces the audiences to musical themes that will occur throughout the evening and can set the tone for the production. The truly wonderful overtures are meticulously crafted and play with the musical themes in sequencing, tempo, and key to produce a thrilling unified musical event. Due to time constraints and changing formats, many contemporary musicals do not have an overture.

2 *Entr'acte*: The entr'acte is a piece of orchestral music played before the start of the second act. Like the overture, it serves as a cue to the audience that the show is about to restart and helps re-establish the environment of the musical coming back from intermission.

3 *Underscoring*: Underscoring is music intended to accompany a scene or dialogue. It plays a pivotal role in the musical scene where song and dialogue are woven together. The underscoring can amplify the emotional current, build tension, or reveal unspoken truths happening between the characters. Some scores have specific line cues to

match up with moments in the underscoring. Even when these guideposts aren't identified, it can become clear how the ebb and flow of the music is meant to match the scene. Underscoring will often house repeats or vamps to make room for the individual timing of each production.

4 *Vamp*: A section of music, usually 1–4 bars, that is repeated until a cue is given to move on, typically by the conductor. Vamps allow for flexibility within the performance. Many vamps, such as those written by composer John Kander in songs like "New York, New York" and "All That Jazz," have become iconic.

5 *Playoff/chaser*: A playoff is a small encore of the song that was just performed and is meant as a device to get the performers offstage and transition to a new scene.

6 *Bows and exit music*: Bows music is composed to accompany the curtain call (see Chapter 12). Exit music follows the bows and plays as the audience exits the theatre.

The score also includes notes on how music should transition from one song to another. *Applause segue* indicates that the music should stop for applause before continuing on. *Direct segue*, *attacca*, or *as one* signifies that there should be no break between the end of one song and the beginning of the next.

Music Through a Dance Lens

Again, it is not crucial that a choreographer read music. However, having some base knowledge empowers one to find hidden clues on the page that can directly translate into movement. Following the contours of the notes on the page reveals the flow of the melody. Is it smooth and connected, seamlessly moving from one note to another, or are there large and jagged jumps in pitches? Does the tune stay relatively within a small note range, or are there extremes of high and low? More ink on the page often means more activity in the orchestra. All of these qualities can be interpreted through the body.

Speaking the same language as the music director or conductor establishes a collaborative atmosphere. One way to do this is to refer to sections of music by the measure number listed above each bar. Measures are counted from the beginning of the piece until the end of that song. Many times, measure numbers are only listed at the beginning of a new section or musical theme. These divisions give clues into shifts in the number. Often sections in the score are labeled with terms used to describe these moments in the original production. While the feel of each section does not need to be replicated, it presents insight into how the build of the number was developed and can reveal the original intention of each theme or passage.

Time and key signatures have direct emotional and movement correlations. Director/ choreographer Susan Stroman, whose notable works include *The Producers*, *Contact*, and *Crazy for You*, described how she, along with dance arranger Peter Howard, manipulated time signatures when building dance music for "Shall We Dance" from the musical *Crazy for You*. If she wanted the characters to be shy and coy, she would play it in a soft shoe rhythm. If she wanted to show them falling in love, it was put in 3/4 time. If they were chasing one another, it was expressed in a fast 2 (cut time). Musical keys come with ingrained cultural significance. Research into the traditional and popular music of the region where the musical is set can deepen the understanding of the narrative housed within a score. For example, within the US American culture, a major key can signify happiness, stability, and joy while a minor key often expresses sadness, contemplation, or turmoil. However, different cultures ascribe meanings to various modes.

Rhythm is the heartbeat of the dance. Movement musicality is the ability to physically manifest the rhythms and accents. When looking at the score, track the rhythm through the time signatures, speed, and accents. Does the song have a steady beat or is the time signature constantly shifting? Is the music simple and unwavering or are the accent marks strewn throughout the measures? These questions lead to insights for the choreographer about the story occurring in the moment and the state of mind of the characters. It can also be a launching point for the underlying vibration of the dance.

What You Hear Versus What You See

When working on a pre-existing musical, the orchestrations and dance arrangements are already established, based on the original (or revival) production. In these instances, it is the choreographer's responsibility to take the existing musical build and translate it through their own physical lens of storytelling. Many shows offer the ability to license several different versions, including the original Broadway version and subsequent revivals, so before beginning work, be sure you are clear on what version the theatre or company has licensed. Then check that all materials, including the score, libretto, and reference cast recordings, match the version that was licensed.

Cast recordings can be useful tools but can also present challenges. Most of the time, cast recordings do not contain the entirety of the dance music. These passages have been trimmed down for time and file size. If using a cast recording as a reference, a choreographer must track in the score where the cuts were made and take note of the music that is not present on the recording. Sometimes dance music or entire songs are also sped up for the recording. Bpm markings are designated in the score; use a metronome to check the speeds against the cast recording. The performers and musicians featured on a recording might have made artistic interpretations of the music that are not reflected "on the page" in the score. Before getting too attached to a phrasing or accent, the choreographer should refer to the score to make sure it is there. Finally, due to budget, time, and space, not all theatres are able to produce musicals with a full orchestra. In these instances, the orchestrations are pared down to a smaller number of instruments. This might affect the sound, tone, accents, and fullness of the music. In these cases, the orchestra rehearsals and sitzprobe or wandelprobe (see Chapter 11) are critical opportunities for the choreographer to hear the music as it will actually sound and make any necessary adjustments to the choreography.

When working on a new musical, dance arrangements and orchestrations may or may not yet exist. They might be written in full or simply have an outline. In new work, the choreographer works closely with the director, music director, composer, and dance arranger to ensure that the musical build matches the story and intention of the movement (see Chapter 10). During these conversations, that base understanding of Western European musical notation will enable everyone to speak a common language.

In most rehearsals, the music is being played on piano (occasionally there might also be drums). No matter the skill and virtuosity of the musician playing rehearsals, hearing a score only on piano is quite different than hearing the full orchestration. The way a piece is orchestrated will greatly impact the tone of the number as well as the choreographer's interpretation of that music. An accent will have a completely different feel and meaning depending on the instrument that voices that accent. Markings in the score such as vln. (violin), drs. (drums), str. (strings), and gtr. (guitar) will communicate what instruments play that part of the music. For this reason, when following along to a score, it is helpful to find a recording of the full instrumentation where the accents can be heard on the specified instruments. Video recordings of other productions can be a resource for hearing the full arrangements. The music director might also be able to create audio files of certain parts of the score. A choreographer can start to assess what instruments lead different sections of the music and how that can affect the physical interpretation of that music.

Musical Changes, Counting, and Cutting

When listening to the orchestrations for dance breaks and production numbers, the musical changes are the biggest insight for a choreographer in outlining the narrative and energetic build of the number. Something happens to cause that shift. In the score, mark these changes with a long vertical line that exaggerates the bar line and separates the music into sections, or beats. These divisions will be utilized when sectioning the number (see page 68).

A choreographer can analyze each section separately, taking notice of the important qualities such as the tone, tempo, key, groove, meter, expression, articulation, and rhythm. This will help determine what action or exploration of a theme, idea, or emotion is transpiring and what movement best serves the moment. A choreographer can also scrutinize the transition from one section to another. Is there a key change that raises the stakes of the moment? Does the music slow down or speed up? Does the groove shift?

Counting the music is a useful tool in communication with dancers. It also can reveal patterns within the music and highlight moments of deviation. If there has been a long series of 8 counts and all of a sudden there is a 6 count phrase, it grabs the attention. In common 4/4 time, most dancers and choreographers break the music into counts of 8. The music, however, is written in 4 beat measures. Therefore, each 8 count typically consists of two musical measures. More complex meters will fall into a choreographer's perceived counts in a variety of ways, so it is important to track the relationship of counts to measures in the score.

Methods of counting are individual to the choreographer. Some choreographers do not work with counts at all, but rather use rhythm and accents to communicate movement and groove at the same time. In pieces with difficult meters or a constant changing of time signatures, clarity can be provided by working out how to count the music. This can be done individually by the choreographer, in collaboration with the music director, or together by the full company. Communicate where new phrases begin and why certain measures were grouped together. One exercise to physicalize the counts is to walk around while listening to the music. Walk on the beat and change direction every time it sounds like a new musical phrase.

In the early and mid 1900s, live theatre was one of the prime methods of entertainment. Audiences were receptive to performances that lasted over three hours. Today's audiences have a much shorter attention span. With the breadth of data available at one's fingertips, people are accustomed to processing larger amounts of information in shorter amounts of time. Many musicals contain lengthy overtures, entr'actes, transition music, and dance sequences. These musical passages are sometimes trimmed or cut for reasons such as lack of time, lack of ability, lack of necessity, or to preserve a steady momentum of storytelling. A producer or theatre must always consult the licensing agency for permission to make any modifications to the script or score.

If granted permission to trim a piece, look first at the desired narrative and energetic build of the number and look for moments that take the energy down, do not continue to move the story forward, or repeat unnecessarily for that particular production. Work with the music director to track the key signatures and make sure that any cuts follow a natural key progression.

Physical Interpretations

Once a choreographer knows a score inside and out, they can begin to create the physical interpretation of that music. The music and dance should be so inextricably linked that it seems as if the movement itself manifested the music into being. That symbiotic relationship can take on different forms. The movement can parallel, exaggerate, or challenge the melodies, rhythms, syncopations, accents, and expressions. No matter the method of interpretation, the music and dance should work concurrently to carry the emotional and narrative load. Too much movement can distract from the music's artistry while not dancing to music with inherent motion can feel unsatisfying.

The coexistence of dance and music runs both directions. If the orchestra hits, the dancers should hit. If a dancer twirls, the orchestra should twirl. A choreographer can examine the music for movement prompts. What instruments are being utilized? What happens if instruments are translated by different parts of the body? Are the drums the hips? The horns the shoulders? Does the dancing cause the music to happen or is the dance in response to the music? Does the music and dance live side by side like parallel streams or are they in conversation with each other?

Lyrics offer a critical component to the makeup and meaning of a song. The lyrics can be assessed when stripped away from the music. What are the lyrics expressing independently? Do they house any references to movement? Do any of the phrases inspire ideas of motion? What is the rhyme scheme? Then pair the lyrics back with the music and investigate their relationship. Are the music and lyrics conveying the same thought, idea, or emotion? Are they challenging each other? What does their harmonious or discordant relationship say about the story or the character? What is movement that interprets the music versus the lyrics? These questions all create sparks of motivation to support the choreography process.

ACTIVITY DISCOVERING THE CUT

Most of the time the cast recording contains a condensed version of dance breaks. Taking the sheet music, follow along with the cast recording and discover where the cuts in the score were taken. Determine which measures are played and which measures are skipped. Even without an extensive knowledge of reading music, certain elements can be tracked to match up a musical phrase with the corresponding transcription. When searching for a musical phrase in the sheet music, look for the following:

1 Beginnings of major musical ideas or sections
2 The shape of the melody line
3 A change in time signature or key signature
4 Major accents
5 Rhythmic patterns or syncopations
6 Long sustained notes versus several fast notes
7 Suggested cuts: some scores will offer options of music to be cut.

ACTIVITY DRAWING THE MUSICAL PHRASES

This activity enables the choreographer to physically diagram the shape and flow of a musical sequence. It can be used as a cheat sheet when creating choreography.

1 Pick a piece of music or an instrumental/dance break housed within a number.
2 Figure out how many counts are in each musical phrase (8 counts, 6 counts, etc.). This might change during the musical passage.
3 While listening to the music, number the phrases along the left-hand side of a piece of lined paper (A). The space to the right of the number will contain markings specific to that musical phrase. Each time a new musical theme, idea, or section begins, draw a horizontal line across the paper and start the numbering of musical phrases over again (B). If the number of counts in a musical phrase changes from section to section, label it at the top of each new segment (C).
4 Give each large section of music a name. This can be based on the feel of the music, the story being told, the build moment, or anything that brings movement motivation.
5 Mark a phrase that is shorter than the established counts with a vertical line that breaks up the row proportionally to the number of counts. For example, if the established phrase is 8 counts and then a 4 count phrase appears, draw a vertical line that cuts that row in half. You can also put the number of counts in parentheses to the right of the vertical line (D).
6 Once the outline is done, start at the beginning of the music and draw your personal interpretation of the music. Smooth lines can trace the pattern of the melody. Steady straight lines can represent an even beat. Sharp lines or jagged peaks and valleys can denote accents (E). When necessary, counts can also be written along the row or just for important accents and syncopations (F).

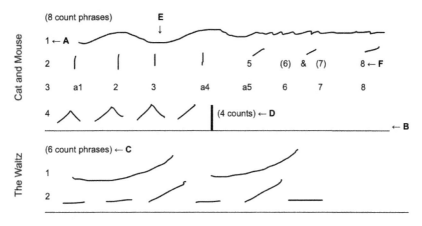

Fig. 4.5 Drawing the musical phrase example.

ACTIVITY SCORING THE SCORE

1 Pick a piece of music and make sure you have access to the proper sheet music from the score. This exercise can be aided if you have a full recording of the song, but is not necessary.

2 At the beginning of each new section, draw a large bracket. Label each section with an uppercase letter.

3 Highlight the time signature and key signature at the beginning of each section and any time it changes.

4 Circle any important markings that would relate to the movement:
   a) Accents
   b) Tempos
   c) Expression, articulation, and dynamic markings
   d) Instrument delineations.

5 Underline any significant words or phrases in the lyrics.

5   Musical Staging

Musical staging is the action of the performers during moments of singing. It includes the performers' position on the stage as well as the physical movement employed. Musical staging is most often used for solos, duets, and small group numbers, but is also relevant to the beginning song portion of large production numbers. Musicals with small casts might primarily feature musical staging and are approached differently by the choreographer than dance heavy musicals with large ensembles. The amount and intricacy of musical staging is dependent on the style of the production. A musical that is hyper-realistic in tone will have less movement and staging than a hyper-stylized musical pastiche. No matter the size or extent of the movement, all staging must be true to the story, characters, and relationships portrayed. In successful musical staging, both realistic and stylized, the movement should feel spontaneously generated from that specific character, world, and experience.

Earning the Song

Humans most typically do not burst into song in the middle of a conversation. Most people do not use singing and movement as a method of communication in everyday interactions. Therefore, these occurrences onstage require an escalation of energy referred to as "earning the song." When a song is "earned," the stakes of a scene leading up to the song become so heightened that singing becomes the only possible release of that tension.

Moments of song and dance are meticulously crafted by musical theatre writers and strategically placed at points of emotional or climatic peaks. Again, song and dance emerge as the mode of expression when words are not enough. The objectives of the characters become increasingly urgent and the pace of the scene might quicken leading into the music. Even when heading into a ballad, the stakes must continue to rise, causing the proceeding dialogue to either speed up or emphatically and purposefully slow down. If equating the energy onstage to a ball being tossed in the air, the performers must give the ball a strong, deliberate push to launch the introduction of a new medium such as song and dance.

Song Structure

Many songs in musical theatre, especially from the Golden Age, follow a standard AABA song structure. These songs are typically 32 bars in length and consist of two choruses, a bridge, and a final chorus. Each song and situation surrounding a musical moment is unique to the show. Additional song structures are also utilized within musical theatre. But some general principles exist surrounding the intention of the AABA song structure.

Many songs begin with an introduction, or verse. The verse acts as the pathway to transition from scene into song. The musical intro sets the stage in mood and tone. The verse musicalizes the experience of opening a diary and being transported to the character's internal world. The verse leads into the song proper, the main body of the song. This is where the AABA structure begins. In the first two choruses, the character goes about obtaining what they want. They try unsuccessfully in two different ways. It is common in songs that start with two choruses, or A sections, that one chorus is more personally connected to the character (I/me), while the other chorus is more connected with the scene partner or outside world (you).

At this point, the character must try something else, leading into the bridge, or B section. Musically the bridge sounds different from the choruses and takes the song somewhere new. The character must explore other ideas, options, or perspectives. It is in this moment that the character goes on a journey and comes out changed. This leads the character into the final chorus, or A section, where they are able to examine their previous desires and go after their objective with an enlightened understanding. Composer/lyricist Jason Robert Brown stated, "That transition out of the B section into the final A—that is the most important point of the song. That is the joint on which the whole song rests. Because that is the point at which a character opens in some way—whether they grow, they learn something, they move forward in some plot moment, something like that. But it's right there" (2013: 43:25).

Stage Moods

The placement of a character onstage directly affects the way the performer feels and the way the character is perceived by the audience. Stage locations come with qualities, or stage moods, that are interpreted through the cultural lens of the audience. The following discussion of stage moods is rooted in the work of Alexander Dean and Lawrence Carra (2009: 135) as interpreted by one of my mentors, director/choreographer Paula Kalustian. It bases the analysis of the stage through a Western cultural lens for an audience that reads text from left to right. The order in which we process information in our daily lives impacts the way we experience composition and movement onstage. These are general observations rather than steadfast rules. Every performance space and design has distinct and individualistic positions of power. This section will illustrate stage moods in relationship to a traditional bare proscenium stage, where the audience is all housed on one side, without any set pieces or levels. Other stage configurations are discussed in Chapter 8.

First divide the stage vertically into stage right, center stage, and stage left. Stage directions are from the performer's perspective, so stage right is on the audience left, or house left, and vice versa. Next divide the stage horizontally into downstage (closest to the audience), center stage, and upstage (furthest away from the audience). The result is a grid of performance areas (Table 5.1).

Table 5.1 Performance areas

Upstage right (UR)	Upstage center (UC)	Upstage left (UL)
Center right (CR)	Center center (CC)	Center left (CL)
Downstage right (DR)	Downstage center (DC)	Downstage left (DL)

AUDIENCE

Center stage holds a high degree of power.

1 *Center center*: When a performer is center center (CC), they are the center of the universe and have every opportunity open to them. The performer can move anywhere and carries strength in all directions they might face (front, left, right, upstage).
2 *Upstage center*: Upstage center (UC) is a position of control or reign. Often this stage area is the location of judges, rulers, deities, and rituals such as weddings. A performer standing upstage center has their body facing front to everything and can look out on the whole stage. Stage moods of this area include critical, judgmental, forgiving, bestowing, taking away, mediating, and balance.
3 *Downstage center*: Downstage center (DC) is also a position of strength, but is more intimate and vulnerable. The performer is closer to the audience, eliciting a different feeling from both the performer and the viewer. When a character is downstage center, they have the inner strength to reveal their most personal thoughts. They can talk to a higher power. They can also become a universal voice that encompasses the other characters onstage as well as the audience.

Stage right (SR) often represents the familiar, or home. Because Western cultures read from left to right, they look to their left, or stage right, first when taking in an image. Entrances from stage right feel natural, comfortable, and expected. Family, friends, and familiar characters tend to enter from stage right. Characters feel at ease and are confident to be themselves. Places where people relax, such as kitchens, bedrooms, and dens, are often established stage right. Musical cues to SR moods include music that is light and whimsical or romantic in feel. Characters look stage right over the audience when thinking, talking, or singing about home, the past, family, friends, or romantic interests.

1 *Downstage right*: The stage moods of downstage right (DR) include friendly, trustworthy, safe, and reminiscent. In some ways, this area can be even more intimate than downstage center. A character positioned downstage right has the safety to show who they really are, reveal a secret, express their desires of love, or muse about their memories.
2 *Center right*: Center right (CR) is one of the spots onstage that is less powerful. A character can enter from center right or travel through it, but it feels unsettling if the character in main focus stays there for too long.
3 *Upstage right*: Upstage right (UR) is a place of confidence and preparation as the hero embarks on their journey.

Stage left (SL) represents the unknown. This can be mysterious, scary, exciting, or comical. Strangers and newcomers to the audience or other characters onstage tend to enter from stage left. A person entering from stage left knows something others do not.

Fig. 5.1 Stage moods. Photo by Bret Brookshire.

Choreographers often use this entrance to shock or surprise the audience. Stage left can be sinister (villains) or fun (comedic foils). Musical cues to SL moods include music that is dark, unsettled, upbeat, or driving in feel. Characters look stage left over the audience when thinking, talking, or singing about adventure, fears, desires, or places they have to go. The results could be tragedy, but they could also be previously unknown joy and fulfillment.

1 *Downstage left*: The stage moods of downstage left (DL) include adventurous, mysterious, night, and wilderness. Things have the potential to go wrong. This can also be an area for highly comical moments, including comedic arguments.
2 *Center left*: Just like center right, center left is one of the spots onstage that is less powerful. A character can enter from center left or travel through it, but it feels unsettling if the character in main focus stays there for too long.
3 *Upstage left*: Upstage left (UL) holds a metaphysical quality. The fog of Brigadoon rolls on from upstage left. This area can house sprites, spirits, and other mythical or mystical elements.

Partners

Duets are a common staple of musical theatre. The physical connection between two characters onstage both in placement and movement tell the audience vast amounts through non-verbal communication about the relationship between those characters. It is the tension created with energy and space between performers that enraptures audiences to invest in the story. When staging duets, take into account dominance and focus. Dominance is the importance or power of a character based on their position onstage, whereas focus is the concentration of stage energy where audiences are compelled to look

(Kirk, Bellas, and Kirk 2004: 101–102). Most of the time the character with dominance also has the focus. However, if the person in response to the dominant character is more critical to the story, then they will receive the focus.

When staging two performers in a duet, consider the horizontal planes on which they stand. Two characters who are sharing equal emphasis can stand on the same plane. In this scenario, they are facing each other and the audience is seeing both characters in profile. The performers can also "cheat out" to the audience by opening up their downstage shoulder so that each performer is standing at the diagonal. Although this might feel unrealistic to the performers, by opening up the intimate interaction between two people, the audience is able to witness the moment more fully.

General rules of emphasis state that the person furthest downstage or the person facing most fully to the front carries the most weight or importance. If two performers are both facing front, the one furthest downstage will take emphasis. But if the downstage performer is facing upstage with their back to the audience, the upstage performer facing front will have the dominance. In a duet where the emphasis volleys back and forth between characters, the performers can "take the stage" (moving to a more dominant position) or "give the stage" (moving to a less dominant position and thereby giving the emphasis to the other performer) (Novak and Novak 1996: 80). Emphasis can be modified with the addition of level and design elements.

Most of the time performers should avoid "upstaging" themselves, or facing their back to the audience, while singing. When this happens, the viewers are unable to track who is singing and cannot fully witness the experience of the character expressed through facial and physical features. The performer who is singing can be placed upstage where they can face out and the character listening can be placed downstage with their back turned to the audience.

The distance between two performers directly impacts the tension held between two characters onstage. When performers are too far apart, there is a lack of tension or stakes. Audience members, unable to see both performers at the same time, have to split their attention. Having partners on opposite sides of the stage might be a helpful image related to the story, but it is hard to maintain for an entire song. On the other hand, if performers get too close to each other, there also is a lack of tension or obstacle. The closeness we hold with others in everyday interactions does not always translate to the stage because the audience is excluded. The space needed to create tension between performers also varies depending on the size of the theatre and the distance of the audience to the stage. For this reason, performers and the creative team must experiment to discover the subtleties of each new theatrical space.

Whenever transitioning from the rehearsal room to the actual performance space, a valuable exercise is to place two performers who have intimate songs or scenes together onstage and the rest of the company in the audience. Start the performers on complete opposite sides of the stage and have them slowly take steps in toward each other. Track at which distance the performers onstage start to feel tension between themselves as well as when the viewers in the audience start to feel the tension. Have the performers continue to move closer together until they lose the tension both from what they feel and what is perceived in the audience. This gives the performers an understanding of the window of distance that will create optimal tension between the characters. Once the exercise is complete, have the

Fig. 5.2 Partners. Photo by Bret Brookshire.

first two performers join in the audience and two other performers execute the exercise. This will allow the first performers to experience the perception of the audience.

Singing and moving are both activities that pull focus onstage. However, as playwright Thornton Wilder noted, "the eye is the enemy of the ear in real drama" (Gelb 1961). Although speaking or singing is powerful, the viewer will most often be drawn to movement or physical activity. If trying to establish a character that is singing as the character with the main emphasis, then they should also execute the movement. In this way, the words and physicality work together to enhance each other. If the person listening is moving, it will take the focus away from the person singing. Exceptions exist when the two partners are moving together, either as a couple or individually at the same time. Also, a choreographer might give the action to the listening partner when the physical movement of the silent character is more critical to the story than the dialogue or song lyrics.

When staging a love duet, it is crucial to map out the physical contact with the performers. Resources, such as the book *Staging Sex: Best Practices, Tools, and Techniques for Theatrical Intimacy* (2020) by Chelsea Pace and Laura Rikard, gives directors, choreographers, intimacy choreographers, and educators clear guidelines and practical exercises to establish a culture of consent, desexualize theatrical intimacy, and articulate boundaries. It also offers a vocabulary to choreograph moments of intimacy in a clear, safe, and repeatable way. Any type of physical contact from a handshake to a kiss, to more involved intimacy should be mapped out and transcribed in detail. Consent for any physical contact must be given freely and continuously in order to ensure the safety and comfort of the performers. Also, a performer has the right to withdraw their consent or change their boundaries at any point, even after the show has opened. By clearly choreographing these intimate moments, the performers are given definitive actions rather than having to improvise. See Chapter 12 for information about approaching moments of contact, intimacy, and fighting.

Mapping out the physicality of a love duet affords the ability to track the build of the sequence. If the characters hold hands or embrace too quickly, then there is nowhere to go and the necessity of the song diminishes. Even specificity in eye contact or lack thereof can communicate the relationship between characters. When studying the progression of a number, take into account the audience's experience. If one side of the audience can only see the face of one of the partners, find staging for the performers to switch sides. No matter the benefit of a certain movement or configuration, everything must be motivated by the story and the characters' objectives. While having the two performers face out (one person is singing to their partner's back or in a coupled holding position) is a great way to invite the audience into the event and emotional journey of the characters, if unmotivated it may feel contrived and false.

Movement While Singing

Staging movement while a performer is singing is a balancing act. The choreographer has to weigh the difficulty of the movement with the intensity of the singing required of the performer. One also juggles finding movement that enhances the song, lyric, story, and experience of the character while avoiding stereotypes and clichés. The choreographer aims to create movement that is fresh, exciting, and narrative while still feeling natural and spontaneous, as if happening for the first time. The choreographer can often be extremely involved in musical staging and yet does not want their presence to be felt by the audience. All the movement should be generated from the character's objectives and the story.

Evaluate how motion affects the singer's voice and their ability to execute the song. Large cardiovascularly challenging movements make it difficult for the performer to sing, especially for a solo vocalist. Even with a large group singing, the dancing should not sacrifice the impact of the vocals. Some musical productions use pre-recorded vocal enhancements to round out the sound during high-intensity choreography. When a lead character has dance followed by a vocal solo, the choreographer can build in space between the end of the dancing and the start of the vocal for the performer to catch their breath. On the flip side, a choreographer can deeply examine how a performer sings and use it to coordinate movement. The singer's rhythms, breath patterns, and phrasing can all be inspiration for choreographic accents and dynamics.

The first step in creating movement for a song is to decide what purpose the movement is serving in relationship to the audience experience. This can dictate the amount of movement incorporated at the start of the number. For more realistic or naturalistic shows, a small amount of movement at the top allows for a gentler transition from scene into song. This leaves room for a gradual build of movement. When there is a large amount of movement at the top of a number, it can generate a jarring change for the audience. This can be extremely effective in moments of heightened theatricality displayed in shows such as *Urinetown*, where musical moments are meant to shock the audience. In musicals such as *Jersey Boys*, the amount of staging and movement is tied to whether the characters are singing in a scene (non-diegetic) or performing in concert (diegetic).

Especially when working with performers who have limited dance training or experience, a choreographer can approach staging from a motivation or idea rather than actual steps.

What are the character's feelings in this moment? What is the relationship between these characters? How can that be expressed through the body? How does the music inspire the body to move? What are the gestures, shapes, and images that convey that story or emotion in our daily life and how can that be heightened to match the stakes of the music? In this way, a choreographer can highlight the everyday movements of people and draw upon personal and cultural movement histories to tell the story.

For soloists, a choreographer can individualize movement to the performer by offering them freedom to explore and play with movement ideas in their songs and then refining the performer's instincts and impulses. The statement "I have a couple ideas, but I would love to see what you discover, and we can edit and tweak from there" gives performers license to create and collaborate while taking the onus of choreographing away from them. By stating that they have a game plan, the choreographer provides a safety net, making the performers feel safe to explore without pressure. Choreographers can also offer a motivation, objective, or imagery for the performer to physically interpret in their own way.

Each person has their own individual rhythms and flow of movement. This is what makes people unique and should be harnessed. However, it can also cause performers to fall into repetitive patterns that dilute moments of emphasis and accent. For example, some people tend to always gesture on the downbeat or use symmetrical gestures where both hands are doing the same thing. Rather than making a performer self-conscious by addressing these patterns, a choreographer can continue to stretch the performer's range by offering movements that break up the pattern. This could include gestures that occur on the offbeat or musical accent as well as exploring movement that contrasts the music.

Performers must energetically fill the size of the space, even if they are the only one onstage. Soloists can use several tools to take up more energetic space. This can be achieved by:

1 Becoming more grounded—this might include taking a wider base with the feet
2 Lifting energy toward the balcony
3 Having a sharper and more intense focus
4 Widening their stride.

In a traditional "song and dance" number, the movement becomes interwoven into the character's mode of expression. Song and dance share the responsibility of storytelling. These characters live in a world where dance is a natural form of communication. When staging a "song and dance" number, the choreographer can fill the notes at the end of phrases as well as musical interludes with movement that transports the character from one place to another both literally onstage and figuratively on their emotional journey.

Motion

Revisiting the concept that "the eye is the enemy of the ear," movement will take focus when done simultaneously with speech or song. When the movement enhances the words or lyrics, this becomes a symbiotic relationship and the physical motions aid in storytelling. However, when the movement is in disagreement with the lyrics or the subtext of the music, the meaning can become muddled. If the choreographer separates the movement and words, order dictates accent. Just like a great joke has a set-up and a punchline, when words and movement are placed side by side, the first is used to bring attention and emphasis to the second. For example, if a character sings a line and then jumps, the lyric becomes the set-up and the jump takes importance. In reverse, if the character jumps and then sings the line, the lyrics are now punctuated by the preceding action.

Contrast can also create accent. When movement or gestures are all the same, they lose their impact. However, an audience takes notice when they view one type of dynamic and suddenly they witness the complete opposite. These moments of contrast carry weight and importance. For example, if a character is gesturing in small contained motions and suddenly flings their arms in a large sweeping fashion, the significance of the large gesture is heightened by the proceeding contrast. Choreographers can use contrast as a tool when building up to a critical moment.

Dynamics, or the variations in *how* a movement is executed, are the tools used to communicate through the body. Dynamics live on a spectrum. Examples of dynamic spectrums include quick/slow, high/low, light/strong, big/small, smooth/sharp, and curved/angular. Dynamics can create texture, mood, intention, or emotion. Using a range of diverse dynamics can add color and definition to the movement. Waving to someone lightly and slowly has a much different meaning than waving to someone quickly and strongly. In musical staging, the size of the movement can depend on the situation of the characters and the style or concept of the production. As stakes heighten and energy builds, more tension is created and the body becomes more physically expressive. A character can increase the size of the movement by engaging more of the whole body rather than isolated parts. The size of the movement should also be in relationship to the size of the stage or playing space.

Repetition is a powerful tool when used properly. Moments of repetition should be chosen very deliberately. Repetition of a movement on a specific lyric can be used to make a point or emphasize that word or phrase. A movement or gesture can be developed into a signature move for that character. Repetition can also function much like reprise. A movement is established in the audience's mind and then brought back later to reveal new meaning.

When employing repetition, the choreographer wants the audience to become familiar with the movement and associate it with a lyric, character, event, or emotion without the audience getting ahead of the choreography—being able to predict what will happen next. For this reason, a choreographer might choose to repeat something three times and then find a variation on the fourth time. Or each time the repetition occurs, the choreographer might play with changing where in the body or how the movement happens. If reversing a movement to the other side, the choreographer can slightly alter the change of weight, timing, or rhythm of the step. The choreographer can play around with which characters execute the repeated movement as an idea starts to spread through the community. As long as the variation of the repeated movement stays true enough to the original for the audience to be able to recognize and track it, the choreographer can get creative.

Crosses

While singing, a character might be compelled to move to another location onstage. These crosses can add tension and excitement for both the performer and the audience. The quality, timing, and direction of the cross all give information about the emotional state and motivation of the character. Darting can be strong, severe, and unsettling, whereas weaving and gliding can feel more contemplative and romantic. A character that walks in a straight line is often perceived as having a certainty in intention. No matter the quality or speed of the cross, it is important that they feel purposeful and motivated by a character's objective (to attack, seek, discover, question, seduce, etc.) rather than a performer wandering around the stage.

Just as areas of the stage carry certain strengths and meanings, different crosses hold varying degrees of power. Horizontal crosses can be useful and compelling, but the flatness of a cross moving parallel with the proscenium arch can grow monotonous. Without the benefit of depth, a two-dimensional, horizontal cross starts to become aimless pacing if it is not used specifically and economically. Many believe that because Americans read from left to right, a cross from stage right to stage left is more expected and natural to an audience, while a cross from stage left to stage right can be surprising or unnerving and can convey tension or struggle.

Vertical crosses can be both strong and weak depending on the context. A performer walking downstage can become more powerful and vulnerable because they are getting larger and closer to the audience. However, at a glance, audience members can't accurately perceive depth. Therefore, a cross that creates depth alone on a proscenium stage, particularly one that is not raked (sloped on an upward angle away from the audience), is sometimes hard to read from the house (audience seating area).

On a proscenium stage, diagonals are the longest and strongest lines on which to cross. This is because the performer is traveling horizontally as well as vertically, creating length and depth at the same time. For Western audiences that read left to right, the cross from upstage right to downstage left is considered one of the strongest crosses onstage. Tying crosses into stage moods (see page 52), a character starting upstage right and traveling down left (the area of the unknown and adventure) may have a sense of purpose, need to escape, or optimistic excitement. In the reverse, a character starting upstage left and traveling down right (the area of home and the familiar) may be looking back on the past with a renewed wisdom or attempting to return to the comfort of home.

Traveling in a curved line can be both visually interesting and beneficial in helping performers "cheat out" to the audience. For example, if the performer in focus is traveling from downstage left to center center, they can curve their cross, passing through center left on the way. This allows them to travel upstage while keeping their face open to the audience. Using a curved line to transition from one location to another is also a tool in proscenium theatre to make the stage look bigger, because the performer must traverse more ground to reach their final destination.

Pay attention to which direction a performer is facing and how that affects sightlines for the audience. A character might cross down right as they remember their loved ones back home. However, once they arrive downstage right, if they keep facing that direction, they are cut off from the majority of the audience. Alternatively, if they arrive downstage right and then open up towards downstage center, technically the performer is visible by a larger majority of the audience, and story-wise the character is able to experience a moment and then share it with the world.

Along with the effectiveness of depth and width in crosses, also examine the influence of height. Level creates a whole new plane on which performers travel, opening up fresh movement possibilities. When level is added to a diagonal cross, the visual impact is again heightened. One thrilling example: a dancer starts upstage right, jumps in the air, lands rolling on the ground, and ends up downstage left.

Gestures

Gesture is a large part of our everyday non-verbal communication. Gestures can enhance the meaning of spoken words or change the meaning altogether when it is in contrast to the words. Many texts have been penned on the interpretation of body language. Although researchers have aimed to codify and define gestures, the explanation and significance of the movement is based on the individual, the societal and cultural views, and the context of the interaction.

Gesture is also a powerful tool onstage. Gestures are a part of theatrical events all over the world. In African and Native American cultures, gestures are embedded in rituals. Indian mudras, or symbolic hand gestures, are utilized extensively in religious contexts, yoga, and dance. Many theatrical forms throughout history and parts of the world, including theatre of Ancient Greece, Commedia dell'Arte, and the Vietnamese form of Tuong Singing, used specific formalized gestures to represent characters and emotions. In Kabuki, performers strike a *mie*, or pose, during moments of emotional intensity (JAC 2019). French singer and teacher François Delsarte categorized the way people physically responded to emotion through a series of gestures. Jacques Lecoq established his school L'École Internationale de Théâtre Jacques Lecoq to train performers in a body-centered approach to acting. Most acting methods have principles based around the use of gestures.

When gesture is paired with singing, it can externalize the intentions of the character and become the physical embodiment of the music and lyrics. The music can have an effect on the tempo of a gesture. A performer may be more natural with quicker gestures that match real life, or may become more lyrical by slowing the gesture down to match the flow of the orchestration. Staccato motions can accent while legato movements expand the time a character experiences that emotion. Using contrast, a mixture of both natural and lyrical, or staccato and legato gestures, can develop a dynamic story. A change from one speed to another can underline a significant moment. Often the size of the gesture correlates with the energetic build of the music. A gesture can utilize the whole body or simply the corner of the mouth. As the musical intensity increases, the size of the gesture equally grows. A gesture that starts with the hand might move to involve the full arm and then the entire torso.

Gesture in song can be realistic, expressive, or indicative. Realistic gestures mimic the natural movements of people in everyday life. Gestures such as waving, reaching, or hugging oneself can reveal information about a character's personality, environment, and intentions by how they are executed. When accompanying music or song, realistic gestures can be exaggerated in size based on the heightened world and style of the musical. A choreographer can take an everyday gesture and find ways to magnify and abstract it. Realistic gestures are affected by the presence or absence of other characters. A person acts differently when alone than when they know they are being seen by others. Smaller, realistic gestures are powerful in moments where the character is telling the audience, other characters, or themselves something of extreme importance.

Expressive gesture communicates a theme, idea, or emotion. In their book entitled *The Viewpoints Book: A Practical Guide to Viewpoints and Composition*, Anne Bogart and

Fig. 5.3 Gestures. Photo by Bret Brookshire.

Tina Landau describe this symbolic type of movement as "those that belong to the interior rather than the external world (of behavior); they express feeling or meaning which is not otherwise directly manifest" (2005: 49). These movements are not a part of a person's everyday physical vocabulary. Expressive gestures can illustrate an important lyric or express how a character is being affected. They embrace ideas such as peace, turmoil, love, loss, fear, isolation, and anticipation. When exploring expressive gestures, a choreographer can examine personalized relationships with these themes and meanings to avoid clichés.

Indicative gesture, or "indicating," is a method by which performers use movement to directly represent words. For example, a character points to their eyes, then their heart, and then to someone while singing "I love you," or places their arms in a circle overhead when singing about the sun. These gestures are similar to those associated with children's songs. In essence, the performer is "showing" the audience the lyrics. This type of movement is extremely stylized and is only successful when used sparingly and knowingly. Indicative gestures might be useful in a show like *You're a Good Man, Charlie Brown*, where all of the characters are cartoons, but would ring false in a more naturalistic musical such as *Dear Evan Hansen*.

Stillness

Stillness is an extremely compelling tool, especially when juxtaposed with robust kinetic energy. As a society, US Americans tend to stay very busy and sometimes do not always utilize the power of stillness. The lack of motion gives the audience time to examine the internal experience of the character. Stillness can demonstrate times of decision-making, indecision, and discovery.

Because movement will take precedence over lyrics, stillness is also valuable when the lyric is the most important thing, such as a patter song where the audience has to listen attentively to catch all of the words, rhymes, and puns. Stillness is also appropriate when the event of the song is too personal and intimate for gesture. When an entire song requires stillness, subtle changes in focus, breath, tension in the body, and even the alignment of the back can express the arc of the journey. When there is a song with a large amount of imagery, fantasies, or memories, the performer can imagine a movie reel out in front of them with the images or scenarios flashing before their eyes.

Stylization

Style is a set of parameters, characteristics, or conventions based on a genre, time period, culture, or artist. It can be outlined in the script or writing style, or dictated by a director and choreographer's concept. Stylization describes *how* those parameters are executed to color the movement. Style impacts how characters physically move throughout the world and the process of the choreographer in creating movement. Style can be expressed in the way performers carry their bodies, move, gesture, and interact with each other. Some musicals or approaches to a production require realistic movement and gestures while others are more "stylized" or heightened in physicality. For example, performers in a musical set in sixteenth-century France would move with a different amount of tension in the body than performers in a musical set in California in the 2000s. The movement in a musical written in the style of hyper-realism would differ in tone and feel from a musical farce. All forms of theatre have different styles that shift as cultural and popular attitudes evolve and artists experiment with new ways to tell stories.

Some styles in musical theatre were heavily influenced by European artistic movements such as realism, surrealism, avant-garde, expressionism, and romanticism as well as literary genres such as satire, parody, camp, and pastiche. Theatrical forms that hold a set of goals, principles, and techniques including melodrama, farce, musical comedy, vaudeville, music hall, extravaganza, burlesque, agitprop, epic theatre, physical theatre, and immersive theatre have also been reflected in musicals. Individual artists and writers can also dictate style. A musical written by Adam Guettel requires different vocal choices and interpretations than an Andrew Lloyd Webber mega-musical.

Expressionism is defined as "an artistic style in which the artist seeks to depict not objective reality but rather the subjective emotions and responses that objects and events arouse within a person" ("Expressionism" 2021). Many of the Golden Age musicals had an expressionist style. Musicals were addressing serious topics such as murder, domestic violence, and addiction in a way that highlighted the impact on the characters. While lyrics became more colloquial, the tone of productions were poetic in look and lyrical in physicality. Choreographers abstracted pedestrian gestures into larger expressive dance.

In the later part of the twentieth century, contemporary musical theatre turned toward realism. Realism is the idea of trying to objectively replicate real life onstage. However, realism is nearly impossible to achieve in a musical because the world is not realistic. Most people do not have arguments through song. They do not dance down the street while heading to work. "Musical theatre is, at its essence, built on the contrast between speaking and singing, between everyday speech and the poetry of lyrics, between walking and dancing" (Wolf 2011: 10). Therefore, it becomes necessary to implement heightened realism. In heightened realism, all of the feelings and behaviors of the characters originate from a realistic place, but the stakes become raised. The characters live in a musical world where singing and dancing are accepted as forms of communication and expression.

Some genres and styles of musicals are self-aware. The characters or performers are in on the joke and know that they are performing or making commentary. There is a tongue-and-cheek air to the material as well as the performance style. Many of these musicals break the imaginary fourth wall placed between the performers and the audience and have direct address to the audience. Satire, camp, and parody can all be self-aware. In these instances, a choreographer might choose to have the dancers "comment" on the movement vocally, physically, or through facial expressions. In these cases, the performers are knowingly demonstrating to the audience the act of "putting on" the character. This convention should be used sparingly and with deliberation. However, it is vital in a world of heightened realism that performers don't begin to veer into self-awareness. For example, the exuberance during a large tap number should feel like a heightened state of realistic joy rather than dancers thinking "look at my cheesy smile!"

Physical Comedy

Movement and dance can be used to increase the humor in a song or scene. In physical comedy, the picture or movement of the body and the facial expressions create a funny situation or reveal the inner thoughts of a character to the audience. Along with illustrating particularly witty lyrics, conventions of physical comedy that have been developed and refined throughout centuries can delight audiences and add an additional dimension to the comedy. Ideas of comedy in every culture and theatrical form throughout history can be mined for use in choreography. For example, a choreographer can study *lazzis* or "bits" from Commedia dell'Arte through vaudeville all the way to Looney Tunes. Pratfalls, sight gags, prop comedy, miming, slapstick, deadpanning, clowning, and pulling faces are all tropes, or "shtick" of physical comedy. A running gag is a comedic bit that is continually executed and expanded on throughout the musical.

Physical comedy can be derived not just from the what, but also the how. The execution of a movement can alter its meaning while amplifying the humor. When changing focus, a choreographer might give a performer a fast take (or double or triple take) that happens sharply and quickly, or a slow burn which occurs smoothly and slowly with maximum intensity. The comedy "rule of three" states that doing something three times is most effective and efficient in capturing the humor. A movement or gesture can also be turned comical through exaggeration or displacement of that movement to a different part of the body.

Timing and cleanliness are the keys to physical comedy. All bits must be carefully planned and rehearsed to extract maximum comedic effect. When the composition creates the humor, the comedy is dependent upon the angle from which it is viewed. This requires the choreographer to take note of the placement and direction of the physicality in relationship to the audience.

The Mini Build

A build is the continuous rise of stakes that contributes to the excitement, energy, and forward motion of a scene, song, or dance. While a sequence can have ebbs and flows in the pace, dynamics, and size, it should steadily drive toward the ultimate climax of the piece. Changes in the amount, size, speed, and placement of movement can all contribute to a build within the staging of a song. The following elements of musical staging can create mini build in a song:

1 Transitioning from the "me" verse to the "you" verse (see page 52) expanding the character's view to the outside world

2 Stillness to movement

3 Broad strokes to pixels: movement every 8 counts to movement every count

4 Changing location onstage to a more powerful place

5 Changing level

6 Increasing the amount, speed, or difficulty of movement

7 Shifting rhythms or accents

8 Adding the involvement of more characters.

Sample Staging Outline: Solo

This sample staging outline is based on the stage moods described on page 52. It is assumed that the stage is bare and does not take into account scenic design, which will have an impact on the location and size of the staging. This example uses the song "Memories of You," with music by Eubie Blake and lyrics by Andy Razaf. The song was featured in many musicals, including *Shuffle Along, or the Making of the Musical Sensation of 1921 and All That Followed*. Reprinted by permission of Hal Leonard LLC.

Chorus A1 ("Me" Chorus)
Waking skies at sunrise,   Center center
Every sunset too,
Seems to be bringing me
Memories of you.

Chorus A2 ("You" Chorus)
Here and there, everywhere,   Traveling downstage right, remembering
Scenes that we once knew,
And they all just recall   Turning focus to audience center
Memories of you.

Bridge B1
How I wish I could forget   Traveling downstage left
Those happy yesteryears
That have left a rosary of tears   Opening up to audience center

Chorus A3

Your face beams in my dreams   Moving with determination to center center
Spite of all I do!   by curving through left center
Everything seems to bring   Coming downstage center
Memories of you.

ACTIVITY NOTATING IN THE SCRIPT

In songs without major instrumental sections or dance breaks, musical staging can be notated directly into the script. Abbreviations such as DL (down left), US (upstage), and X (cross) create a shorthand. Differentiate between prescribed movement and prompting questions for the performers. As practice, choose a song with musical staging and map out the staging in the script. Consider where the characters are onstage, interactions with the design, and prompts to ask the performers that might lead to movement ideas, and steps.

1 Obtain the libretto pages for the song or print out the lyrics. Make sure it is single-sided. When bound or stapled, the lyrics appear on the right with a blank sheet to the left.

2 On the blank page, write any important information about the scene, the character's objective, the story, and practical needs of the number.

3 To the left of the lyrics in the margin, write any prompts for the performers that will prepare you to create movement together in the rehearsal room (such as "How does your character feel about that?").

4 To the right of the lyrics, write any specific movement, choreography, or blocking.

5 If a movement occurs on a designated lyric, circle the word and draw a line to the movement.

6 If there is an instrumental or dance break, write out the choreography to the far right and draw a bracket connecting it back to the script.

No matter how much a choreographer plans in pre-production, there is a required openness and willingness to change depending on the performers' interpretations, the progression of rehearsals, and the needs of the production. The version created initially will shift, change, and adapt. For this reason, update notes in the script so that there is a record of the most current version of the staging.

6   Production Numbers

Production numbers are large sequences that include a majority of the cast. They create energy, spectacle, and heightened emotions as solo and group singing evolve into dance. Many production numbers feature one or multiple dance breaks. These numbers occur during climactic moments in the musical. They can drive a story forward as characters take action or make discoveries. These numbers can physically embody the coming together or change in a community. They can inject entertainment, humor, joy, drama, excitement, and variation from individual or two-person scenes and songs.

Quite often production numbers are lengthy and therefore require a constant growth in stakes and forward motion in order to hold the audience's interest and attention. The creative team never wants the narrative momentum to stop, even in moments of energetic entertainment or levity. It is also undesirable to allow the audience to get ahead of the material, predicting what will happen next. It is a mistake to underestimate an audience. People go to the theatre to be moved, entertained, and challenged. Production numbers should be crafted with a build that serves the story and keeps audiences invested.

When devising a large production number, it is important to visualize the overall picture in addition to creating the details. Choreographers work in different ways, but I personally find it best to work from big to small. This ensures that the number tells the story, gives the audience the right information, and serves the musical as a whole. Spectacle both in design and performance is a prominent part of the art form and can be used to elicit excitement from the audience. However, impressive special effects or beautiful dancing can be perceived as hollow if it does not help support the story.

The first step in building a production number is to identify the context and function of the number within the show. Consult your movement arc (see page 33) and review answers to key questions about the number's story, concept, and purpose. Dance is an integral part of storytelling in musical theatre and often the physical events that take place are essential to the character's journey. If not specified in the script, the choreographer works in collaboration with the director (and writers on a new musical) to devise the action occurring in the dance breaks. Often in new works, the choreographer's ideas of movement narrative become part of the fabric of the show and are included in the final script.

To help define the movement story, consider the role of the ensemble in the production number (see Chapter 3). Are they individuals populating the world? Do they collectively represent a larger emotion or idea? Are they acting as tour guides or facilitators? This role can change throughout the production number. Understanding the purpose of the ensemble in each moment of the number helps the choreographer decide how to unearth and capitalize on the ensemble's power to direct audience focus and give clues on how to feel about or engage with the story. Then begin to assemble the build of the number. Break the piece down into sections by locating moments within the number where a shift occurs or something new happens. Laying out the progression and sequence of the number will ensure that the audience is following the plotline and that the energy continues to have a forward trajectory without dipping or lagging.

Once the choreographer has broken down the number into sections and established the build, the next step is to sculpt the stage pictures through formations and movement patterns. The stage configuration will largely dictate a choreographer's approach (see Chapter 8). Document the stage pictures and how performers transition from one place to the next taking into account elements of composition including emphasis, balance, level, width, depth, shape, contrast, spatial tension between performers, pattern, direction, placement, and unity. The choreographer can then track what the audience sees and confirm that the images onstage support the story and build.

The very last phase is the creation of the actual movement. This is not to say that a choreographer cannot begin a creative process through an exploration of movement. The discovery of a step might in fact be a choreographer's way into a sequence, a number, or even the physical approach to the entire musical. However, knowing the motivation and meaning of the dance will make the creation of movement infinitely easier and will imbibe the steps with specificity and purpose. It is through this work that choreography transcends from a string of generic, meaningless steps to powerful, organic, and expressive movement storytelling.

Sectioning the Number

When structuring the build of a production number, I find it useful to employ Stanislavski's units of action. Not only does this help narrow in on the story, but it also divides the number into bite-sized morsels. Once parceled out, the creation of a large number doesn't feel quite as daunting. In order to structure a build within a production number, break the number down into sections, or beats. According to Stanislavski, a beat is the smallest unit of action. Whenever there is a beat change, it is a clue that something new must happen onstage. A beat shift typically occurs when:

1 A character enters or exits

2 A character achieves, loses, or changes their objective (what they want)

3 A physical or psychological event changes the circumstances, environment, or actions of the characters (O'Brien 2011: 10).

This last factor can encompass a myriad of events. A physical event can range from small (two characters make first eye contact from across the room) to enormous (a volcano erupts). A psychological event prompts the characters to have a change in perspective. A character might make a discovery, receive new information, or change tactics to achieve their goal.

With a production number, one of the biggest clues for the location of beat shifts is the music. Robert Benedetti describes locating beats within a scene: "Each change in action, whether there is a change of objective or not, can be felt as a change in the rhythm of the scene" (2001: 101). This directly translates to musical changes in a song. A beat shift often happens at the beginning of a new verse, but can also be represented by changes in key, tempo, groove, melody, presence or absence of vocals, and a switch in character singing. Re-examine "Scoring the score" for the musical number (see page 49) and make any adjustments or additions to the sections. Then begin to examine not just *where* the music changes, but *why* the music changes. Any perceived transition in the music happens because the character or story advances. Label each new section in the score with a large letter for sequence and a description of the action that transpires.

Examine how the placement of the dance music impacts the flow and narrative of the number. Referring back to the roles of choreography discussed in Chapter 3, is the dance break infusing energy? Showing important action? Diving deeper into an emotion, theme, or idea? Creating tone and environment? Dance music can appear at the top, middle, or end of a number, or re-occur several times throughout. Each position requires a different approach by the choreographer on the intention, feel, and energy of the movement. Notice how vocals are juxtaposed with instrumental music. If there is a dance break that leads into another singing section, the choreographer must align the build of the dance to maintain the momentum.

How to Create a Build

A build is essential to propel the journey of the character. Over the course of the musical, there must be constant and evolving conflict that leads the characters to the ultimate climax and final resolution of the story. Without conflict the characters lack purpose and therefore the story lacks meaning. Within a production number, the build can advance the narrative or open up a deeper understanding of an event or emotion. A build happens when there is a continual rise in stakes. This is caused by an increase in elements including energy, tempo, tension, volume, intensity, size, and amount of movement. However, the increase of one element does not necessarily equal the increase in all elements. For example, a choreographer might increase tension and intensity by decreasing the number of people dancing from a large group to an isolated person. In these moments, the soloist should take up the same energetic space as the group that preceded them resulting in a forward momentum of energy and story. A build in a production number leads to a climax. This peak occurs toward the end of the number and could be the button itself. When a choreographer knows the destination, the road to get there becomes clear.

The build is also crucial in capturing the attention of the audience. There is a difference between offering the audience a moment of levity from high emotional intensity and having a drop in energy or stakes that causes the audience to tune out. A river might ebb, flow, weave, turn, widen, narrow, rush, trickle, deepen or shallow, but it is still constantly flowing in one direction. The goal is to keep the audience invested and engaged throughout the entire number as well as the length of the musical. Just as a musical and the performers must "earn" the transition from spoken word into song, the musical must also "earn" the transition from song into dance. Moments of sustained dance, such as a long dance break, encompass a pinnacle of emotional and physical expression. Without an effective lead in, the dance might feel false or jarring. Building into the dance also gives the performers an opportunity to gear up physically, mentally, and emotionally for the movement.

Types of Builds

There are endless ways to create a build to a production number. Each build is unique to the story of the musical and should reflect the emotional arc of the characters. Types of build moments that might occur throughout a production number include (but are not limited to):

1 *Soloist*: A single dancer.

2 *Duet*: Two dancers either dancing together or simultaneously but separately.

3 *Small group*: three to six dancers.

4 *Partnering*: Several couples socially dancing or partnering with lifts.

5 *Add-on*: The methodical and continual addition of dancers.

6 *Call and response*: This can be done between groups, individuals, or one person calling and the group responding.

7 *Contagion*: A movement that begins with one person or group and travels as each person or group starts after the one next to them. This creates a wave or ripple effect.

8 *Canon*: A movement or phrase that is executed by individuals or groups at different times. This can be accomplished with a staggered start or dancers starting together but at different points in the phrase.

9 *Challenge*: Two dancers or teams in competition.

10 *Clump or amoeba*: The clump can remain stationary, advance toward the audience, travel horizontally from one side of the stage to the other, or travel in a unique movement pattern. There can be one unified clump or several clumps (Figure 6.1).

Fig. 6.1 Clump. Photo by Bret Brookshire.

11 *Passes*: Dancers traveling across the stage (either individually or in a group) one after another. They can all travel the same path, or begin and end on different parts of the stage.

12 *Improvisational jam out*: All the dancers onstage improvising or having a large dance party.

13 *Freezes*: Alternating movement with freezing either in poses or in tableau.

14 *Slow motion*: Dancers slowing down or suspending time through the slow motion execution of the movement.

15 *Travel section*: Dancers moving in a specified pattern, such as a figure 8, throughout the section.

16 *Peel-off*: Dancers peeling off from a straight vertical line, or two vertical lines, in alternating directions.

17 *Horizontal or vertical lines*: Stationary or moving and passing in geometric patterns.

18 *Featured dancers*: This section highlights one or more virtuosic dancers. Other members of the cast can also be moving with coordinating gestures and movement.

19 *Specialty sections*: This section houses special skills including tumbling, tricks, jumps, aerial, and lifts.

20 *Circle moment*: A circle can be a coming together of a community, such as a ring shout, or a circle of social dancing, such as the waltz or polka. Circles can also symbolize traveling or a whirl of motion. Dancers can form one circle or multiple circles.

21 *Dancers as objects, events, ideas, concepts*: Dancers become the physical embodiment of objects (a car), an event (showing the memory of an earlier time), an idea (freedom), or concept (the main character's inner demons).

22 *Prop*: This section of choreography features interaction with and manipulation of a prop.

23 *Full group: individual movement*: Everyone is dancing but with different choreography. This creates a sense of organized chaos.

24 *Full group: unison/mirrored movement*: Everyone is dancing the same choreography. Also known as an all-skate (Figure 6.2).

As a choreographer constructs the layout and build of a large production number, they look for the build moment that most effectively physically expresses the meaning or action of each section. Take into account which characters and ensemble members are dancing and what it means as additional members of the community launch into or halt action. The order of the build and the transition from moment to moment is paramount. The transition of characters beginning in a circle and expanding into an all-skate reveals a different story than characters who are initially dancing an all-skate before being pulled together into a circle. The order has a direct effect on the build of energy as well as the interpretation of the narrative.

Groupings

The placement of people onstage and the architectural structure of those configurations impart information to the audience about the identity and experience of the characters. The

Fig. 6.2 Full group unison. Photo by Bret Brookshire.

response of the ensemble can also prompt the same response in the audience. In their book *Choreographing the Stage Musical*, Margot Sunderland and Ken Pickering describe the differences and advantages of naturalistic groupings versus formal groupings as summarized below (1989: 63). In naturalistic groupings, the performers are staggered into various sized groups throughout the stage. They are bundled together without a clear, identifiable shape. Each performer might have their own physical position, level (sitting, standing, leaning), and focus. The characters are individuals having their own unique experience and response to the events of the story. These types of formations mimic live crowds and gatherings.

Formal groupings are stylized with performers spaced into perceivable shapes, or formations, and frequently embody the same physical position, level, and focus. In these instances, the dancers share an identity (either an external or internal force directly impacting the main character) or an experience (everyone collectively feeling the same emotion or reaction to an event). Formal groupings do not typically occur spontaneously in life, but hold power onstage because they are quickly processed and interpreted by the viewer.

No matter whether the placement of performers is naturalistic or formal, the space between individuals or groups is vital to the visual significance of the image. Similar to the space between partners discussed on page 55, if groups are too close together, the audience is unable to distinguish between them. Inversely, if groups or individuals are spaced too far apart, the audience is unable to take in the entirety of the stage picture. A straight line when adopted precisely can persuade focus and wield power. However, during moments of observation onstage, performers have a tendency to unwittingly drift into straight lines. The flatness and unnaturalness of this formation should be avoided unless explicitly chosen by the director or choreographer.

Eliciting Applause

Typically, an audience applauds at the conclusion of a musical number. The creative team gives cues physically (big arm gesture), vocally (a strong cutoff), and technically (a light bump) that signals the end of the number and invites applause. At times, a director may not want applause after a number in order to keep momentum flowing. In these cases, the physical, vocal, or technical energy must continue so as to not create a break where audiences have time to respond. A creative team must be very deliberate in how they solicit audience interaction so as not to cause confusion. Previews are helpful in testing out the viewer's reactions to the production.

In exceptionally powerful moments, the audience might be compelled to applaud in the middle of a song or production number. Audience members become invested in watching characters struggle and succeed against all odds as well as witnessing the power and skill necessary for performers to execute a difficult song or dance. There are two types of moments in choreography that have a tendency to elicit applause. The first are those feats of seemingly superhuman ability. This includes impressive tricks, large quantities of turns, and daring lifts. The second type of moment is the convergence of a community becoming one. Dancers suddenly come together dancing one recognizable, unifying step. Most of the time this step is not particularly complicated, but rather one that requires a maximum amount of energy and synchronization. In tap dance, trenches are one of the easiest steps to execute and yet prompt the most applause when there are twenty dancers trenching in unison.

The most frequently applauded step is a kickline. It combines the elements of a community coming together while demonstrating incredible skill. A kickline can have its own mini build. For example, the kicks can start crossing over, then move to straight on, and finally to jump kicks. A kickline that starts at the back of the stage and travels forward adds to the intensity and impact as the performers advance on the audience. Theatre legend has it that sixteen kicks will result in the largest audience feedback with applause beginning around kick number eleven.

Viewer feedback is a valuable tool. Choreographers should be cognizant of how and when audiences react to a dance number. A climactic moment early on will cause a number to peak prematurely. If the audience seems conflicted on when to respond, the choreographer can experiment with ways to give clearer clues. If applause or laughter eclipse an important plot point or lyric, the choreographer must make adjustments to redirect the audience's focus.

Buttons

Composer, lyricist, and actor Lin-Manuel Miranda defined a button as "the bump at the end of a song that lets you know it's okay to applaud" (2018). A button usually includes a light cue, an orchestra bump, and a final movement of the performers. It is most successful when all the elements align. The two most difficult moments for a choreographer are determining how a number begins and how it finishes. The button is the last image that an audience sees. It can be a joyous celebration with all performers striking a large pose with expanded gestures, or it can be a devastating statement as a character suddenly collapses to the floor and is left alone in a dramatic pin spot. A powerful button can cause audiences to gasp, cry, shout, or erupt into applause.

Fig. 6.3 Button. Photo by Bret Brookshire.

The first question is whether the button will grow or pull down in size. In a button that grows, the lights get brighter, the orchestra hits a loud final blast, and the performers put an extra hit of force into the final pose (Figure 6.3). A button that pulls down in size must still continue to grow in energy or intensity. Dancers who are spread out around the stage might pull together for the last image of a tight, unified cluster. Even though the picture itself gets smaller, the characters gain more power as they connect. The most dramatic type of a pulled down button is a blackout on the final beat of the music.

When constructing the architecture of the button, a choreographer must take into consideration the placement of the performers. Are they spread out all over the stage? Are there any levels? Do performers end in the house? Are they isolated to one specific location? How does the final picture interact with the scenery? Then a choreographer must consider the physical architecture of the dancers. Is the focus out to the audience? To each other? Toward one centralized person? Is everyone in the same pose? Does the pose fan out from high to low (for example, performers upstage have their arms up while performers downstage have their arms down)? Is the picture symmetrical? Most critically, ask what the final image conveys to the audience. Once the choreographer has determined how a number ends, they can reflect backwards to assess how the journey begins.

Nuts and Bolts

Nuts and bolts are the practical tools used by choreographers to assemble a framework that houses the choreography. They help a choreographer balance an audience's inclination for order with the desire for compositional variety. They build upon human and societal understanding of pictures and movement structures to forward the narrative of the musical. These tools allow a choreographer to create emphasis onstage as well as explore three-dimensional stage images.

Focus

Manipulation of focus is the most important tool in a choreographer's toolbox. No matter the brilliance of the movement, if an audience does not know where to look, the story becomes muddled and the movement loses meaning. In film, the director picks and chooses what a viewer gets to see. With live theatre, a choreographer must intentionally guide the audience's attention. There are several ways to direct focus and create emphasis onstage:

1 *Color*: Colors can dictate focus with brightness, juxtaposition, or contrast. Color can make certain performers stand out while blending others together.

2 *Light*: The intensity of the light equals weight. The brightest area of the stage will pull the most focus.

3 *Level*: Level can include body position (lying down, sitting, standing, jumping) as well as scenic elements that contribute to the height of the performer (chair, stairs, platform). Typically, the performer with the highest level has the most compositional emphasis. The exception is when one person is in contrast (one person lying down while everyone else is standing on chairs). In this instance, the divergent person takes focus.

4 *Position on the stage*: Placement can create focus through strong stage areas (refer to stage moods on page 52), framing formations (a semicircle with one performer in center), or isolation with one person or group drastically separated from others onstage.

5 *Contrast*: Anything that is different will draw an audience's eye. Contrast in movement, dynamics, shape, and placement can highlight a performer.

6 *Movement versus stillness*: Generally, movement will always take focus unless everyone moving is contrasted with one person in stillness. When a specific movement needs emphasis, surrounding it with stillness can draw the audience's eye.

7 *Direction*: The directional facing of the performers will not only inform who the audience looks at, but also which part of the body becomes the focus.

8 *Focus of others*: The performers onstage can steer the audience's gaze based on where they look. They can send focus, or "pass the food," to other members of the company by throwing their attention in that direction. This can be accomplished all at once or the energy can be passed down the line from person to person or from one part of the stage to another.

Many production numbers begin with a soloist surrounded by other lead characters or members of the ensemble. In these instances, the choreographer aims to place the soloist in a position of emphasis where all audience members can view the singer and the soloist can interact with other performers without upstaging themselves. The physical response of the other people onstage offers the audience clues about the state of the soloist as well as the collective and individual attitudes of the community.

All of the above-mentioned techniques can be utilized to highlight the soloist. The soloist can be placed in a brightly colored costume, put in a spotlight, or staged on a higher level. A choreographer can create a frame by placing a soloist in a position of strength using the ensemble to direct the audience's attention by sending their focus to the singer. Some options include centering the soloist while the ensemble members surround (in a semicircle, a "V" formation, or a clump), or positioning the soloist downstage center while others onstage create formations behind. The soloist can contrast the ensemble by dancing different choreography or with a juxtaposition of movement and stillness. This last alternative may be achieved in two ways. The first is to have the lead remain still while the ensemble is active. The other is to leave the ensemble stationary while the soloist weaves around them.

Within its many uses, choreography can demonstrate the central action or create environment and texture surrounding the main characters and embodying the world of the piece. Dance that is the central action should be highlighted using focusing techniques. The surrounding movement becomes atmospheric and prompts the audience's emotional response or suggests how the characters are feeling.

Rules of emphasis will draw focus whether the choreographer intends them to or not. For instance, if the full stage is dancing in unison but one person is contrasting by dancing on the wrong foot, that person will "steal focus." During a group number, moments occur where the solo vocal jumps from person to person. Because movement draws attention, it is helpful for each singer to make a gesture when they begin singing that pulls the focus in their direction.

Direction and Level

The direction a person faces onstage has influence over their emphasis as well as the center of the audience focus. The person facing most downstage will take the most focus. As Tony Award winning director and choreographer Andy Blankenbuehler explains, "If I'm facing forward, the audience is going to look at my face. If I'm facing sideways, they're absorbing my body language and looking past me to the lead character, who's standing right there" (Cramer 2013: 37). Facing upstage can fade a character into the environment of the scene becoming a part of the subconscious feel of the moment rather than the conscious focal point of the event. In this case, the people facing upstage have an impact on the main character and also show the audience the impact of events on the community at large. When a performer faces upstage, they can also continue to narrate as if their shoulder blades were eyes. Finally, certain shapes are more impactful when viewed from a specific angle (Figure 6.4).

Play around with the direction a dancer faces during movement and what that communicates to the audience. What happens if a physical phrase is turned sideways? What happens if all dancers face different directions and then dance a phrase all facing the same way? How many ways can this choreography be viewed and how does that alter the meaning? Adjusting direction can add clarity of focus as well as complexity and build in the production number.

Level plays a critical role in manipulating focus onstage. The rule of thumb states that the person on the highest level will draw the most focus. For a number to build, there must be continuous forward motion. It is easy to perpetuate a build by finding more and more height within a production number. However, going from a high level to a lower level can cause a loss of energy. In this case, another type of increase is necessary to keep the energetic ball in the air.

Fig. 6.4 Direction. Photo by Bret Brookshire.

Repetition versus Variety

Just as reprise is a useful tool in familiarizing and recontextualizing the music for the audience, the ideas of theme and variation can be used in dance motifs to create a language for the audience to further understand the meaning of the movement. Repetition can be used to create a signature move for a lyric, song, or character. Movement motifs can remind audiences of important actions, themes, or ideas. These thematic movements might reappear throughout a song, or evolve over the course of the entire musical. The audience develops associations with the movement that can be used to reiterate an emotion, give a deeper look at the internal experiences of the characters, and offer a new perspective on events.

When establishing a movement motif, the choreographer wants to use body positions, movements, and gestures that are recognizable to enable audience recall later on. The first time the motif occurs, it should be highlighted and given focus. Allow the motif to imprint on the audience. Once it has been established, the motif will take on a different meaning each time it appears. This can be achieved by changing the story context in which the movement is performed or by morphing and evolving the motif as it is repeated. Variations of motifs can be achieved through changes in action, quality, space, and relationship (Smith-Autard 2010: 47). The motif can be executed by different characters, dancers can face different angles, the movement can alter in time and quality, or the steps can change. A choreographer must be intentional with repetition in order for it to be effective rather than predictable. A choreographer should also track the amount of time between motifs. If too much time passes before the reappearance of the motif, an audience might lose track thus diminishing the impact.

Over the course of a production number and subsequently an entire musical, a choreographer finds ways to create compositional variety. Continuously repeating a step or a formation will cause the audience to tune out. If equating special moments to a deck of cards, once the choreographer has spent a card, it is no longer available to them, unless it is going to become a running theme or gag. Variety in formations is crucial not only to the engagement of the audience, but also the progression of storytelling. Stage pictures and formations are extremely important communication tools. If a large production number remains in the same formation the entire time or if every number in a musical ends with a straight line, the characters are not advancing on their physical journey.

Formations constantly evolve to keep the routine visually stimulating. Variety can be accomplished both in transitioning to a new formation as well as establishing a movement pattern within the formation itself. In the proscenium, while change is important, it should not happen too quickly or there is no time for a formation to be established and its effect fully realized. During a number, there is a balance between allowing a picture or formation to register while still having enough variation to avoid monotony. These changes should occur during a beat or musical shift that is driven by the story.

As a choreographer devises steps for a group of dancers, the question of opposition is important to consider. Within the picture frame of the proscenium arch, choreographers often create variation by having dancers stage left of center perform the same movements as the dancers stage right of center, but in the opposite direction. If stage left reaches out with the left hand, stage right reaches out with the right hand. This opposition can create interesting compositions that breathe a new life into the dance steps.

Individual versus Unison

One way for a choreographer to create visual interest is to have each group or individual dance different movement. When there are many things going on at the same time, the audience member cannot take in every exact movement, but rather subconsciously absorbs a feel of the moment. Conversely, dancers all performing in unison signifies a group of individuals coming together to have a shared, collective experience, or the dancers all having the same identity representing one unified emotion, theme or idea. Unison versus individualized movement, paired with formations, movement style, facing, and lighting, can signify changes in the role of the ensemble over the course of a number.

When delineating the narrative of a number, look at the order and impact of unison versus individualized movement. Is it more powerful to transition from individual movement to unison movement or vice versa? Does the dance move from chaos to organization, or from a singular idea that branches out in different directions? Typically, the move from individualized movement to unison movement creates a more effective build because all the characters unite to overcome the obstacle. Consequently, many production numbers end with a unison all-skate. However, the opposite might be more appropriate and impactful for a specific moment.

Balance: Symmetrical versus Asymmetrical

A choreographer aims to create visual balance in stage pictures, where both sides of the stage or the pictures have equal weight. This weight can come in the form of people, set pieces, and amount of movement. Balance can be symmetrical or asymmetrical. With symmetrical balance, everything to the right of center is identical to everything left of center. Symmetry onstage communicates stability and security. Although at times this can be powerful and visually pleasing, if used too much, symmetrical balance can feel unrealistic and forced.

In asymmetrical balance, both sides of the stage are visually different but still balanced. For example, there might be a large clump of six dancers stage right and two clumps of three people stage left. Both sides of the stage have the same number of people but the formations are less predictable. Set pieces add to the visual balance. The main dancing might be occurring stage right with tables of observers placed stage left. A choreographer can also purposefully utilize an unbalanced stage picture to elicit a feeling of unease for the audience.

In order to establish balance, the center line of that balance must be determined. Most of the time the center line is center stage. However, if only part of the stage is being utilized, then the balance is based off of the center line of that performance area. A choreographer can also explore moving the center line of balance to take the characters off of their normal axis. Choreographer Merce Cunningham played with changing the center of focus. As Susan Cooper described in her book *Staging Dance*, "Merce Cunningham revolutionized the traditional notion that the centre of the action is in the centre of the stage. In his works, the centre of the action can be anywhere on the stage and, indeed, may have several centers focused simultaneously" (2016: 25)

Formations

Formations give a production number structure, visual aesthetics, and a progressive build as the transition from one formation to another signifies a change in character or story. Each new section should cue a formation change, although some sections can house multiple formations. When beginning a number, a choreographer can listen to the music on repeat and allow their mind to visualize the number as a whole. Movements, patterns, and formations often reveal themselves in these moments of open exploration.

After defining the sections of the build, the choreographer can start laying out the various formations. The choreographer should keep in mind what the narrative of the moment is and how a stage picture can aid in communicating that story. What formation best serves the build moment? An add-on can result in a straight line or a wedge. A canon might work best in staggered horizontal lines. The choreographer must determine where the formation is located onstage. Not all formations have to be based off of center or face downstage. Refer back to the stage moods on page 52. Who are these characters and what is their relationship with each other? Are they individuals having a collective experience or representative of one unified theme or idea? These questions will lead to a series of formations that enhance the production number. All of the formations discussed are based on a proscenium stage configuration. See Chapter 8 for adaptations to alternative stage configurations.

Lines

The straight line is a clean and ordered formation that can effectively captivate the audience's attention. They are ideal for a contagion or ripple movement as the audience can track the

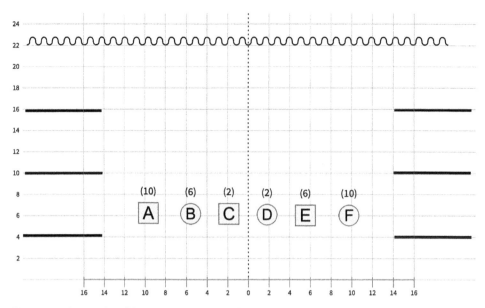

Fig. 6.5 Horizontal line. Diagram created using Stage Write.

pattern. A *horizontal line* is a strong formation because it follows the line of the proscenium arch. When the audience sees all the performers side-by-side, it makes a riveting visual (Figure 6.5). The horizontal line represents a unified wall, or a coming together. In these moments, there is a sameness of the characters or their intentions. A typical use of a horizontal line is the kickline. While a horizontal line is powerful, it can become flat and monotonous if overused or held for too long. Variation in the movement, level, or facing of the individuals within the line or the entire line itself can add complexity (Sunderland and Pickering 1989: 76).

The *vertical line* gives the choreographer the ability to manipulate focus. Because the audience cannot perceive depth, a large group of dancers can seemingly turn into one. This gives an anticipatory feeling that something is coming. A choreographer can reveal more dancers within the vertical line through a stacking of varying levels, dancers branching out in alternating directions, or arms splayed at different heights. This is a fun transitory formation but cannot be sustained for a long period of time. The *diagonal line* combines the power of both the vertical and the horizontal line. The compelling, asymmetrical formation has depth but the audience can still clearly see all of the performers. The focus of the dancers in the line can pass the emphasis to the person at the most downstage or upstage point of the line.

Multiple lines create a repetition of pattern, depth, and meaning. These formations bring together a full ensemble and are often used during the eleven o'clock moment of the number. *Multiple horizontal lines* can be executed with dancers stacked directly behind the initial person and therefore also create multiple vertical lines (Figure 6.6). This formation has structured unity that is reminiscent of the military or drill teams. *Multiple horizontal lines* can also be formed utilizing the windows between performers. Housed within staggered horizontal lines are also diagonal lines that can be employed in moments of canoned, rippled, or grouped choreography (Figure 6.7).

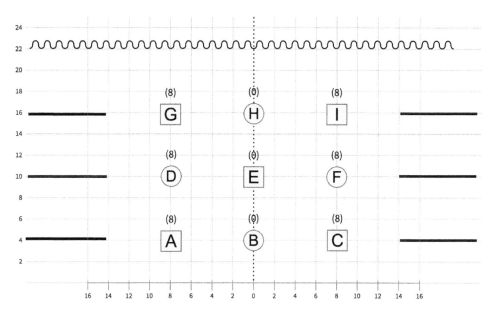

Fig. 6.6 Multiple lines stacked. Diagram created using Stage Write.

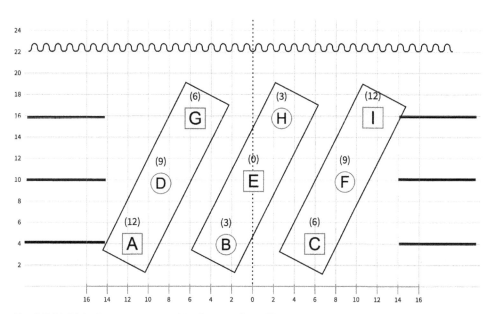

Fig. 6.7 Multiple lines staggered with diagonal lines. Diagram created using Stage Write.

The "V" formation is the coming together of two opposite diagonal lines. This stage picture offers depth, and the two lines automatically draw focus to the point, which may be the furthest downstage or the furthest upstage depending on what message the choreographer wishes to convey. When the point of the "V" formation is downstage, the image sends energy forward in a presentational manner aimed at the audience. This can be

Fig. 6.8 Wedge with point downstage. Photo by Bret Brookshire.

rotated so that the forward energy is directed toward another character or point of the stage. When the point of the "V" formation is upstage, the energy is pulled toward the person at the peak, drawing the audience in. A *wedge* is a filled in "V" formation, similar to the structure of bowling pins. The wedge combines the collective strength of a clump with the formal unity of straight lines. This formation is powerful and balanced (Figure 6.8). Additionally, in staging a trio, a triangular formation helps share the focus.

Curves

Curves can both offer a sense of flow due to the circular nature of the shape as well as conflict or tension as the curves of the formation juxtapose the walls of the space. A *circle* formation creates the feeling of movement. Circles are a large part of many cultures utilized in rituals, celebrations, and social dance. A circle formation can include one large circle, or several layered circles that can face different ways, cross in and out, or travel in opposite rotating directions. On a proscenium stage, circles can sometimes be a difficult formation because they intrinsically exclude the audience members, who are not part of the circle. When employed, the choreographer should track the audience's experience in relationship to the formation. The directional facing of the dancers in the circle will also dictate the impact on the characters and the audience. A *semicircle* has the community inclusiveness of a circle, but incorporates the audience as a part of the circle. This enables the viewers to be a part of the collective experience. Semicircles cast focus into the center and therefore are useful in framing a soloist or main character.

Other Formations

A *staggered* formation has performers spread out across the entire stage in windows with no structured lines or curves (Figure 6.9). This formation allows the dancers to take ownership of the space and have a united experience while retaining their individuality of character. While the formation has no apparent order, it must be repeatable. A choreographer can give performers marks based on a number line (see page 150), identifiable architectural elements, or floor spikes to ensure that the same formation is achieved every time.

A square, or box, is an extremely stylized formation that can be problematic for an audience to recognize unless the stage is raked or the audience has stadium seating that gives the viewer some overhead perspective. A choreographer should take into consideration the meaning of each line making up the box and how they interact with each other as well as their relationship to the center of the box. This formation can represent a confining space in which a character is trapped. The square can also highlight varying goals or opinions. It has four distinct lines rather than the smooth curve of a circle and demonstrates that the four sides have different points of view.

A *pose* or *stationary tableau* can tell an entire story through one picture. Compositional elements of emphasis, balance, level, width, depth, shape, contrast, spatial tension between performers, pattern, direction, placement, unity, color, and light give the audience a vast amount of information both consciously through overt images and subconsciously through the tone and mood of the tableau.

Placing performers in the house (where the audience is located) has both advantages and disadvantages. The audience becomes fellow members of the community. This interaction can thrill viewers as well as force them to ponder their own place in the world of the piece. With performers in the house, audience members can be inspired into action

Fig. 6.9 Staggered. Photo by Bret Brookshire.

such as clapping or even dancing along. However, if large numbers of performers onstage suddenly go into the house, the number of performers in view of the audience dissipates and can cause a loss of energy, affecting the upward mobility of the build. The choreographer can choose to start off with dancers in the house who then add to the stage and thereby increase the energy. If the dancers head into the house in the middle of a number, the choreographer should consider making adjustments to staging or technical elements onstage to compensate for the loss of dancers in the space.

Multiple Formations

As part of the build, a choreographer can divide a formation into multiple formations. When the choreography grows in complexity of form, multiple formations can enhance the visual interest as well as reinforce themes or ideas. A repetition of the same formation with the same choreography can magnify a statement and make it visible to all parts of the audience (Figure 6.10). Multiples of the same formation with canon choreography can illustrate how ideas are passed down. A repetition of the same formation with different or modified choreography demonstrates the individuality of each group's personality, experience, or perspective.

When a choreographer aims to combine two or more diverse formations, placement, size, and definition of those formations are paramount to the audience's perception. If two formations are too close together, it becomes difficult to discern them apart. An angular formation combined with a curved one can mute the impact of both formations or can be exploited to showcase tension and conflict.

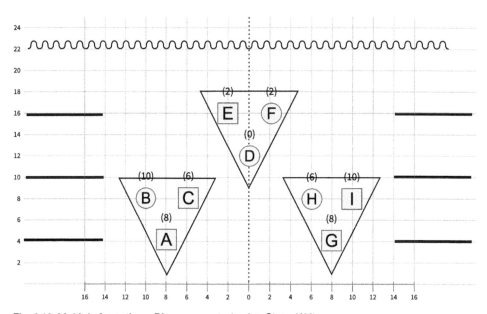

Fig. 6.10 Multiple formations. Diagram created using Stage Write.

Movement Patterns

Transitions and movement patterns are equally essential in telling a clear story. Within a choreographic routine, transitions are the movement from one composition to the next. Movement patterns are tracks dancers travel within a formation. Movement patterns should always be motivated by the intentions of the characters. Transitions best occur with a change in tactic or dramatic action, transforming choreography from a progression of random steps to narrative movement.

Any time a stage composition changes, find ways to transfer energy rather than losing momentum. Compelling transitions hand off the energetic baton from one formation to the next. When performers are leaving the stage, the choreographer must find a way to replace that energy loss with new entering performers, broader movement, or heightened intensity. As always, level adds a new dimension to movement patterns. Leaps, slides, and lifts can generate punctuation, surprise, and excitement adding to celebration or chaos. Let's study movement patterns through the lens of the formations previously discussed. All of the movement patterns are described for a proscenium stage. See Chapter 8 for adapting these patterns into another stage configuration.

Lines can be accompanied by many movement patterns. A single line can split into two lines with people alternating front and back. It can also split into multiple lines at varying depths. A choreographer can switch lines with a passthrough. Lines can box around each other by pairing dancers with a dancer in the line in front or behind them. During a peel-off, dancers in a vertical line peel off in alternating opposing directions (Figure 6.11).

When lines travel or pass through each other vertically, it gives the feel of a busy city. When lines travel or pass through each other horizontally, the movement resembles waves. A *tidal wave* occurs when horizontal lines continue to come downstage and split like the surf at the front of the stage as the lines behind move forward. Those dancers that split at the

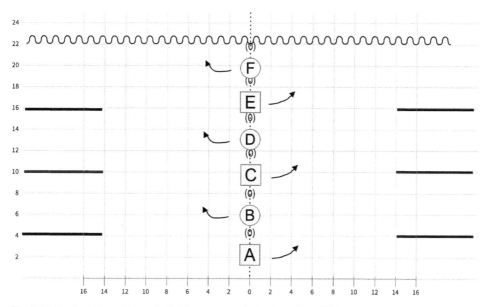

Fig. 6.11 Vertical line with peel-off. Diagram created using Stage Write.

front can cross around to the back making a new line so that the tidal wave continues unendingly. This pattern gives the audience the feeling of wearing 3D glasses as the formation seems to spill over at the front of the stage. It can demonstrate a charge or the feeling of being overwhelmed. At this point, the characters can no longer be passive.

A *pinwheel* adds motion to the straight line. A two-spoke pinwheel is one large line with half facing the front and half facing the back. A choreographer can also establish a four-spoke pinwheel for added flare and complexity. Pinwheels are presentational with an air of pageantry and can be useful in moments of extreme celebration. They can also be militaristic and demonstrate the marching or advancing of different factions.

A single line of dancers *snaking*, or traveling in curved patterns, can have several connotations based on the intent of the performers. It can be festive or conversely feel predatory. It can also show a passage of time. Dancers might even physically connect to each other by holding hands or holding onto the shoulders or waist of the dancer in front of them.

Theories of stage moods (see page 52) and crosses (see page 59) discussed for individuals also apply to groups. For example, a diagonal cross is powerful because it maximizes distance by combining the power of both depth and width. A *figure 8* can be built with two opposite diagonal lines that cross at center (making an X). Once dancers reach a downstage corner, they head upstage and feed back into the diagonal line. This pattern is very celebratory and the focus is continually passed to whomever is crossing at center.

Soul Train is named after the famous music and dance television program that ran for thirty-five years. In this movement pattern, dancers form two parallel vertical lines. Then the two dancers at the upstage most points of the line come into the center and are featured as they dance down the middle. Once finished, they rejoin the sidelines at the most downstage point. This progression is part of a social custom where the dancers in the middle get the focus while the others root them on.

A clump traveling together signifies a unified purpose. The clump can start upstage center and advance directly downstage with a clear intent. It can travel horizontally from stage right to stage left or vice versa. While in the clump, dancers can form an amoeba changing the size and the shape of the clump by varying body angles and positions.

The circle has been discussed as a formation, but dancers traveling around in a circle offer an entirely new level of visual interest. Multiple layered circles can travel in alternating directions (Figure 6.12). In European ballroom dances, a couple revolves around each other clockwise, but the entire circle formation rotates counterclockwise. Therefore, a circle traveling clockwise will give the feeling of stilted flow or unease. This can be used purposefully by the choreographer to portray a reversal of time or to make the audience feel unsettled.

Circular movement patterns can also give the sensation of dreamlike fantasy, magical transformations, or showmanship. A *Ziegfeld circle* is reminiscent of the flashy numbers in the Ziegfeld Follies revues. It occurs when dancers rotate facing out away from the circle. As the dancers move downstage, they take a low level and when they reach the upstage point, they take a high level. This pattern is typically amplified using arms or a prop such as feather fans (Figure 6.13). A *whirlpool* has a looser structure than a circle, but the performers are drawn into a spiraling movement pattern. The whirlpool can symbolize unstable chaos as energy is gathered at the center. The final resolve of a whirlpool leaves the world of the characters changed in some way.

Fig. 6.12 Multiple circles. Photo by Bret Brookshire.

Fig. 6.13 Ziegfeld circle. Photo by Bret Brookshire.

The *wave* is a contagion where performers, in a circular formation, execute a movement, such as raising their arms, in sequence, one after the other. For many, this pattern evokes images of sporting events, where a wave of people standing and lifting their arms travels around the sports arena. The wave pattern demonstrates people all being inspired at different times as the revelation is passed along. This movement progression is not as effective in a proscenium, because the audience is excluded from the shape. The upstage side of the circle is further away from the spectators, so the movement loses impact when it travels around. However, it can become quite powerful when executed in a semicircle as the contagion travels from one side of the stage to the other. The contagion can also start at center stage and radiate out.

Cinematic transitions take concepts of film and apply them to the stage. Each of these patterns is designed to trick the eye and leave the stage transformed after it occurs. In a *swipe*, dancers travel across the stage horizontally either from one side of the stage to the other or from opposite sides and crossing when they travel. The picture that they swipe in front of changes by the time the dancers leave. Characters or set pieces can be added or taken away. An *iris* is a closing in from all directions on an image. This can be accomplished with dancers as well as added technical elements to close in the image from the top.

In a *reveal*, the dancers magically make something or someone appear. Dancers are placed in a clump or formation in front of the final image and then pull away simultaneously or one at a time to reveal the composition behind them. *Fanning in* describes when all the dancers move toward a central location. This can be executed in lines, circles, or a full stage image. *Fanning out* occurs when all the dancers move away from a central location. Fanning in and out signifies a need for change. The ensemble comes together to make up their minds and get on the same page. Then they disperse back out to share the change with the rest of the community including the audience. This effect can also cover up a costume quick change as the character at center is unveiled in a new look.

An *advance* describes movement where dancers incrementally continue to get closer to one central location or character. This builds energy and excitement by putting pressure on the main character to take action. The advance can also be toward the audience, breaking the fourth wall and driving the viewers into participation with the musical event.

A single formation can grow or diminish over the course of a choreographic phrase. During an *add-on*, dancers are slowly added to a formation. This might start with a single dancer and end in a large formation such as a wedge. In a *dissolve*, dancers are slowly taken out of the formation as it gradually disperses.

Diagrams

As a choreographer structures a production number, diagrams of formations including movement patterns and transitions will give the choreographer a clear sense of the build as well as a playbook to reference when it comes time to stage the number with performers. There are several methods used to create diagrams both by hand as well as digitally.

If the design is already completed, it is helpful for the choreographer to use a pared-down overhead ground plan of the stage and the set to draw diagrams. This gives the choreographer a chance to see how formations are informed by the space. The simplified ground plan can be copied so that several appear on one page as the choreographer tracks through the number. A choreographer can request this outline from the set designer or stage manager. These mini ground plans can assist during all stages of pre-production (see Chapter 9) and rehearsals (see Chapter 11).

Each choreographer develops a diagram shorthand with an accompanying key. Performers or characters might be listed by their initials or color-coded. Groups might be distinguished by shape. Each diagram should be labeled with an uppercase letter corresponding with the section in the production number. If there are several formations within one section, the letter should be followed by a number (e.g., F3). Once the formation is drawn, arrows denote the movement pattern within the formation or the transition to the next formation. If the characters are color-coded, the arrows should also be drawn in the respective color. If there is a canon of movement or groups are doing different choreography, numbers can signify order or which choreographic sequence is being performed.

The choreographer can also use digital software, such as Stage Write, to create charts of formations and movement patterns. Stage Write was developed by Jeff Whiting and is used by many Broadway, regional, and international productions as well as training institutions. It allows the user to upload a ground plan or draw their own. From there the choreographer can track formations and movement patterns throughout the show. It also has the ability to store videos and has a digital script where cues and blocking can be notated.

When designing formations in pre-production, especially with a large ensemble, choreographers can also use three-dimensional options. Many choreographers will use buttons, pennies, figurines, or even color-coordinated paper stick figures to represent all the people onstage and explore formation options. Ideas for final formations can be documented with overhead photographs. A 3D model provided by the set designer helps the choreographer visualize how the formations translate to the stage.

ACTIVITY ANALYZING THE BUILD

A choreographer can gain an incredible amount of insight by analyzing the work of others and investigating what did or did not work. Find a video recording of a production number from a musical and complete the following:

1 Title of the Number:
2 Show:
3 Year:
4 Choreographer:
5 Briefly describe the story being told in the number.
6 List the steps of the build.
7 Was this build successful? Why or why not?
8 List the formations used.
9 What energy or story did the formations convey?
10 List the movement patterns.
11 Did the pace of changes in formation or movement pattern work? Why or why not?
12 What tools were used to direct focus?

ACTIVITY BUILDING THE BUILD

1 Choose a large production number (more than five people) from a musical. Start by scoring the score (see page 49). By the end of that exercise, the number will be divided into sections, or beats. The rest of this activity can be notated in the score, separately on paper, or in a digital document.

2 For each section list:
   a) Uppercase letter label.
   b) Description of action that transpires.
   c) Build moment (solo, all-skate, canon, partnering, challenge, improvisation, etc.)—a section may contain multiple build moments.
   d) Role of the ensemble.
   e) Draw a diagram of each formation present in that section. Every build moment should have an accompanying formation. Some build moments might have multiple formations.
   f) In the diagram for each formation, draw arrows that illustrate any movement within the formation or transitions to the next formation.

3 EXAMPLE:
   a) Section D.
   b) Our protagonist is struggling to continue forward as the naysaying voices in his mind and his own self-doubt start to pull him back.
   c) Down the aisle—soloist heading downstage with ensemble alternating crossing as he passes.
   d) Ensemble represents the voices in his mind.

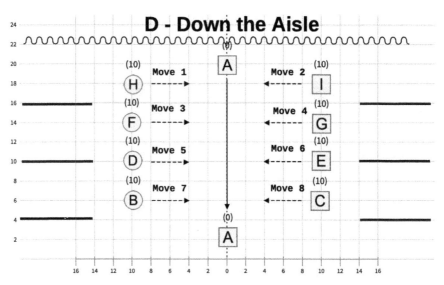

Fig. 6.14 Building the build example. Diagram created using Stage Write.

7 Creating the Steps

Many people believe that the job of a choreographer is simply making up steps. However, the concept of the creation of movement in this text isn't addressed until Chapter 7, and is only one out of thirteen chapters. Although the responsibilities and work of a choreographer are so much more extensive than the decision of arm placement, the actual movement is the main essence of the choreography. It is the language through which the choreographer communicates to the audience.

This book does not pretend to be the ultimate text on how movement is created. Entire books have been written on creativity as well as the act of developing choreography in various contexts by diverse artists. The goal is to take a look at several different approaches to the making of movement through the lens of musical theatre in the hope of adding tools to a choreographer's toolbox that can be used or thrown out at their discretion. You can refer to Chapter 9 for additional insight into the pre-production process. Whatever one's method, within the framework of musical theatre, the movement becomes an integral part of the storytelling. Because dance is the most heightened element used in the medium, it becomes the emotional truth of a piece. In addition, the relationship between the movement and the music contributes to the cohesion and meaning of the musical.

Process

Every choreographer has their own process. Some choreographers are inspired by the rhythmic and melodic elements of the music while others first latch onto the energy, shape, and dynamic of the driving emotion. Different cultures approach the creation of movement from different vantage points. As described by Nyama McCarthy-Brown, "Within an Africanist context, improvisation is a communal experience wherein lines between performer and audience are explicitly blurred for the enjoyment of the community. Movement, even when being improvised, is shared and developed as an interactive device. This is in contrast to a Western approach to improvisation that focuses on the movement invention of an individual and encourages an introspective physical experience" (2017: 97).

Creativity is an elusive friend. Often in commercial theatre the creative team is working on tight timelines. However, the creative process cannot always be rushed. This means a choreographer must be disciplined in leaving time for movement development. On the other hand, high stakes of limited time can spark incredible imagination in the moment. Therefore, in creativity exists the dichotomy between structure and openness to play. One must be willing to take big risks while also willing to change and adapt on the spot. In pre-production, a choreographer must not be too quick to focus on the final product. Many times, the first idea sits at surface level and can lead to clichéd movement. A choreographer needs to be comfortable exploring messy and potentially terrible ideas. Aim big and be willing to fail in order to see how a moment can work. If the choreographer never explores what it could be, then they will never find what it should be. Sometimes this entails holding space for several ideas and playing them out until the right one reveals itself. Settle for nothing less than the movement that moves people. Creation is also rarely a solo act. When a choreographer is receptive to other people's visions, worlds, ideas, and movement truths, it allows the movement to become rich and vibrant. Inspiration can come from deep discussions and explorations with members of the creative team, associates, and cast.

The Six Questions of Dance

As the choreography begins to take shape, an examination of the six questions of dance will ensure that the movement is telling a story, creating character, and expressing emotion. These inquiries are built around the work of Doris Humphrey, who in her seminal text *The Art of Making Dances*, broke down the ingredients of choreography into design, dynamics, rhythm, and motivation (1987: 46). These six questions are derived from those ingredients and give choreographers a place to begin developing the movement and return to when hitting roadblocks.

1 *What*: What the dancer is actually doing. This includes the design of the body. A choreographer should consider the line and shape of the movement and what that expresses. Is the design linear and angular or curved and circular? How does one shape flow into the next?

2 *Who*: What character or group of people is executing the movement? How does movement manifest in their unique body? What event or emotion are they experiencing? What is their attitude toward that event or emotion? What is their relationship to each other?

3 *Where*: The placement of the movement in space. Where on the stage or in the performance space does the movement occur? Consider what the direction and level of the movement communicates.

4 *When*: The rhythm of the movement. Take into account the accents or the syncopation of the movement in relationship to the music.

5 *Why*: The reason behind the movement. Action requires motivation to convey meaning.

6 *How*: The dynamics of the movement (see page 59). These dynamics create the link between the *what* (action) and the *why* (motivation).

Intention

Questions raised in Chapter 3 about the narrative of the movement and the function of the choreography must be understood on a deep, fundamental level as the physical manifestation takes form. In the beginning, these questions are raised in the macro sense about entire numbers. But as the choreographer works their way through a number, these questions must be asked about every moment — every move. The function of the choreography can shift over the course of the number or occur simultaneously with different groups of dancers. A character might be dancing their literal action and then turn to express what is actually going on inside their head. Although the movement's relationship to the music, lyrics, and stage design is essential, the choreography should be able to convey the story even when all of those pieces are removed and the dancing is left to stand on its own.

Choreography designed to be naturalistic will differ greatly from presentational choreography. The basis of naturalistic movement is typically derived from abstraction or augmentation of pedestrian movement while presentational dancing is typically more centered in traditional steps of a dance genre. Presentational choreography often displays moments of unison dancing and precise, linear formations, while naturalistic choreography places dancers in more realistic groupings. Again, no matter the intention of the choreography, it must serve the greater story at large. If rooted in truth, movement can be intensified to become a flashy and thrilling spectacle while still having meaning.

Style

Style is not concrete steps, but rather a color through which all movement is filtered. Style describes attributes such as lines, shapes, patterns, placement, tension, tempo, dynamics, movement qualities, carriage, size, rhythms, and devices that are consistent throughout a dance or an entire show. The style creates a framework that holds all of the movement ideas.

Dance genres have stylistic and technical elements associated with the movement. Dancers performing hip hop, jazz, ballet, flamenco, Bharatanatyam, salsa, Irish step dance, or danza will all embody attributes idiosyncratic to that form of dance. Some choreographers gravitate toward specific movement qualities that seep into all of their work. Movement style can also be dictated by the style of the music. Time signatures, keys, rhythms, tempos, accents, and articulations all impact the correlating movement.

While many codified dance forms dictate style, the reverse can also be true. Guidelines of a style can dictate the movement. A choreographer can take the dynamics of a style and apply it to everyday movements. This elevates simplistic actions to stylized dance. If looking to generate cohesion throughout a number or a musical, the rules of style (or styles) should remain consistent. If a rule is broken, it should be intentional and for a meaningful purpose. Otherwise, the audience will be taken out of the world of the show. If the rules are established right at the beginning of the number or musical, the audience becomes familiar with the language spoken and knows how to translate the choreography.

Economy

Economy in the movement as well as the entire storytelling process is crucial to retaining audience attention. You never want the audience to get ahead of you. If a statement can be made with one word or motion, it does not need an entire number. The act of editing is essential, although it shouldn't happen too early in the creative development. A choreographer must be willing to experiment in order to find the most satisfying result. As the show is reaching full fruition in rehearsals, consider trimming anything that stops the forward motion of the narrative. This might require a choreographer to "kill dreams," or let go of things that are personally significant but that are not working. A step might be thrilling to watch or hold sentimental value, but if it does not continue the storytelling and serve the script then it must be changed or cut.

The length of a dance sequence can have a direct impact on its effectiveness. Audiences make connections quickly. Choreographers must weigh how much information is truly necessary in order to produce the desired story or audience response. This requires trust that the audience does not need to be spoon fed every detail. At times one can present the audience with morsels of truth and leave them to arrive at their own conclusions. A choreographer need only be truthful to the story and emotion of the moment rather than try to indicate to the audience. Conversely, a choreographer's goal may be to invite the audience to sit in an experience longer than they would make room for in their normal lives. Stay ahead of the audience by not directly repeating a step multiple times unless the repetition is for a specific purpose or building up to something. Work to discover slight variations, canons, or evolutions of the movement.

Within the movement arc of the entire show, a choreographer does not want to peak too early. If they give the audience all of the movement ideas, conventions, tricks, and metaphors in the beginning, they have no more cards to play. A choreographer can pique the audience's interest while leaving room for the dance to bloom and develop over the course of the performance. Refer back to your movement arc (see page 33) to track the movement trajectory.

Creation

For any creative act, starting is the hardest part. No matter how much research, planning, and charting is accomplished, at some point thought must be put into action. This might require forcing oneself to hunker down in a dance space for a set amount of time, even if literally just sitting. One may end up with a single step to show for the time. True creation requires the patience to hold space for unanswered questions and the willingness to fail forward. Every possibility creates an avenue to explore. It can be an emotionally and mentally fatiguing process, so choreographers must continue to find ways to fuel their energy with projects that fulfill them as well as rest time to allow ideas to marinate. Asking questions is more valuable than trying to impose answers. Rather than attempting to replicate or rearrange something that has already been done, a choreographer can use their individual movement truths to advance the art form forward. Research, abstraction, physical representation, dance journaling, movement prompts, efforts, objectives, zones, and centers are just a few paths choreographers can take toward creating original movement.

Research

Research (see Chapter 2) becomes the contextual background for the work of developing steps. Movement true to the time period, location, culture, and characters of a musical create authenticity and establish the world of the piece. The audience might not directly track the research but rather sense it in the energetic accuracy, depth of character, and subtle detail in the movement. The movement will contain a wider color palate if the choreographer does not just employ standardized steps. Dig deeper into the movement and dance steps of the communities by finding videos of non-professional dancers and visiting locations to soak up the culture. Additionally, instead of applying research at face value, one can examine the elements and dynamics that make the referenced work exciting. A choreographer working on a musical set in the 1970s can survey the stylistic attributes of dances such as the boogaloo, voguing, and the hustle and apply them to original steps. Choreographers can use their character analyses to decipher how each character might interpret the same movement in different ways. Find connections between the dances of then and current movement vocabulary. In this way, a musical can have the tone of the period while employing a fresh and modern vocabulary. When describing his process of creating a movement vernacular for *Shuffle Along: The Making of the Musical Sensation of 1921 and All That Followed*, choreographer Savion Glover explained, "It's adding the steps and style of the past to the rhythms and sounds of today. It's performing an old-school step with a new-school style—or maybe you take a step from today and execute it in a style from the past" (Green 2016).

Choreographers can also mine their research of other visual mediums and investigate how it can be translated to the stage. What is it about that artwork that connects to the piece? What about it perfectly articulates the feeling and poignancy of the moment? Is it the composition? The color? The tone? The angle? Once a choreographer understands why they are inspired by something, they can apply it to their own art through the lens of their personal choreographic voice.

Anachronism is an "error in chronology" (Merriam-Webster.com Dictionary 2021). If a musical is set in Victorian England and all of the movement is based in historical dance forms such as the Viennese waltz and tango, a contemporary step will feel out of place. However, if the choreographer establishes in the first dance steps of a musical that although the show takes place in the 1850s, all of the movement will be stylistically modern contemporary dance, the audience will accept the convention and start to look for connections between those two time periods. This decision is most impactful when the anachronistic movement style highlights an important aspect of the story or a connection between then and now. Anachronism can also be used as a tool to bring the audience's attention to a character or event that conflicts with or is otherworldly from the ordinary world of the musical.

An artist will know that they have done extensive research when they no longer have to think about it. They have absorbed not just the information, but the full scope of the world they are preparing to inhabit. The research is a great place to return when a choreographer hits a roadblock. At some point, however, the choreographer must step away from the research and trust that it will infuse into the work.

Abstraction

Abstraction is taking a literal action and reinterpreting it through modification. Abstraction is critical to step away from indicating (gestures directly representing speech) and transforming ordinary movement tasks into expressive dance. "A dance that is an abstraction brings forth the essence of the original inspiration. It contains a semblance of reality that we can identify but cannot put into words" (Minton 2007: 87). Through abstraction and embracing the unique truths of specific characters, choreographers can heighten pedestrian movement while avoiding generalized clichés. The degree of abstraction impacts the audience's perception and understanding. When abstracting movement, starting with a basis in the underlying literal or behavioral movement and gradually increasing the level of abstraction will help the audience track the meaning of the movement. "There is no time to delve into depths to find hidden resemblances to the natural, these should appear easily and very quickly" (Smith-Autard 2010: 34). However, if the abstracted movement is more environmental and not part of the main action, then even by stepping far away from the literal form early on, the audience will sense the overall tone of the movement without the direct association to its origins.

The foundation of the abstracted movement can be based on personal movement histories. How a person walks, cooks dinner, puts on clothes, writes a letter, and gestures while speaking can all be choreographic fodder. It can also be structured around recognizable human reactions: shivering when cold, impatiently tapping a foot, or gasping when frightened. Abstraction can also be applied to group movements: the jostle of people on a subway car, the hustle of people walking down a city street at rush hour, or the beautifully artistic patterns of sports players moving around a field.

The most common form of abstraction is to take an ordinary movement and exaggerate or heighten it. This is appropriate to the art form of musical theatre since musicals already take place in a heightened reality. Other alterations to the movement include, "changing the shape in space, performing with different body parts, backwards or upside down, larger or smaller, slower or faster, on a different level, in a different direction or a different pathway, [and] changing dynamic qualities" (Sunderland and Pickering 1989: 28–29).

Physical Representation

With physical representation, dance symbolizes a larger meaning. Dance can illustrate the way the breeze blows through the trees. The movement can express the emotion of a character, reproduce an abstract version of an important event, or embody an obstacle such as the pressure of society. Dance can personify the subconscious desires or the inner dialogue of a character. Dance can become a physical actualization of the lyrics. Through physical representation, a choreographer can also begin to build any movement motifs (see page 77) that will be reintroduced throughout the number or show.

There are countless ways to physically suggest an idea. Experiment with shapes and dynamics that embody the lyrics or larger ideas within the context of the number. Delve into personal connections with the themes, emotions, or ideas and individual movement truths to break out of generalizations. Physical representation becomes less about the performer as a character and more about the body as a mode of expression so the choreographer can manipulate the direction and angle of the dancer.

Dance Journaling

Dance journaling is the act of improvisation, or freestyling. It is the body's stream of consciousness. Dance journaling allows the choreographer to tap into their physical impulses without the constraints of a desired outcome or the pressures of an audience. It can free up choreographers to get out of their analytical head and begin to trust their movement instincts. One can use the music of the musical or any soundtrack that conveys the idea, emotion, rhythm, or message of the moment they are developing. One of the best ways to utilize dance journaling as a choreographic tool is to film the improvisation session and then view the video for steps or sequences that are particularly stimulating.

Sometimes during improvisation, dancers begin to fall into comfortable patterns, repeating the same movements or employing only one dynamic quality. Creativity lies within limitations. When every option is a possibility, it becomes difficult to choose a path. However, if a dancer is given the limitation of telling the story only using their fingers, they can discover an infinite number of ways to articulate with their hands. When faced with an improvisational rut, limitation exercises can help break out of habitual movement patterns. These exercises can include movement initiated from one part of the body (movement initiated from the chin), traveling along a specific plane (movement that travels forward versus backward), or an objective with an obstacle (trying to jump into the air but weighed down). A choreographer can also experiment with the physical manifestation of an image (a marionette puppet with strings on the wrists and knees) or embodying the physical essence of an animal (a cheetah versus a sloth). These exercises will open up a new range of physical ideas that are still true to the choreographer's original movement quality.

Movement Prompts

Movement prompts enable the choreographer to collaborate with the performers to find the movement organically in the rehearsal room. While this process can be very rewarding, it also requires more time to delve into the movement as a group. The choreographer must take that into account when scheduling rehearsals and use this process strategically and economically based on the amount of rehearsal time allotted to a production.

Structured exercises lead the performers in coming up with physical material. From there, the choreographer transforms into a curator by observing patterns and pulling out pictures, movements, or sequences that speak to the moment. When deciding on a movement prompt, take into account the story or character experience being portrayed as well as the performers executing the movement prompt. All dancers work differently and have unique movement qualities and instincts that can be further mined through the right movement prompt. Imagery of motion frees the artist to explore their own personal interpretation. For example, a choreographer might investigate a character's inner turmoil by instructing the performers to try and hold still while a tornado is swirling inside of them. The choreographer can also assign a prescribed sequence such as "advance, twirl, leap, fall, recover, reach" that dancers can physically manifest in their own way.

Efforts

Rudolf Laban was a pioneer in modern dance, choreography, movement analysis, and research. Laban believed that a person's inner attitude was directly linked to their movement: "The source whence perfection and final mastery of movement must flow is the understanding of that part of the inner life of man where movement and action originate" (Laban and Ullman 2011: v). An examination of Laban's theories can present an avenue for choreographers to create story and character-based movement. This book presents a brief overview of the idea of efforts. Many texts are available on Laban's methods and how they can be put into practice.

One of Laban's principal theories is the concept of "efforts." An *effort* is the quality, or dynamics, of a movement during action. It describes the feel of the movement both for the person executing the movement as well as people observing the movement. The effort of a movement communicates *how* an action is executed. The same step performed with a different effort will change the character intention as well as the audience's interpretation of meaning. "Our choice of the type of muscular energy, or from now on EFFORT, which determines how we carry out an action, is the result of previously experienced inner impulses. Coupled with our chosen spatial direction it produces a definitive expressive movement quality" (Newlove 2001: 13). In the book *Laban's Efforts in Action* by Vanessa Ewan and Kate Sagovsky, the concept of efforts is compared to how people perceive color. Efforts, like color, add a specific quality to its subject. They can appear separately or be skillfully woven together (2019: 9–10).

Laban observed three motion factors: weight, time, and space. Each of these factors can be measured on a continuum between two opposing elements (Newlove 2001: 75). Weight ranges from strong to light. Time ranges from sudden to sustained. Space ranges from direct to indirect (flexible). The various combinations of the motion factors produce the eight basic efforts shown in Table 7.1.

Efforts help the choreographer and performer create three-dimensional characters onstage. When experimenting with the efforts, one should refer to the characteristic factors. While the names of the efforts are useful, they also come with certain movement connotations when in reality these efforts can be performed with any part of the body. The effort describes the *dynamics* of the movement rather than the movement itself. As a tool to generate movement ideas, a choreographer can first experiment with the effort that most emulates the intention of the character and the feel of the music. Then the choreographer can make new discoveries by applying an opposite effort to the same movement. One can even pull apart different musical elements: what effort are the drums versus the strings? The underscoring versus the lyrics?

Table 7.1 Laban's eight basic efforts

Effort	Weight	Time	Space
Thrust	Strong	Sudden	Direct
Slash	Strong	Sudden	Indirect
Press	Strong	Sustained	Direct
Wring	Strong	Sustained	Indirect
Dab	Light	Sudden	Direct
Flick	Light	Sudden	Indirect
Glide	Light	Sustained	Direct
Float	Light	Sustained	Indirect

In addition to the effort of a movement, take into account the *flow*. Flow is the continuation of movement. It speaks to the tension and order of transfer from moment to moment. Flow can be free or bound. This concept can be articulated in a multitude of ways. Laban describes it in terms of outward versus inward initiation: "Movements originating in the trunk, the centre of the body, and then flowing gradually out toward the extremities of the arms and legs are in general more freely flowing than those in which the centre of the body remains motionless when the limbs begin to move" (Laban and Ullman 2011: 18). Jean Newlove outlines it as: "Flow is considered to be bound when an action can be stopped at any given moment . . . Flow can be considered to be free when it is difficult to stop suddenly" (2001: 48). Free movement has an absence of tension while bound movement is characterized by resistance in the body. Think of free movement like a child skipping through a field of flowers while bound movement might feel like swimming through peanut butter. When stakes or intensity are raised, the body requires more sustained resistance to communicate the gravitas of the situation.

Flow can also be simultaneous, where the whole body is moving at once, or successive, where the movement travels from one part of the body to another. Simultaneous and successive movement only describes the path of the movement transition, not the quality. Both pathways can be smooth and continuous or jerky and interrupted (Newlove 2001: 46). Finally, the intention and feel of the movement can be affected by the planes on which we travel. These planes include forward versus backward, high versus low, inward versus outward, and the diagonals created by combining these planes. For example, a movement traveling forward can feel like an attack while the same movement traveling backward can be perceived as a retreat.

Objectives

The principles of objectives, tactics, and obstacles can all provide choreographers with movement ideas. All characters have an *objective*, or something they want from someone else under the given circumstances of the musical. Tactics are the means by which the character attempts to achieve that objective. When one tactic fails, the character must attempt a new one. These tactics can be described using action verbs such as: to intimidate, to befriend, to soothe, to entertain, to manipulate, to charm, to threaten, or to provoke. The book *Actions: The Actor's Thesaurus* (2004) by Marina Caldarone and Maggie Lloyd-Williams is one of several resources that offers a wide range of action verbs. Obstacles are physical and psychological roadblocks that get in the characters' way of achieving their objectives.

Choreographers can use action verbs as inspiration for movement. They can explore how a character would physically actualize the verb. This is dependent on the characteristics, manner, temperament, and tendencies of the character. Rather than finding a stereotypical way to seduce, the choreographer can determine how that specific character in those circumstances would carry out the action of seduction.

Zones and Centers

One of François Delsarte's principles divides the body into three zones. The head is the mental, intellectual zone. The upper torso, or heart, is the emotional, moral, spiritual zone. Some practitioners connect the arms to this zone. The lower torso, or gut, is the vital, physical zone (Shawn 1963: 32). Knowing which zone a character is functioning from can provide the initiation point of movement and a place to begin exploring choreographic ideas.

Michael Chekhov was an actor and director who developed his own acting technique that stressed the imagination and a physical embodiment of the character. Chekhov believed in the connection between the physical and psychological. He described his concept of imaginary centers as such: "Imagine that within your chest there is a *center* from which flows the actual impulses for all your movements. Think of this imaginary center as a source of inner activity and *power* within your body" (Chekhov 2002: 7). This imaginary center can move and emanate from any part of the body depending on the character. It can also change in quality. Imagine how a character moves differently if their imaginary center is a large, soft, warm center at the back of the knees versus a hard, small center at the tip of the nose (Chekhov 2002: 81). A choreographer can physicalize the imaginary center of the movement as a launching point for choreographic inspiration. As the event or emotion intensifies, the movement can continue to expand outward.

Fundamentals

A return back to basics gives choreographers new perspectives on movement that can be incorporated into choreography.

Initiation and Force

Based on the motivation, the physical initiation point of movement changes the execution. For example, a flick initiated from the wrist has a different tone and quality than a flick initiated from the shoulder. Once movement is initiated, it can retract back toward the initiation point, continue to grow, or hit and hold to establish a picture. All three options say something about the character's frame of mind and their approach to the situation.

As a rule of thumb, choreography that begins with the upstage foot or arm opens up the movement toward the audience. Dancers entering from stage right typically start to move with their left foot and vice versa. Gesturing or posing with the upstage arm high and the downstage arm low ensures that the audience can see the image and that the performers do not block their faces.

Just as the stage requires balance, symmetrical or asymmetrical, the body also requires equal but opposite forces in order to stay balanced. As a dancer executes a high battement with the right leg, the left leg is equally pressing into the ground. During a backbend, the head and shoulders are traveling back while the hips travel forward. This opposition is fundamental at a technical level but can also be capitalized on from a narrative sense. What are the two conflicting or harmonious forces driving the character to action?

Shapes and Transitions

The *shape* of a movement refers to the stationary images created by the body. When looking at a shape as if it were a still painting or snapshot, the audience can infer story, character, and emotion. The physical alignment of the body as well as the negative space, or space in between parts of the body that the audience can see through, all contribute to the overall meaning. The shape of the movement can be defined based on the position of the performer's body as well as that performer's relationship to structural pieces and other performers (Bogart and Landau 2005: 9).

"All shape can be broken down into either lines, curves, [or] a combination of lines and curves" (Bogart and Landau 2005: 9). Lines and angles communicate a different emotion and intention than curves and circles. Certain characters might move more predominantly in one than the other. A character who is narrow-minded might transition from angular movement to more circular moves as they start to open up their mind to other possibilities. Some shapes are easier to sync up in precision with other dancers and therefore are more conducive to unison group dancing.

Transitions detail how the dancer transfers from one shape to the next. This connective tissue communicates the driving force of the character and illustrates how the character navigates through the world and fights for what they need. While many performers focus on the power moves such as leaps and turns, it is the connective tissue, the preparation and the landing, getting in and getting out of these power moves that propels the story forward.

Choreographing the Eyes

As the common truism goes, "Eyes are a window to the soul." The direction and intensity of the eyes speaks volumes about the intention and emotional state of a character. A choreographer can exploit this power by choreographing the gaze of the performers along with the body. Fosse expert Deb McWaters refers to "bullet eyes" where dancers bore a hole through the back wall with the intensity of their stare (McWaters 2008: 161). One movement can have a totally distinct meaning based on the focus of the dancer's eyes. A slow développé with the dancer looking over their shoulder communicates differently than if the dancer is staring down their scene partner.

When a dancer is turning, spotting (or maintaining eye contact with a fixed point) helps with balance and orientation. The eyes are the last to leave and the first to return. Likewise, characters with a purpose lead all changes in direction with their eyes. When the body precedes the gaze, a character seems lost or off-kilter. With each change of focus, the performers must actually look at something and see an image (either real or imagined) for the audience to see it too. These shifts should be purposeful and precise. When a dancer looks down, it cuts off the emotional truth of the performance from the audience and should be avoided unless for a very specific reason.

Speed, musicality, and syncopation

Just as certain musical styles or grooves have a tempo in which they are usually played, emotions, objectives, and action verbs have a coordinating speed that matches the intensity and drive of the moment. A placating movement will have a different tempo than a movement meant to warn. Additionally, dance has the ability to alter time. A choreographer can transition from slow motion, to normal speed, to organized chaos with dexterity as a means to punctuate the story or surrounding environment and mood.

The connection of the movement to the music is paramount to the successful communication of the story. As a choreographer breaks down the various components present in the orchestration, they can start to attribute musical phrases or instruments to different characters, emotions, ideas, or events. For instance, during a character's solo, the percussion might represent their racing heartbeat while the strings articulate their attempt to stay calm. The lyrics might express what the character wants the world to know while an arpeggio in the flute portrays the character's subtext. Once these elements are pulled apart, the choreographer can be selective about what the audience needs to witness. The movement of the entire body can start following the percussion and then jump to the strings. Alternatively, the choreographer can assign instruments to various parts of the body.

Syncopation adds texture and surprise to the movement. Avoid only placing movements on the main counts or repeatedly choreographing in 8 count phrases. Switching up the rhythm keeps the audience engaged and prevents viewers from getting ahead of the action. Syncopation can also be used to set apart and highlight an important or flashy movement.

Contrast, Isolation, and Accent

The power of contrast has already been mentioned, but is worth taking into account as the steps are being created. When a dance is performed with one consistent dynamic, nothing becomes important. Contrast can build up to or highlight a climactic moment. If the choreographer wants the audience to key into a high movement, place a low movement directly beforehand. Isolation can also be utilized for subtlety and to manipulate the audience's focus. If the choreographer wants to draw the eye to a particular part of the body, everything else must remain still. If the rest of the body is motionless, the audience will be able to tap into the isolation of a single shoulder roll or grasp of the fingers. In comparing the body to an orchestra, "It is important not to play the 'full orchestra' all the time, otherwise the specific beauty of some 'instruments' may not be fully appreciated" (Sunderland and Pickering 1989: 31).

Accent can be achieved any time an inverse dynamic is suddenly introduced. If the movement is slow and sustained, a sudden and quick movement will stand out. Impressive, eye-catching movements that require maximum physical effort will also create accent and focus such as large leaps, flips, and kicks. Another way to generate an accent is to utilize a physical glottal. A glottal attack is an explosive, grunting sound caused by a build up of and then release of air from behind the glottis. A physical glottal is an explosive burst of force or energy at the top of a movement to add emphasis. When physical glottal initiates a hit and hold of the movement, the choreography becomes sharp and specific.

Suspensions, Freezes, and Sounds

Moments of stillness are just as vital to choreography as movement. Suspensions, or a delay of action, and freezes leave room for breath, absorption, interpretation, and tension. Groups fluctuating and trading off movement and stillness frees up the audience's eye to bounce around the stage like kids in a candy store, taking in glimmers of detail in every direction. A succession of poses paints a visual backdrop to surround the main action. As director and choreographer Andy Blankenbuehler describes, "You have to create pauses so the audience can take in the picture. Our responsibility in that pause, or in that picture, is to make the meaning clear" (Cramer 2013: 37). Movement that stops and starts can illustrate a pause in time to focus on a single moment.

At times, the most powerful choreography during the final moment of a song or an entire show is stillness with the full cast singing straight out. Especially when paired with soaring vocal arrangements, the coming together of the community of characters toward one united goal can delight and uplift in a way that no amount of movement could accomplish. A choreographer must know when to use movement, but also when movement hinders and stillness is a stronger choice.

During moments of group exuberance, encourage dancers to add in vocal sounds and calls. Additionally, a choreographed unison shout, hiss, cry, or exclamation of a word can add a level of sonic impact that amplifies the movement. These group chants should be used sparingly and strategically or else the significance will diminish. Sounds produced by the body, including clapping, snapping, and slapping, can physically manifest the driving beat of the music or add a strong acoustic component to the dance that stimulates the audience both visually and aurally.

Dancers as Objects

Along with physicalizing characters, ideas, emotions, events, and obstacles, dancers can also represent inanimate objects. Dancers can use their bodies to create trees. They can work together to form the walls of a room or a chair. Bodies in motion can demonstrate vehicles such as trains or cars. Characters onstage interact with the representative object as if it were the real thing.

This convention forces the audience to use their imaginations. It is useful in many situations: a small theatre that does not have the space, budget, or resources for elaborate sets; theatre in an arena configuration where set and furniture pieces would block the view of the audience; a traveling company; a musical that changes locations and time too fast to facilitate actual scenic changes; or a musical that is largely character and ensemble driven.

Crowd Movements

In heavily populated production numbers, a choreographer can use theme and variation to communicate the same feel and sense of movement to varying degrees of difficulty. While a group of dancers executes a complex dance break downstage center, the surrounding performers can employ coordinating head or arm movements that mimic the direction, flow, shape, and rhythm of the choreography. This background choreography (named by a performer in one of my productions based on the sweeping motion of the arms as "spraying the corn") can also include changes of motion (bouncing), weight (swaying), direction (facing toward or away from center), and level (squatting or standing on a higher level). These crowd movements can accompany or comment on the main action, such as in a call and response. They can also demonstrate the attitude of the surrounding society.

Utilizing the Design

The design of a production is integral in creating the world of the piece as well as the dimensions of the characters. A choreographer can harness the design to enrich staging and choreography in a way that adds depth and a cohesion to all elements of a production. Characters must inhabit and interact with their surroundings in a way that is truthful to the character, time period, and story. Ideas of how to incorporate sets, costumes, and properties into dance and musical staging may be introduced by any member of the creative team. This stresses the importance and value of rich discussions and strong collaboration.

Level is one of the main tools a choreographer can use to direct focus, build energy, and offer complexity in stage pictures. Set pieces such as chairs, benches, beds, tables, couches, stairs, ladders, and platforms all present opportunities for level. Performers can interact with set pieces to alter the position of their body, enhancing their physical expression. A character leaning on a lamppost is having a very different experience than a character swinging around that same lamppost. Performers can sit, stand, lie down, jump, lean, twirl, wrap around, and dance with scenic elements. A chair alone can be utilized in countless ways. Along with sitting and standing on the chair, a performer can lift it, balance it, crawl under it, straddle it, face it in different directions, drag it, and break it. Chairs can be positioned together to create other objects and places. Doors are another scenic element rich in possibilities. Doors allow characters to disappear and reappear. They can make it feasible for the audience to witness two sides of an event unbeknownst to the characters. Doors are key to many comedic bits. The sound of the door closing can also add percussive accents.

Costumes not only add dimension to characters, but also can become extensions of the movement of those characters. Costume pieces with a large amount of fabric such as skirts and capes add a flow both from the movement of the performer, such as spinning, and the physical manipulation of the costume piece. Other costume pieces like hats and gloves can be taken off, put on, and used for accent. Even the type of shoe can be incorporated into the musical staging. A character strutting in a four-inch stiletto has a very different movement quality than a character stomping in work boots.

Properties, or props, can contribute to the accentuation, meaning, spectacle, intensity, size, or comedy of movement. Some props are linked with a time period, such as fans and handkerchiefs. These props carry certain rules, practices, and meanings established by the society of the time. As a choreographer researches these conventions, they can choose to exaggerate or reinterpret them. Some props are inspired by the setting of the scene. A song that takes place in a library might incorporate books and rolling carts. Umbrellas integrated into a street scene can speak to the weather, but also the mood of the characters or the pressures of society surrounding them. Props can also be woven into character personality traits. A character might walk with a cane, carry a pocketbook, or never go anywhere without their teddy bear.

A character can interact with the prop as a literal object or use it to provide an accent and intensify the line of the body (Sunderland and Pickering 1989: 108). The choreographer should experiment with how many different ways one prop can be utilized. If a prop is going to become a main component, one should attempt to find at least three different ways to use the prop or incorporate it at least three times during the span of the show. A choreographer might also explore how the meaning shifts when the prop changes hands to another character or is positioned on a part of the stage.

Notation

A choreographer must have a way to notate and recall the steps they have developed. Choreography might be created days, weeks, or months before rehearsals begin. Video has become the modern form of dance notation. However, choreography in written form can be quickly accessed in the middle of rehearsal and shared with other members of the choreographic team. It can also more easily be modified as changes are made.

There is no established form of notation for musical theatre choreography. While some movement notation systems such as Labanotation exist, they are not prevalent in the industry. Some original choreography for licensing is written out in long paragraph form and can be difficult to decipher. Many times, a choreographer's shorthand is not detailed enough to be coherent after a long period of time or to other people attempting to recreate the staging. Licensing organizations are now working with companies such as The Original Production that create video tutorials to accompany choreography license and performance rights.

The following notation system has been developed as a way to thoroughly transcribe steps, taking into account the shape and direction of the body, the relationship to the music, and the intention of the movement. The choreographer can input data into the grid by hand or digitally. In conjunction with staging diagrams to notate formations and movement patterns, this system will provide choreographers with a means to document and preserve their work. See below for an explanation of the grid as well as a sample 8 count.

A: The count of 8 (or count of 6 if in 3/4 time)
B: The intention behind the movement
C: The counts: these are the actual counts on which the movement falls as opposed to writing out all the counts present in the 8 count. One can also circle a number if the beat is accented
D: Steps
E: Direction or footing
F: Arms

Table 7.2 Notation grid and example

A	C											
	D											
B	E											
	F											
1	1	&	2	3	4		5	&	6	7	&	8
A pot boiling	Chassé			Ball – Change			Chassé			Chassé		
over	R (Facing US)		L	R			L			R (Facing DS)		
	Press to side			Cross front body	Up splayed					Out splayed		

ACTIVITY STEPS NOTATION

1 Choose one section from the production number outlined in "Building the build" (see page 90).

2 Using research, abstraction, physical representation, dance journaling, movement prompts, efforts, objectives, zones, or centers, create two counts of 8 of movement.

3 Using the grid below, transcribe the movement.

4 BONUS: Show the grid to someone unfamiliar with the choreography and test how well they are able to reconstruct the movement. Make any necessary adjustments to the transcription.

8 Adapting to Various Spaces

Since choreography is movement through space, the space in many respects dictates the movement. No matter the stage configuration, dance can be used to create atmosphere, demonstrate changes of location and passage of time, reveal the inner thoughts of the character, manipulate the audience's focus, and, most importantly, further the story.

Types of Spaces

As described by Stephen Joseph, "[Proscenium theatre] is characterized by its picture-frame stage and the architectural separation of the auditorium space from the stage space. The proscenium theatre has two 'houses,' divided by the proscenium wall" (1967: 11). A proscenium stage can be flat or raked, where the stage floor is lower downstage and gradually gets higher as the performers travel upstage. This can give the audience added perspective and a clearer, more overhead view of the entire space. However, a tilted stage can be difficult in the execution of certain moves such as turns and landing jumps safely. The Actors' Equity Association has safety rules regarding the approved steep of a raked stage. If a stage is raked, the choreographer should work with the performers to ensure comfort and safety.

Differing from the proscenium stage, open stages have no separation between performers and the audience. The type of space is determined by the location of the audience. An alley stage has an audience on two sides. This mimics a street or the view of a parade. A thrust stage contains spectators on three sides. This can often be the most complex configuration because it has the compound strengths and issues of both proscenium and theatre-in-the-round. The depth of the thrust ultimately determines the choreographer's approach to the space. Some proscenium stages have an extended apron that in essence turns it into a thrust configuration.

Theatre-in-the-round, also referred to as central staging, arena staging, or circular staging, is the most extreme form of an open stage, where the audience surrounds the action on all sides. Many theatres are built specifically for theatre-in-the-round, while others offer adjustable seating, where the stage configuration may be changed depending on the needs of the production. In arena theatres, the stage space takes on a variety of shapes including a circle, an ellipse, a square, or a rectangle. To help with audience sightlines, many times the audience is raked above the stage floor or the stage itself is raised. The latter creates a distorted vantage point for the first few rows of spectators if the seats are located right at the edge of the stage. To solve this issue, sometimes there is space between the stage and the first row of audience members that can be used for lighting or for performers to walk on the ground level.

In theatre-in-the-round, vomitoriums, or voms, are the entrances and exits from the stage. Although the concept of these entrances dates back to fifth-century Athens, the word "vomitorium" originated in Ancient Rome, when it described large passages used to enter and exit an amphitheater. Today, these aisles are oftentimes also used as entrances for the audience. However, voms may alternately lead performers offstage by passing under the audience.

Arena staging is not a new concept. Children instinctively play in the round. They create environments that expand in all directions. Sports arenas, bullrings, and circuses all offer entertainment in the round. Communal activities such as social dancing and sitting down at a dinner table all occur in configurations with people on all sides. Theatre-in-the-round is often thought to be the first form of theatre, developing before speech or written word. It began with storytelling and tribal dances as spectators instinctively surrounded the action. African and Native-American theatrical rituals are still performed in the round. Today there are numerous professional and university theatres that are either built for theatre-in-the-round, or can be adjusted to arena staging. Some notable theatres include Circle in the Square in New York City and Arena Stage in Washington, D.C.

Site Specific Theatre

Site specific theatre is a performance piece that takes place outside of a traditional theatrical space. The location is unique to the material being presented. The site usually has a relationship with the musical's setting or themes. The Tooting Arts Club mounted a production of *Sweeney Todd* in Harrington's Pie and Mash Shop—one of the oldest pie shops in London. The production transferred to the West End and in 2017 the pie shop was recreated in the Barrow Street Theatre to bring the immersive production to New York City (Broadway World 2018). Any setting can be transformed into a theatrical space including an office building, junkyard, forest, hotel, boat, or playground. The theatrical experience is often interactive and immersive for the audience. This type of theatre by nature is unpredictable and allows room for unexpected events to transpire.

In site specific work, the space becomes a central component for the making of movement. Rather than a suspension of disbelief, viewers are seeing how the literalness of the space directly correlates to the dance. The creative team must decide if the audience is collected in one location or if they travel to various spaces. Also determine whether audiences are guided through the experience or left to explore on their own. All of these elements will impact the timing, perspective, and order of physical storytelling.

Benefits and Challenges

All stage configurations inherently have benefits and challenges. The proscenium stage allows the director and choreographer to clearly control the picture viewed by the audience. Compositional elements can translate to direct information because all audience members are seeing the same image from the same angle. Contrary to the singular viewpoint offered by a proscenium theatre, one of the main challenges for creating on an open stage is the fact that the surrounding audience is viewing the action from multiple perspectives. As Irvin J. Atkins describes, "The audience sees different relationships between the actors on stage and so interpret differently. The inability to perceive an intended relationship is the chief difficulty the director must overcome on the multi-perspective stage" (1976: 232).

However, central staging offers numerous unique benefits. The fact that every audience member views a different performance means that each audience member has a unique, personal experience. Because little or no scenery is necessary, theatre-in-the-round is cost-effective and offers the performers and creative team the opportunity to find imaginative ways to establish an environment. Also, arena staging allows more audience members to be seated closer to the action onstage. This creates an intimacy between performer and spectator and enables the performer to aim their performance equally to all parts of the audience. Arena configuration also allows theatre owners to maximize the audience capacity for a space, increasing ticket sales.

When transitioning from choreographing for a proscenium stage to creating movement for theatre-in-the-round, a choreographer alters their mindset and adopts different techniques. The creator evolves from a painter to a sculptor. If a production is being remounted for various stage shapes, the choreographer should think of the subsequent productions as adaptations rather than direct translations, keeping the essence of the piece while breathing new life into it.

Performance spaces that deviate from the traditional proscenium layout offer new challenges that compel choreographers to conceive inventive and imaginative solutions. The process of finding innovative answers leads to the development of new creative styles. A change in stage configuration allows theatre to evolve. Although theatre-in-the-round is thought to be the oldest and most primal form of theatre, the majority of the art form has adhered to a proscenium configuration for centuries. Theatre-in-the-round as well as stage orientations not yet attempted open the door to experimentation that has the potential to progress the art form.

It is important to continue experimenting with open stages as these spaces offer an intimate form of storytelling that cannot be experienced with television or film. Especially in the current, isolated, technology-driven culture of social networks and streaming, theatre-in-the-round invites an audience to become more actively involved in the events unfolding onstage. Open stages have the possibility to advance the art form while returning to the intimate goal of theatre: to evoke an emotional response from the audience.

Even if a choreographer's career mainly involves productions in a proscenium theatre, working in various spaces, such as central staging, helps the choreographer think about new and interesting stage patterns and shapes. When a choreographer becomes adept at creating movement in non-conventional spaces, they can use those principles to expand the boundaries of traditional proscenium theatre.

Tricks of the Trade

Whenever working in a new space, a choreographer should attempt to do a preliminary walk through of the space before beginning any choreography or staging. Examine the perspectives and sightlines of all parts of the audience as well as the performers. Choreographic ideas should match the size of the space. By knowing the strengths and weaknesses of each performance space, a choreographer is able to make informed choices on how to creatively craft stage pictures, design exciting movement patterns, effectively stage a song, and address the needs of physical comedy. Every space has its own unique and incredible theatrical capacity, just waiting to be mined.

In an arena stage configuration, the audience no longer observes an enclosed picture, but rather surrounds the action. They become part of the performance in two major ways. The first is that a spectator will not only be able to watch the activity onstage, but also the audience members seated on the opposite side. Therefore, the audience can witness the characters' journeys as well as the impact of those journeys on fellow audience members. Secondly, spectators become involved in the story, and sometimes the action onstage affects the audience in the same way as the characters. For example, in a challenge dance where two groups are on opposite sides of the stage facing their opponents, all audience members are positioned behind one of the teams. The audience subsequently becomes divided, visually siding with the group standing before them. Therefore, in theatre-in-the-round, the role of the audience changes from passive spectator to active participant.

During any production process, it is important to develop a common language that describes the parts of the stage. This allows the director and choreographer to communicate their vision with the performers and designers. In a proscenium theatre, words like upstage, downstage, center stage, stage left, and stage right help to define areas onstage. However, these descriptions all refer to the relationship between the performer standing onstage and the audience out in front. Therefore, when creating stage compositions in the round, a different vocabulary is necessary.

There is not one definitive method for labeling the circular stage, but the most common approach is to number the parts of the stage like the face of a clock. For example, if there are four equally spaced out voms, those would be located at the 12, 3, 6, and 9 positions. Another approach is to refer to the areas of the stage as a compass with North, South, East, and West directions. Sections of the audience must also be labeled for clarity. The various sections can be assigned numbers or letters.

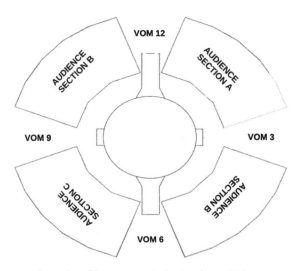

Fig. 8.1 Arena stage configuration. Diagram created using Stage Write.

While a choreographer works in proscenium staging by looking directly at the picture from the front, for an open space it is beneficial for the choreographer initially to place themselves not as an audience member, but rather as the subject onstage. Become aware of what is being projected to the onlooker and in what direction. Once the image is complete, it is vital that the creators sit in various parts of the theatre and view their work from multiple perspectives. This ensures that all audience members are able to follow the story being told.

Opposition of choreography can be a useful tool in proscenium to add symmetry and complexity to the movement. In the round, however, opposition is not as effective or as necessary for visual intricacy. Because each audience member is seeing the dance from a different angle, the point of view is constantly shifting. The dancers are changing what side of the audience they are facing and stage pictures continuously transform, so there is less need to create distinctions within the steps themselves. Opposition can even become distracting and confusing in this stage configuration. Spectators do not all see the same composition, so the pattern of opposition is lost.

In the round, symmetry is no longer gauged on a two-dimensional plane with a line down the middle. Rather, it is viewed three-dimensionally, initiating at the central nucleus and emanating outward. The nucleus does not need to be positioned at center stage and can be moved throughout the space to create asymmetrical, yet balanced images. A choreographer can also have multiple nuclei around which symmetry is established.

Formations

Distinct stage spaces require different approaches when visualizing and creating choreography. In a production number, it is important to ascertain what story is being communicated through the dance, and what images the audience needs to witness in order to understand that story. How formations are used to control the spectator's focus is very different depending on the stage configuration. The following will explore building formations for the arena stage.

For every formation in the round, there are three options, each of which impacts the audience in a unique way. The first is to create one picture or action onstage and allow each member of the audience to observe it from a different angle. This affects primary and secondary focuses because the changes in perspective will highlight various parts of the action. Some will see performers straight on, while others will ascertain different expressive information by viewing the performers' profiles or backs.

The second option is to establish a singular vantage point by staging movement in one vom. When a performer has their back to an aisle, the whole audience views the picture from the same angle. This technique works best when trying to accomplish an image where the perspective is critical to the interpretation (e.g., a reveal).

The third option is to provide every audience section with its own version of the formation. Each section has a dancer or a group of dancers that are performing the same steps in the same formation as the dancers facing the other sections. This option works well with unison dancing and is useful at moments in the show when the performers are trying to directly relate to the audience.

The areas of strength onstage change depending on the space. Formations such as lines, circles, and wedges are standard on all stages, but their strength differs depending on the theatre configuration. There are several variations of the line that could be used in arena staging. The first is a line from one vom to the vom directly opposite, such as clock position 6 to clock position 12, with the dancers facing every other way (Figure 8.2).

A second approach is to have two lines back-to-back. Surprisingly, this composition is not as strong if the two lines run from one vom to the opposing vom, such as clock position 3 to clock position 9. In this scenario, most of the audience members experience the formation from an angle because in actuality, the two lines are facing the aisles at clock position 6 and clock position 12. It is more effective to have the two lines run from the center of an audience section to the center of the opposing audience section, for example, from clock positions 1½ to 7½. This way, two audience sections are given a full view of the line. Then if the choreographer switches up the orientation of the formation, from 4½ to 10½, the remaining two sectors receive a full view (Figure 8.3).

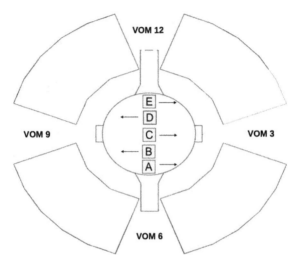

Fig. 8.2 Line variation 1. Diagram created using Stage Write.

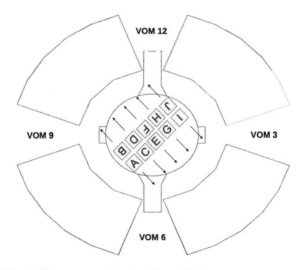

Fig. 8.3 Line variation 2. Diagram created using Stage Write.

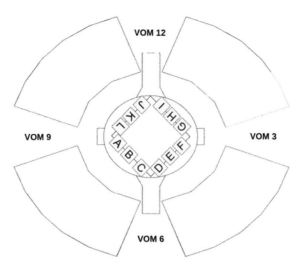

VOM 12

VOM 9

VOM 3

VOM 6

Fig. 8.4 Line variation 3. Diagram created using Stage Write.

A third approach is to give each group of spectators its own line. If you looked at this formation from a birds-eye view, it would resemble a square inside of a circle (Figure 8.4). This variation allows each audience member to receive the full visual impact of the line. However, this line does not carry the same strength that a horizontal line in a proscenium theatre inherently possesses. In proscenium, a horizontal line mimics the border created by the proscenium arch. In the round, the straight line fights against the curve of the stage and may be unsettling for the audience. This formation is also difficult for performers to achieve, because they will instinctively want to follow the rounded edge of the stage.

While it can be difficult to make a strong statement with a circle formation in proscenium due to its exclusion of the audience, this formation is fundamentally effective in the round. It is powerful because the audience is, in essence, fully involved in the shape. When a choreographer creates a circle with performers facing out, it allows every audience member to see a performer directly facing front. This is one of the strongest formations in the round because the performers can fully relate to the audience.

In the round, the wedge, or "V," is a challenging shape, but when used properly it can be compelling. There are three different ways to adapt the wedge formation, employing the three ways to design any stage picture in the round. The first, where each spectator views one aspect of the whole picture, is established by one wedge in the center or two wedges that are back-to-back and face opposing voms. The choreographer may either choose to have all the members of the "V" formation face the same direction or have the two sides cheat out toward an audience section, so that only the point of the "V" is facing the aisle (Figure 8.5). The second variation, where the important focus point is put in one of the voms, is also applicable to the wedge. This is achieved when the point of the "V" is put in one vom and the two lines fan out onto the stage (Figure 8.6). The third alternative involves presenting each audience section with its own version of the formation (Figure 8.7). This configuration works well for final stage pictures.

Since each audience section in open stages views the action from a different angle, compositional variety is possible not only by completely changing the formation, but also

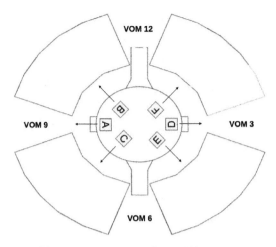

Fig. 8.5 Wedge variation 1. Diagram created using Stage Write.

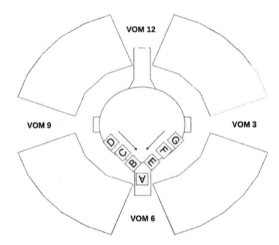

Fig. 8.6 Wedge variation 2. Diagram created using Stage Write.

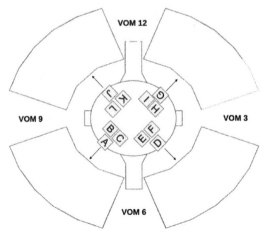

Fig. 8.7 Wedge variation 3. Diagram created using Stage Write.

by taking the same formation and moving it to a different part of the stage. For example, a "V" formation established in one vom for a section of a number can be moved to another vom to create a new visual statement. A choreographer can also maintain the same formation but trade out performer positions to give audiences a new cast of characters.

Movement Patterns

In looking at movement patterns and transitions from one stage picture to another, stage configuration is crucial in determining rate and quality. In proscenium, a choreographer takes time to fully realize a stage image. When staging in the round, formations must constantly change to make sure that each audience member is able to see and absorb what is occurring onstage. Most formations cut off a clear view to someone in the audience, so they must continually adjust and evolve. A production number staged in the round will most likely have a significantly higher number of formations and transitions than the same production number staged in a proscenium theatre.

When fashioning transitions, the stage space not only dictates "when," but also "how." Crossing patterns carry different dramatic weight depending on the stage configuration. Also, the involvement of the audience as active participants changes the way onstage crosses affect the audience. In the arena setting, if one character charges at another onstage, the moving performer is not only advancing toward a fellow performer, but also toward the spectators seated behind that performer. Similar to the proscenium stage, diagonal lines carry the most power. However, in central staging, diagonal crosses from one aisle to another give the feeling that the dancers are traveling through the audience.

It is an established perception on a proscenium stage that a character who crosses in a straight line has a strong power of intention. One that moves in a curved pattern is less determined. "Dancers who execute movement in straight paths appear strong and direct . . . Curved pathways lack the strength of movement performed in straight paths; when a performer follows a curved pathway, the body facing changes constantly, and the visual impression is less forceful" (Minton 2007: 47–48). Yet the weakness of the curved line on a proscenium stage is exactly what makes it an effective and powerful movement in theatre-in-the-round. Because the angle of the body is constantly changing, more people are able to see the performer's face and the surrounding audience can observe the choreography from all angles.

For movement patterns, a choreographer can look for shapes and patterns that match the architecture of the space. In a dance sequence, the choreographer may create variation on a proscenium stage by having multiple horizontal lines moving in opposite directions. The same cinematic swiping action is achieved in arena staging by using a circle. In the round, it is especially exciting to have two circles, one inside the other, traveling in opposite directions.

One movement pattern that is more suited to the proscenium stage is having multiple vertical lines that travel and cross each other. Because the audience is able to see the entire picture from the front, the design of straight lines and the militaristic movement sequences of precision dancing are compelling. In theatre-in-the-round, these straight lines lose impact because viewers are seeing them from an angle. Another pattern that is more successful in proscenium is an advance. In the round, advances are ineffectual because as a group of performers gets closer to a location or central character, they block the view of the audience. An advance can be successful in the round if level is added. Two ways to accomplish level are to place the main action on a platform or have the advancing dancers crouch down.

There are movement patterns that are fundamentally successful in a circular space. For instance, theatre-in-the-round, particularly when the stage is low and the audience is raked, is conducive to kaleidoscope effects. Dancers move like spokes of a wheel, traveling in and away from center. These movements are reminiscent of Busby Berkeley films where moments in the dance sequences were shot from overhead. Additionally, the pattern of a line dance was built around the notion of performing in the round, because the same sequence of steps is repeated in all four directions. The wave is another pattern that resonates in the round. While a full circle wave is not as effective in proscenium, in arena staging, this pattern follows the shape of the stage and the audience is included by being equidistant to each part of the wave.

Creating Focus

It can be challenging in the round to highlight a single performer among many, because audience members view the action from different perspectives. The choreographer must find a way to integrate the ensemble as tools of focal manipulation or remove them from the equation. Costume and lighting designs become crucial in controlling the audience's attention as well as establishing time and place, since large set units are not effective on an arena stage. Level on a proscenium stage creates compositional variety and can help to focus the audience's attention. In arena staging, level becomes even more crucial; not only for focus and variety, but also to make sure that every audience member retains a clear view of the important action onstage. By placing the soloist on a higher level, the ensemble can surround the featured performer without blocking the view of the audience.

Another way to bring focus to one performer in the round is to place them in one of the voms. This provides all audience members the opportunity to clearly observe the performer's face from the same angle. One problem with this formation is that action on the stage may block the audience's view of the vom. In order to remedy this, the choreographer can position all performers in a vom. It does not matter if the ensemble members are in the same vom as the soloist or spread out amongst the remaining voms. Another remedy is to situate the highlighted performer on a higher level than the rest of the cast onstage. The soloist can either stand on a level in the vom, such as a platform or chair, or the people onstage can attain a lower level by sitting or crouching.

The differences in highlighting a soloist in proscenium versus in the round will also affect the choreography. In a proscenium setting, the lead performer may be part of a group by executing the same movements as the ensemble, but they may also stand out with different, featured choreography while the ensemble becomes texture. In the arena staging, however, the soloist becomes the centerpiece of the entire sculpture, making it harder to vary movements without becoming visually muddled. Because the soloist is fully incorporated into the image the audience sees, they often have to execute the same choreography to maintain clarity.

Musical Staging

When developing musical staging for the soloist, duet, or trio, a choreographer must always consider the principles of focus and dominance. However, the methods for creating visual emphasis differ depending on the stage configuration. In proscenium, performers can remain stationary for long periods of time only shifting in breath, focus, or gesture. Partners can stand relatively close together and still maintain tension. In theatre-in-the-round, the singer must continue to move or change direction so everyone in the audience sees their face. Also, if two performers get too close to each other, the audience is blocked from viewing the interaction.

When a performer is alone on a proscenium stage, they undoubtedly have strength standing center and traveling downstage to down center. However, in the round, the areas of strength differ. Center stage is still quite powerful, but as a performer travels toward the audience, they lose emphasis because fewer audience members can see their face. A soloist placed center stage in the round must continually change body angles to open up to all the audience sections. These changes of orientation should be dramatically motivated, occurring at a change of beat, a reaction to something onstage, or a tactic shift so as not to appear artificial.

The most compelling way to accomplish these shifts is to have the performer face an audience section and then turn to the audience section directly opposite. For the third move, they choose which of the two remaining sides to face, and then finally sing to the remaining opposite audience section. By playing to the opposing sections and not just revolving in a circle, no one spectator goes for too long without being able to see the singer's face.

In duets, compositions must have enough distance and negative space for the audience to be able to see through the picture and observe both partners. One way to open up a duet for the audience is to place the two performers at an angle instead of singing directly toward each other. Seating can often facilitate this without the image feeling contrived. For example, with a bench placed on a diagonal, one character can sit facing vom 6 while the other sits facing the opposite vom 12. Then the performers can direct their focus over the shoulder so they connect with their fellow performer while still being visible at multiple angles.

In the round, some audience members are watching the dominant action, while others are viewing the reactions of the secondary character. When the performers change body angles, the audience focus also switches, and spectators become more deeply involved in the cat and mouse game occurring onstage. Also, arena stages tend to be more intimate, so the audience can view more of the stage simultaneously.

During a duet, there should be distance between the singers, but the choreographer must be keenly aware of the tension being created. If performers are too close or too far away, the tension dissipates. In the round, the perfect distance to create tension is different than on a proscenium stage. The performers must stay further apart so as not to block the audience's view, which might seem contrived during intimate moments. However, because the audience is more directly drawn into the action, it is possible to maintain tension even as performers stand at greater distances.

Other techniques for staging a duet in the round include placing the performers in opposite voms resulting in distance between them, or keeping one singer stationary center stage while the other travels in a circle from vom to vom. The circle offers a sense of freedom of movement while the voms guarantee anchoring guideposts to find moments of stillness. Without that grounding factor, performers can start to wander unnecessarily. Usually, the performer singing is shifting while the one listening remains still. This principle can be reversed if the action of the silent character is more important to the story than the lyrics that are being sung. Even though more movement is usually necessary when staging in the round, all the shifts in position must continually be motivated by the characters' actions.

In staging a trio, the principle of placement in a triangular formation translates to most stage configurations due to the three-dimensional qualities of the shape. In the round, the performers may either face each other, allowing space for the audience to see, or they can all face out. The performers can also continuously trade positions within the triangle so that every audience member has a chance to see each of them. Again, these changes of position must happen at logical and motivated moments.

Many physical comedy bits were developed or refined in proscenium vaudeville houses. These bits were created with the intention that they would be viewed from a specific angle. The composition of the picture is what often created the humor. Issues arise when trying to stage physical comedy in the round, because the audience is viewing a composition from many different angles. A comedic bit such as a character being hit on the head, sinking lower with each strike, might best be viewed from the front and therefore placed in a vom.

In vaudevillian duets such as "All for the Best" from *Pippin* or "Bosom Buddies" from *Mame*, it is important to keep the two characters working as a team, even if they need to constantly shift orientation or trade positions. Sharp, quick transitions from facing one another to facing toward the audience can aid in giving the number the polished slickness of a vaudeville routine. However, anytime there is a physical gag or a side-by-side dance step, it is best to put both performers in one vom, creating a presentational vantage point to everyone in the audience. Traveling dance moves have more impact when both performers execute the step facing one way, and then switch directions in unison rather than having each individual facing opposite sides. In this type of comedic duet, it is stronger to keep the pair working together and playing off of one another.

Storytelling

The successful accomplishment of choreography furthering the plot is largely affected by the stage space. When choreographing in the round, plot-advancing sequences such as "Satisfied" in *Hamilton* or "Buenos Aires" from *Evita* can be daunting. It is hard to control the audience's focus on a specific series of events when action is taking place on other parts of the stage.

Lavish scenery is not viable in arena staging because it would block the view of the audience. Therefore, many times in large production numbers, the dancers are needed to establish setting, atmosphere, and story; but the audience must still be able to follow the central action. A change of location can be signified by a simple change in the body angle. Dance sequences or traveling steps can represent the passage of time. Dance can also draw attention away from parts of the stage to accomplish a set piece or costume change resulting in audience surprise at the transformation when the focus reverts.

Movements must be designed so that the spectators' eye follows the important storyline. One tool is to position dancers in the voms to create atmosphere while the important events are occurring onstage. The dramatic action can be interspersed with moments of dance that then transition in a way that draws the eye. Cinematic swipes can reveal an important picture. A contagion of movement can end with the lead character as the audience tracks the progression to the important plot. Levels are also a reliable way to direct the audience's attention and help them track the main story while other activity occurs onstage. Drawing attention to one vom or part of the stage and then suddenly shifting focus to the opposite vom or stage position can create surprise, organized chaos, and a sense of excitement or pandemonium. During the most critical moments, having everyone freeze and throw focus to the central action guarantees the audience's view of the story.

The choreographer can manipulate the audience's focus from observer to a character's point of view in order to help the audience understand the story being told through dance. For example, a female lead character can start dancing as others join in, forming a line. As the character reaches a vom, she witnesses her partner flirting with another girl. The audience switches from tracking the female lead to seeing events from her perspective.

ACTIVITY FROM PROSCENIUM TO THE ROUND

Take the production number outlined in "Building the build" (see page 90) and transition it from a proscenium configuration to an arena stage configuration. The sections of the number as well as the story being portrayed will remain the same, but the build, formations, and movement patterns are likely to modify. Remember that in the round, formations may change more often than in a traditional proscenium stage. Diagram the formations, movement patterns, and transitions on the following stage layout with four equidistant voms and four audience sections.

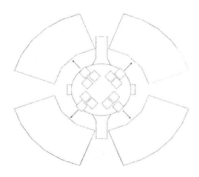

Part 2 The Practice

The following chapters will address how the artistic creations of the choreographer are put into practical application. They will walk through the entire production process from pre-production through the final curtain call outlining the specific expectations and obligations of the choreographer.

9 Assembling Your Team

For most productions, the choreographer chooses the choreographic team. The level of the production will often dictate the size of this cohort. Every contract and theatre are different, and requesting associates can be a negotiation point for a choreographer when accepting a job opportunity. For a regional contract, the choreographer might be allocated one company member to serve as dance captain and/or associate choreographer. On a large-scale Broadway production, the choreographer may have several team members including multiple dance captains and an associate choreographer who later may serve as the resident choreographer.

Choreographers are tasked with creating a choreographic vision that serves the script as well as the director's concept. While the choreographer is focusing on the overall picture and story of the movement, associates concentrate on more specific details. The most important element to keep in mind when hiring team members is to find people with whom you are comfortable being vulnerable. A choreographer wants someone who can see them at every phase of the creative process—even the moments when there are no answers or ideas. There has to be the freedom to look foolish and a willingness to try even the worst ideas. Oftentimes, brilliance comes out of complete failures. A skilled associate is patient, observant, picks up choreography quickly, and inherently understands the choreographer's movement quality. Often during pre-production and in rehearsals, choreographers will create a step in the moment but not be able to replicate it. Associates should be tuned in to the choreographer and be able to repeat the steps back.

A choreographer should also seek an associate who can offer new and exciting ideas that push the choreographer's creative boundaries. Collaborating with people who have different strengths and viewpoints expands the overall choreographic vision. Associates tend to be analytical, able to refine and document movement down to the minutia. Finally, a big part of an associate's job is working directly with the performers. Communication, teaching skills, and an ability to give notes constructively help associates find the best way to collaborate with each individual. Many choreographers have associates that they work with for years and even decades because they have developed a strong, symbiotic creative relationship.

Musical theatre is most dynamic when there is a diversity of voices creating the work. Choreographers hold a position of power and can harness it to hire choreographic team members from traditionally under-represented communities to counter the pervasive practice of hiring all white cis-male creative teams. It is also vital that choreographers treat their associates as creative equals and advocate that the members of their choreographic team be fairly compensated for their time and credited for their work.

Members of the Choreographic Team

Specific duties for each member of the choreographic team will change from contract to contract, so it is important for the choreographer as leader of the team to establish these roles and communicate expectations from the beginning. Empower team members while also making sure that decisions serve the production and are unified in one choreographic point of view.

Dance Captain

It is the job of the dance captain to uphold the choreographic vision both in accuracy and intention. A strong dance captain is detail-oriented and organized. While the choreographer is busy looking at the large arc of a number, the dance captain is making sure that all the performers are executing the movement precisely. They are looking for timing and counts, proper arm placement, correct footing, and accurate spacing onstage. A dance captain is usually a member of the performing company either onstage or offstage doubling as a swing (a person who covers several ensemble tracks). In shows that require a great amount of partnering or that have a large ensemble, it can be helpful to have multiple dance captains who can demonstrate both sides of the partnering.

Once the show is open and the creative team leaves, the dance captain is responsible for keeping the choreography accurate and as close to the original intention as possible by taking notes on the show. The dance captain should observe the show at least once a week either from the house (audience) or from the wings for numbers in which they are not performing. Then the dance captain makes notes related to timing, execution, and spacing either for the full company or for individual performers. Notes can be posted on the callboard, given to the stage manager to email to the company, left at the performers' make-up stations, or given verbally one on one or in a note session. A dance captain must never give notes after "half hour" is called (30 minutes before the show starts).

The dance captain also works alongside the stage manager to run or assist with understudy, swing, and put-in rehearsals (see page 172) as well as cleaning, or brush-up rehearsals with the cast (see page 151). Depending on the production and length of the run, brush-up rehearsals can happen regularly, or only as needed. During a long run, dance captains may additionally train new company members.

Assistant Choreographer

The assistant choreographer can be a member of the performing company or a part of the creative team that is hired exclusively for the pre-production and rehearsal process. The assistant choreographer and dance captain can share similar responsibilities such as noting the show and running or assisting with understudy, swing, put-in, and brush-up rehearsals. It is important at the beginning of each contract that specific duties are clarified. Many times, the assistant choreographer is hired in advance of the start of rehearsals so they can aid the choreographer in pre-production.

The assistant choreographer often takes on administrative tasks, such as creating the Show Bible. This is a large and arduous job and can be assigned to a specific person or as a collaboration of the entire choreographic team. The Show Bible documents every moment of choreography and stage movement in the show. This includes stage diagrams that demonstrate formations as well as traffic patterns, notation of choreography, and important storytelling elements. The Show Bible can either be recorded by hand and housed in a three-ring binder or generated digitally using software such as Stage Write. Video has also become a part of archiving a production. The Show Bible must be precise, thorough, and easy to understand even months later. During rehearsals and previews, the show can morph and change rapidly, so it is also important that the Show Bible remain up to date with the latest version of the choreography until the show is finally frozen (no more changes allowed — this typically happens after opening night). This document is then utilized to train new company members and to specify in cleaning and brush-up rehearsals. For major projects, it can be referenced months and even years later to recreate the choreography in touring and regional productions. See Chapters 6 and 7 for further details on notating choreography and stage formations. In addition, the book *Broadway Swings: Covering the Ensemble in Musical Theatre* (2015) by J. Austin Eyer and Lyndy Franklin Smith offers wonderful insight into creating a Show Bible through tracking sheets and stage charts as well as outlining the duties of a dance captain or assistant choreographer with guidance on how to successfully execute those responsibilities.

It is important that the assistant choreographer develops an understanding of the choreographer's style and point of view. Frequently while the choreographer is teaching new material, the assistant runs a second rehearsal room cleaning learned choreography. During these ancillary rehearsals, the assistant is entrusted to make necessary changes or modifications in a way that upholds the integrity and intention of the movement and remains true to the choreographic vision of the piece.

Associate Choreographer

An associate choreographer serves as artistic colleague and sounding board for the choreographer and is usually separate from the performing company (Fierberg 2017). Many productions have only an assistant *or* an associate. While duties might include items outlined under the dance captain and assistant choreographer, the associate choreographer most often spends the entire rehearsal, technical, and preview process alongside the choreographer offering support, insight, ideas, and solutions. During runs, the assistant or associate choreographer sits with the choreographer and takes notes. A shorthand is quickly developed that allows the choreographer to be able to read and understand the notes, including separating performer and technical notes. For long runs such as Broadway productions, the associate choreographer can transition to resident choreographer. The resident choreographer becomes the voice of the choreographic team once performances begin and maintains the movement integrity, motivation, and precision in long runs, especially with the addition of new cast members.

Pre-production

Pre-production happens before rehearsals with the cast begin and it is the time for the choreographer to hash out ideas and plans. During the pre-production process, choreographers should delve into concepts outlined in Part 1 including research, analysis of the script and score, creating the movement arc, working through musical staging, crafting the build of large production numbers, developing a movement vocabulary, and investigating the benefits of each performance space.

The most difficult part of any creative process is beginning. In her book *The Creative Habit: Learn It and Use It for Life* (2003), choreographer Twyla Tharp makes several suggestions for the start of a new process including finding a morning ritual that inspires one to take action, getting rid of distractions, and physically writing down personal goals for the new project. Choreographers can spend large amounts of time in pre-production. Some of this time might include listening to the music on repeat or sitting in an empty room for hours visualizing stage pictures, painting images in one's head, and creating charts. It is difficult to be creative in a void, so many choreographers bring in their associates during this process. Choreographers will also hire dancers for the day, who may or may not end up as part of the performance company, to come in and bring the choreography to life. This is especially important if there are large moments of partnering. A choreographer wants associates and dancers who will live in the stylistic world of the show, but who will also make completely different choices from them. This opens up a collaborative dialogue and can spark new and exciting ideas.

If there is a specialized dance requirement, such as break dancing, roller skating, or flamenco, the choreographer should study and immerse themselves in the technique, culture, history, and style of the specific dance form. It is also recommended to bring in an expert at this stage who speaks the movement language of the piece to consult and ensure authenticity. They can take a choreographer's impulses and narrative and translate them into the desired style and technique. It is always important to give credit and proper compensation to anyone who is aiding in the choreographic process.

A choreographer wants to enter the rehearsal process feeling prepared with a direction to lead, but not over-prepared where they are unable to incorporate new ideas or make changes. With live productions, things evolve very quickly all the way until opening night. It is not uncommon for numbers to be added, cut, or entirely reconceived during previews. A choreographer might plan for one movement, formation, or concept, but holds onto the inkling of several other possibilities that can be implemented quickly if needed.

The amount of pre-production depends greatly on the amount of rehearsal time and the experience of the performers. In a summer stock contract where there is only one week of rehearsal time to put up the entire musical, the choreographer must come in with everything planned out, making only minimal and necessary adjustments in the room. However, if a choreographer is afforded six weeks of rehearsal, there is more time to explore and develop movement in the rehearsal room. This presents the opportunity for inspiration based on the dancers' interpretations of character and allows the choreographer to tailor movement for the specific performers. Similarly, highly skilled dancers are quicker to pick up choreography and tend to be more facile at making numerous changes and adjustments. Therefore, a choreographer can experiment more in the rehearsal room and open up moments to improvisation. With less experienced performers, a choreographer might plan movement in advance and be open to making accommodations based on the individual. It is important to remember that a choreographer's job is to tell the movement story and serve the vision of the director while making the performers look good. The performers are the ones at the end of the day executing the movement. They should feel confident and the choreography should align with their movement impulses and abilities. The movement should seem to naturally stem from the characters onstage.

It is crucial that choreographers have access to full orchestrations or the entirety of dance breaks. When mounting a pre-existing musical, cast recordings may not contain enough information as they typically comprise condensed versions of dance music and are oftentimes sped up from show speed. When working on a new musical, choreographers might only have access to demo tracks which may include ideas for orchestrations or may only be the piano. Sometimes choreography precedes the creation of dance arrangements. In these instances, the choreographer should stay in communication with the composer, orchestrator, and dance arranger about important movement moments that would benefit from accentuation. See Chapter 10 for collaboration with a dance arranger.

Documentation during pre-production is imperative. With advancement in video technology, this task has become increasingly easier and more accessible. Many choreographers will set up a camera and tape an entire pre-production session as they play music while improvising or experiment with different types of movement vocabulary. Video record any pieces of choreography developed solo or with assistants and dancers, and be sure to label them with the date to keep track of changes. Write down ideas for formations and movement patterns. See Chapter 6 for information on creating stage diagrams.

Auditions

One of the most critical times during a production is the audition process. With the right cast, the path of transforming a musical from the page to an exciting, surprising, entertaining, and moving piece of live theatre is clear. It is vital that all the members of the creative team know the demands of each role going into casting, but also actively seek new and interesting ways a character can be portrayed based on what performers bring into the audition room. Never place limitations on roles based on age, race, body type, culture, gender identity, ability/disability, or national origin unless it is absolutely paramount to the narrative of the show. Instead, focus on the energy of the character, important personality traits (that are not based on stereotypes, damaging clichés, or inherent biases), and required skills.

If working on an established piece, let go of ways that the show has been cast previously. Create something new and relevant to the current moment. Let the performers auditioning surprise you. Someone who differs from the way it has been traditionally played in the past might come in and perfectly capture the essence of the character and material. Remember that when assembling a cast, the creative team is not only choosing performers that are best suited for the parts, but also artists who will collaborate in the rehearsal room and function well as a company. Seek to find those artists who will inspire you as well as bring joy and generosity to the process.

The director and choreographer must have a deep understanding of the piece and the impact of performance practices on the trajectory of the characters. How does a performer of a certain race, ethnicity, gender, or disability inform the character's point of view, history, and experience? This can open up wonderfully rich conversations between the cast and creative team.

Audition Breakdown

Before auditions begin, a choreographer should look through all the dance numbers in the show and decide what necessary skills are required of all the characters and the ensemble. The choreographer will work with the producer and director to create the casting notice and breakdown released ahead of auditions. When pertinent, the casting notice should contain:

1 Style or genre of movement required (tap, swing, pointe, etc.)
2 Any preferred skills (tumbling, proficiency in salsa, etc.)
3 Requested footwear for the dance call (character heels, ballet shoes, jazz flats, etc.).

These can be listed in the main breakdown pertaining to the entire cast or under individual character descriptions.

Dance Calls

There are several different types of dance calls that are utilized in auditions. Depending on time allowances, size of the cast, intensity of dance in the musical, and numbers of different types of styles encompassed, there might be one general dance call or several dance calls, with cuts happening in between. Under a union contract, a production will hold ECC (Equity Chorus Call) auditions for both singing and dance. The union for stage performers, The Actors' Equity Association, has guidelines for how ECCs and EPAs (Equity Principal Auditions) operate. For principal roles, unless dance is a prominent part, the dance call will be housed within the callback process. There might also be a movement callback for principal roles or ensemble that are not required to dance. In non-union contracts, there are not as many mandated guidelines, but most auditions are run in a similar fashion and should always be respectful of the time and energy of auditionees.

The most common type of dance audition is a combination that the choreographer generates. It can either be movement from a specific number in the show or an amalgamation of dance steps and styles portrayed throughout the entire musical. If it is necessary and possible to have several dance cuts, the choreographer might do several combinations that each test different skills, styles, or techniques. These combinations are taught and performed in groups based on the size of the audition room and the amount of space required to execute the movement. It is mandatory that all the groups at one audition call receive the same combination.

Sometimes when there is a large turnout at an audition or the production team is pressed for time, choreographers will first use a dance skill cut. The skill used for the cut should be something that is imperative to the choreography of the show rather something arbitrary. Examples include a double pirouette, a time step, an 8 count of improvised break dancing, or a sustained développé with a specific leg. Typically, dancers will line up and step forward one at a time slating their name and executing the requested skill. A choreographer can gather information about a person by how they walk into the room and the confidence with which they state their name. A dance skill cut is a quick way to narrow down the playing field to performers with the proper technical skills for the dance elements of the show. However, it does not give the choreographer ample time to hone in on the dancers' individuality or artistry and should only be used when absolutely necessary. Another type of preliminary dance cut is to ask dancers to demonstrate an exercise across the floor. Examples would include a ballet grand allegro or an improvisation based on a character, story, or emotion to see the natural movement instincts of the performers.

With the rise in virtual auditions, sometimes the preliminary dance audition is through video submission. The choreographer sends a video teaching the combination and dancers submit a video of themselves dancing the movement. Be respectful of dancers' time and resources, as often in this scenario, the financial burden is placed on the auditionee. Keep the combination short and include only what is truly necessary to see in a first audition round. For the length of the combination, consider only how long you are willing to watch from every single audition submission. Save longer combinations for in-person callbacks. If possible, arrange dance space where performers can record their submissions.

Audition Combination

When creating an audition combination, a choreographer should look at the overall movement needs of the musical. The first step is selecting the piece of music to dance to and finding a cut, usually between 40 and 90 seconds. If using pre-recorded music, it is helpful to produce a separate track that only encompasses that one musical passage. While moves housed within a combination will vary depending on the show, a choreographer can receive invaluable information by making sure the audition combination contains the following:

1 A turn or rotation

2 An extension (kick, battement, développé)

3 An elevation (leap, jump, hop, sissonne, assemblé) or change of level

4 A change of weight (particularly important in a mover call)

5 A change of direction

6 A change of rhythm

7 Story and performance elements.

These are also good guidelines when developing a more generalized dance audition for an entire season or holding recruiting auditions for a performing arts program. In addition to these broad criteria, a choreographer should also include components pertinent to the specific piece such as:

1 Specific genre (hip hop, West African, contemporary, jazz, salsa, flamenco, tap, ballet)

2 Special skills (power jumps, multiple turns, tumbling)

3 Improv (several counts of 8 for the dancers to improvise story and character)

4 Partnering

5 Change in character (for a track that plays multiple parts or are auditioning an entire season with one combination).

Confirm that anything asked of the dancers is safe in the space and that dancers have the proper amount of time to learn the skill. Tumbling should only be demonstrated in an audition if the room has safe conditions and the dancer feels properly warmed up. Any time a choreographer requires partnering in an audition, they must create an atmosphere where the dancers have license to freely give or remove their consent without fear of retribution and that personal boundaries are communicated and respected. The health and safety of the performers in the audition must always be paramount.

In the Room

As a choreographer prepares to teach an audition combination, they should have a clear understanding of what they are looking for and how much time they have to complete the entire round of auditions. It is a balancing act making sure everyone receives the information necessary for casting while staying on schedule. In Equity auditions, auditors are required to see all Equity performers that sign in to audition by the posted audition start time. When the choreographer teaches the combination, especially in callbacks, they are able to see how dancers respond to their method of communication. However, as the dancers repeat the combination, it is also useful to have an assistant who can demonstrate so that the choreographer can watch.

Auditions are a nerve-wracking time for performers. The choreographer can aid this process by leading the dance audition room with confidence, clarity, joy, and humor. It is useful at the beginning of the dance audition to explain the story or character development happening in the specific combination. This gives dancers valuable insight that allows them to make strong performance choices and helps the creative team discover performers that are not only able to technically execute the movement but also bring the characters and story to life.

Everyone learns differently, so when teaching it is beneficial to address steps, counts, and rhythm while always coming back to the narrative. For example:

1 Step: "Your right foot drags across your body, then stomps."
2 Counts: "Drag 1, 2 Stomp 3."
3 Rhythms: "Swish . . . Bam!"
4 Story: "The character is drawing a line in the sand and then standing their ground."

The more explicit the choreographer is while teaching, the more specificity and nuance the dancers will be able to achieve in a short amount of time. It will also save time by limiting the number of clarifications requested. Take time in breaking down transition steps and run the connective tissue between sections always relating back to the story. Continuously switch lines of dancers so everyone has the opportunity to see the choreography and leave time available for questions.

In the audition room, the choreographer must shift their attention from personal (focusing on what they are doing) to a *soft focus* that enables them to take in the energy of the room. "*Soft focus* is the physical state in which we allow the eyes to soften and relax so that, rather than looking at one or two things in sharp focus, they can now take in many" (Bogart and Landau 2005: 31). Even while demonstrating movement, the choreographer can assess how well the dancers are absorbing the information and determine whether it is necessary to slow down or speed up the teaching process. One can also witness the energy, attitude, and learning habits of the performers, which will be valuable information when making final casting decisions. Some useful observations include how quickly dancers take on the style, their attention to details, their ability to make strong choices rooted in character and narrative, and how they share space. Once the combination is taught and questions have been resolved, the choreographer should give the dancers an opportunity to dance the combination in three to four smaller groups. This will offer performers the space to dance the combination full out and provide the creative team another occasion to observe the ability and energy of the dancers.

Making the Cut

Finally, the time comes for the dancers to audition. Decide how many dancers should perform at one time based on the size of the room, the number of dancers in a group, the amount of time available, and how many people the choreographer can watch at one time. This tends to be three to six dancers per group. At this point, the members of the creative and casting team present are invited into the room. The production team must also determine if they want performers to face the mirror or away from the mirror when dancing. Facing the mirror can aid in dancers remembering the choreography but facing away from the mirror can empower dancers to focus less on steps and more on story.

As dancers are called, either by name or audition number, set them up in a formation from stage right to stage left staggering upstage and downstage. Set up the dancer's materials (either headshot and resume or audition card) in the same formation in front of you. Before the dancers begin, take a quick scan of their resume. Take note of shows that utilize a similar movement style or skillset, directors and choreographers they have worked with (people can be contacted for a reference), dance training, and any special skills that might be useful. When the music begins, observe how the dancers utilize the musical intro to establish groove, emotion, environment, or character. Each choreographer develops their own shorthand system for taking notes during auditions. A sample scoring system would be to rate dancers on a scale from 1 to 5 on qualities such as Performance (P), Execution (E), Style (S), and Rhythm (R). You should also include any quick notes that will be important to reference later. The result might look something like:

P - 5
E - 3
S - 4
R - 4
Made strong acting choices

If the choreographer has all the information needed, they can move on to the next group. Otherwise have the dancers switch lines and dance again. Direction can be given that aims to improve their physical specificity ("hit sharp pictures" or "attack the movement"), amplify their storytelling ("use this movement to intimate" or "really explore the feeling of loss"), encourage their creative instincts ("dance this movement like a lion" or "think of the movement as the color red"), or demonstrate their ability to take notes ("This character is making new discoveries throughout" or "try playing an opposite dynamic choice").

While evaluating the dancers, remember that steps can be taught during the rehearsal process. An audition is not a memorization test. The choreographic team wants to make sure they cast performers that will embody the characters, have the necessary skillset, generate the diverse world of the piece, inherently understand the style of the movement, bring joy to the rehearsal room, and offer fresh and exciting ideas. Take note of dancers who are unable to make adjustments or disrespect other dancers in the room. For an opportunity to interact with the performers on a personal or individual level, hold an "interview" portion of the audition by asking dancers a question such as the town they are from or their favorite ice cream flavor. If the performer has a silly special skill on their resume, such as a celebrity impersonation, you could ask for a demonstration.

During the callback process, the choreographic team narrows the talent pool down to a group of people that all have the technical and stylistic abilities to perform the choreography. At that point, casting becomes about assembling the right group of people to create the world of the show while offering unique perspectives. Strong diverse representation is essential to the casting conversation.

One important trait is how dancers function together as an ensemble. Director/choreographer Michael Balderrama, associate global supervising choreographer for *Hamilton*, has developed a technique he terms "fuzzing the eyes" that he uses extensively in auditions and rehearsals to take observations from a micro to a macro level. Fuzzing the eyes and looking just above the performers takes away direct vision and helps activate the peripheral vision. One can also shield one's eyes or wear a brimmed hat to achieve a false proscenium. The choreographer can then view the overall, unified picture. Does the movement of all performers blend together? Does any movement negatively pull focus? This technique does not necessitate that all dancers be perfectly synchronized but rather ensures that as dancers bring their individuality to the movement, the dancing as a whole achieves the right tone, frame or focus of the number.

Once the auditions are complete, the creative team works together with the producers and casting director to make final decisions. A choreographer must collaborate with the director, music director, and producer to determine how important dance ability is for each track. The choreographer should advocate for performers that will be vital to developing the movement world of the musical.

ACTIVITY THE DANCE AUDITION COMBINATION

1   Look through the script and select a song that will work best for the dance audition.
2   Designate a 40–90-second cut of the music. Produce a new audio track of just the audition cut.
3   Create a dance audition combination that contains:
a)   A turn or rotation
b)   An extension (kick, battement, développé, etc.)
c)   An elevation (leap, jump, hop, sissonne, assemblé) or change of level
d)   A change of weight (particularly important in a mover call)
e)   A change of direction
f)   A change of rhythm
g)   Story and performance elements
h)   Any other elements vital to the production such as a specific dance style or genre, improvisation, or partnering.
4   Once the combination is complete, make an archival video for reference.

10 Collaboration

Musical theatre is one of the most collaborative art forms. The number of people required to conceive, write, design, produce, rehearse, build, and perform a musical is extensive. The creative team is comprised of the composer, lyricist, and book writer (when developing a new work), director, choreographer, music director, and design team. It could also include a fight director and/or intimacy choreographer/coordinator. Often the producer and/or artistic director also becomes a main collaborator in the creative process. The design team typically consists of the set designer, costume designer, lighting designer, and sound designer. The design team could also include people with specialized skills such as properties, projections, and pyrotechnics designers. The production team encompasses everyone responsible for bringing the production to fruition. Along with the creative team, this also includes but is not limited to the managing director, publicity manager, stage manager, casting director, technical director, costume shop manager, lighting supervisor, sound technician, house manager, master electrician, and assistants.

Qualities of successful communication include organization, knowledge, and empathy. Team members will have diverse and sometimes differing methods of working and communicating, but in a successful collaboration, it is acknowledged that everyone has the same goal of creating great theatre and people are treated with mutual respect. Differences in opinion, when embraced, can unlock new avenues and often results in a product that is greater than the sum of its parts. As collaborators, there is a balance of sharing ideas and brainstorming without overstepping the boundaries of another member's area of expertise. Mutual respect within the creative team fosters an environment where ideas and suggestions can flow freely.

Choreographers must work closely with the members of the creative team to create a cohesive story and a unified style as well as develop the environment of a production that serves the overall vision and functional needs of the production. Choreographers should strive to speak the language of their collaborators. Know how to read measure numbers in a score when communicating with the music director and musicians. Understand the dialogue around building a light cue during technical rehearsals. Become familiar with the intricacies of reading a ground plan. Learn the qualities and textures of various fabrics. This is a sign of respect and will help ensure clear communication.

Design and Production Meetings

A large amount of work goes into arriving at the opening night of a musical. Meetings on a regular basis help guarantee that all creative and design elements are unified, questions are answered, and budgets are met. There are several types of meetings that occur over the course of the production process. As one of the main members of the creative team, it is vital that the choreographer is present and understands the purpose and expectations of each meeting. Producing entities might have different titles for the meetings listed below, but the goals are consistent.

Creative Discussions

Before any meetings begin, the choreographer should complete their research and script/ score analysis components (see Chapters 2–4). As the choreographic vision starts to take shape, the choreographer will want to brainstorm concepts and get clarifications from the director, music director, and other members of the creative team. Questions might include which characters the director wants to take part in a dance sequence and discrepancies in the script and score with regards to lyrics or dance breaks. A choreographer might have musings regarding items wanted for a dance sequence such as large coins to tap on (42nd Street) or moveable typewriter desks (Thoroughly Modern Millie). Ideas might also present specific lighting opportunities (dancers using flashlights) or costume needs (dancers on roller skates). All of the other members of the production team will be gathering similar thoughts and inquiries, and collectively these will aid in beginning a dialogue. Some of these topics can be discussed early on in conceptual meetings while other more specific items are better suited for later design meetings or break out meetings with individual members of the creative team.

Creative discussions happen at the very beginning of the process once the creative team is hired and typically several months before rehearsals are slated to begin. This is the time for the creative team to have preliminary conversations about the musical. The director usually presents their vision to the team while designers communicate their ideas, questions, and emotional responses to the piece. Some creative teams will have a separate *research and imagery presentation meeting* where all members will display their individual explorations and research materials. Visual communication is beneficial to this process. Talking about something does not offer the same clarity as seeing a visual representation. A choreographer may share some initial thoughts about the function of movement in the show as well as display a visual lookbook or play a movement reel (see page 23).

During this early phase of production, the creative team should discuss dreams before reality. It is important to imagine what could be before deciding on what will be. As the production process progresses, these ideas will be refined to what is necessary and achievable for that particular production. By the end of these early conferences, the creative team ideally reaches an agreement about the story, concept, style, and period of the production.

Design Meetings

Over the next several months, designers will incorporate the information presented into concrete designs. The creative team will have a series of design meetings most often including a preliminary design meeting, a design revision meeting, and a final design meeting. It is vital that the choreographer is present at all of these meetings. The choreographer never wants an element of the design to be a surprise that arrives in technical rehearsal. The *preliminary design meeting* is the first time designs are introduced, usually as sketches or drawings. This opens up conversations around the aesthetic, concept, and practicality of the design. These meetings can be inspiring for the choreographer and often spark new movement ideas based on the designers' visions. At the same time, issues or concerns about the functionality of a design should be expressed. Examine not only what design elements will look like, but also how they will be utilized. The design greatly impacts how movement is perceived and executed. It is preferable to work through issues and make any changes to a design early in the process rather than after elements have been purchased or built. *Design revision meetings* reflect tweaks and modifications based on feedback. Budget meetings also occur to verify that plans are financially feasible. By the *final design meeting*, the creative team has arrived at the design blueprint that will become reality on the stage.

Break Out Meetings

During the design process, the director and choreographer will often have break out meetings with individual members of the creative team to discuss relevant items in depth. The director and choreographer might meet with the costume designer and discuss each character to identify important personality traits reflected in the clothing as well as practical costume needs. A meeting might occur with the set designer and properties supervisor to go through a prop list and brainstorm the best method and materials for construction of props based on usage. A discussion with the lighting designer will include any preliminary lighting ideas including defining key terms to better understand the desired visual. This is the time to really delve into the fun and juicy details of technical elements as well as address grand ideas and discover what is realistically attainable. It is critical that these ideas are discussed early in the process as specific planning and often collaboration between departments is required to successfully transition these concepts from the page to the stage.

Production Meetings

Production meetings occur weekly once rehearsals are underway and contain most members of the production team, or a representative from each department. They are most often led by the stage manager or production manager, depending on the theatre. All members of the production team receive the daily rehearsal report that contains updates, questions, and concerns for each department. Production meetings are the main opportunity to discuss these items as a collective group. Typically, the director presents an overview of what was accomplished in rehearsal that week and then each department has the opportunity to give updates and to ask questions of other departments. These meetings allow unforeseen problems and discrepancies to be addressed and are essential to a successful collaboration.

Designer Run Through

Once the show is staged, there is a dedicated run through specifically for designers to see the work on its feet. The director, choreographer, music director, and stage manager are able to answer any questions that come up and it is a time to clarify any storytelling moments occurring in the production that are not intrinsically present in the script.

Collaborating with the Director and Music Director

While the director is responsible for the overall vision of a show, the director, music director, and choreographer must all work together to produce a musical where the dialogue, song, and dance blend mellifluously, live in the same conceptual "world," and serve a unified story.

The Director

The director captains the mounting of a musical. They interpret the work of the writers while integrating all the performance and technical facets into one cohesive production. The director and choreographer work very closely together in and outside of the rehearsal room. Oftentimes in a fruitful and fulfilling collaboration, the line between director and choreographer dissolves and there is a freedom to respectfully share thoughts and opinions. The audience should not be able to tell where the director's work left off and the choreographer's work began.

Along with the entire creative team, the director and choreographer examine and agree on the story, style of that particular production's approach, conventions to be utilized (such as the ensemble moving all the scenery in transitions, or having "dream" dancers that express the characters' inner thoughts and desires), and the role of dance in the piece. When discussing specific numbers, it is helpful for the director to share conceptual ideas ("in this number I imagine a phoenix rising"). This enables the choreographer to understand the director's point of view while permitting the choreographer to interpret through their own creative lens. The director is able to maintain a consistency through the piece while trusting the skills and ability of their creative colleagues. The director also articulates what has to be accomplished during the course of a dance number both in the narrative (all the citizens escape the approaching enemies) and practically (during the course of this dance the scene must transition from the living room to the office).

In a new collaboration, it is also beneficial for the director and choreographer to consult about duties and method functioning in the rehearsal room. Some directors desire to set musical staging and then turn the number over to the choreographer when the dance break begins. Others prefer to put the choreographer fully in charge of staging any musical moments. There are times where it is valuable to work simultaneously in the rehearsal room to stage something jointly. Over the course of the rehearsal process, other moments might arise where the director will ask for assistance from the choreographer such as transitions, physical comedy, and group scenes.

The Music Director

The music director supervises all musical elements of the production and might also serve as the conductor, orchestrator, and/or arranger. It is the music director's job to make the vision of the composer and lyricist come to life. Before rehearsals begin, the choreographer and music director should confer about the following:

1 The musical sound and style and how that impacts the movement style

2 The story surrounding musical moments

3 Setting tempos for dance moments

4 Deciding how to count certain complicated musical sections or songs to create a seamless language with the cast.

Frequently the cast recording contains condensed dance breaks, reduced orchestrations, sped up tempos, and artistic performer interpretations that differ from the musical notes written in the score. The choreographer should connect with the music director for clarity around discrepancies in the score versus cast recording. When licensing a musical, the creative team must obtain written permission before making any changes or cuts to the material. In shows that have had prominent revivals or are part of the public domain and potentially have multiple cast recordings (such as operettas written by Gilbert and Sullivan), everyone on the creative team should clarify they are referencing the same recording.

The choreographer and music director must be in constant communication to harmoniously combine song and dance. If the music director permits, it is always valuable for the choreographer to be present at music rehearsals, especially during a sing through of an act or the entire show. An interpretation choice that the music director and performer have explored might inspire a different take on the choreography. In the rehearsal room, the director, choreographer, and music director will work together to make decisions about tempo, musical repeats, vamps, and underscoring. When staging dance sequences and adding musical staging, be aware of how the movement affects the performers' ability to sing. Avoid staging people facing upstage or with heads down when simultaneously singing. Similarly, the choreographer should build in rest time after heavy dancing for vocal soloists to regain breath support before singing. As previously mentioned, some musical productions will use pre-recorded vocal enhancements, or "sweeteners", to amplify the sound during moments of intense choreography. Make reference to measure numbers when describing musical moments or announcing where in the music to begin. However, choreographers frequently will nickname sections of a dance (the kickline, the blob, the all-skate) and intuitive music directors or rehearsal pianists will make note of where these moments fall in the score. If the music director is agreeable, the choreographer might also want to sit in on orchestra rehearsals. This is the first time the choreographer will be able to hear the orchestrations played live and affords the opportunity to make adjustments in the choreographer's physical translation.

The Dance Arranger

A dance arranger composes music to support the moments of dance in the show. Dance arrangements can be variations on the themes present within a single song, a hit parade of songs and motifs from the show, a melodic transformation of the composer's work, or an entirely new composition (Chase and Weinberger 2021). These arrangements often take existing material and transform it into something new. In the development of a new musical, the choreographer works very closely with the dance arranger. This ensures that the dance music matches the physical movement in style and forward motion. In the truly spectacular dance arrangements, one can envision the story, style, and energy of the dance just by listening to the music. In preliminary conversations, the choreographer and dance arranger step through a number moment by moment, discussing the story and feel. This might include plot (she is literally swept off her feet), tempo (this moment feels frenetic), time signature (this moment goes into a loving 3/4 waltz), length (this moment needs another 8 bars), or style (this moment transitions into a tarantella). The dance arranger and choreographer should decide the length of each section of the dance break (either in counts or seconds) and find any musical motifs or grooves that equal the energy of that moment. The choreographer and dance arranger become co-authors of the dance moments.

Each collaboration is unique and sometimes steps precede music while other times the music is created first and steps follow. Often when creating new unorchestrated choreography either in pre-production or during rehearsals, the choreographer will work simultaneously with the dance arranger. It becomes a team sport where the movement molds to fit the music and the arrangements bend to match the choreography. As the beat is often the driving force behind movement, it can be helpful in these sessions to also have a bass player and/or drummer present to establish groove. The dance arranger will also orchestrate certain dance elements such as a drum crash on a large kick or choosing specific instruments like strings or brass to match the physical energy of the movement. The ultimate test is how the music feels to the dancers embodying it. As dance arranger David Dabbon stated, "I can read dancers' bodies very well, and I can hear when music's not jiving" (Fierberg 2018). In truly great collaborations, the dance arranger understands the choreographer's movement instincts and the choreographer is attuned to the dance arranger's rhythms.

Collaborating with the Design Team

The design team invents the environment in which the characters live. Each designer is responsible for a specific element, but the design as a whole must be aesthetically cohesive, serve the main vision, support the writer's story and message of the show, and be achievable within the means of the producing organization. If a choreographer has ideas related to that environment, they can empower designers to add their own artistry by offering abstract concepts rather than prescribing outcomes.

The Set Designer

The set designer is responsible for designing and supervising the creation of the scenic elements of a production including all set pieces, furniture, set dressing, and properties. Sometimes there is a separate properties designer or a properties supervisor who can design, build, purchase, rent, or pull props from stock. In this situation, the set designer collaborates with the properties designer so that all sets, furniture, and props are part of one unified design. While the set establishes playing spaces for the performers, it also projects the period and location, evokes mood, helps define the parameters of style, and actualizes the atmosphere of the musical. A dynamic design encourages movement, provides opportunity for strong stage pictures, and energizes transitions.

Once design meetings commence, there are some important questions for the choreographer to examine with the set designer to inspire movement ideas as well as understand the intention and functionality of the design and ensure the safety of the choreography. Elements to consider:

1 *Set pieces*: Is it a unit set (one set that can be representative of several different locations) or multiple sets? Are set pieces moved by performers, stagehands, or automation? How do the sets transition from one to another? Is the main curtain used for transitions or do scenic changes happen in the audience view? Are sets stationary or moveable? If moveable, does it move with casters, hydraulics, other? How do you stop moveable pieces (brakes, drop pins)? How many performers populate the stage at one time?

2 *Entrances and exits*: Where are they located? How many performers can fit through an entrance at one time? Where are the sightlines? How much wing space exists at each entrance? Are there any obstacles to watch out for such as lighting booms, speakers, or set pieces in the wings? (This discussion might include several designers.)

3 *Levels*: How high is each level? What are the dimensions of the playing space on the platform? Are there any sightline issues? How do performers get onto the levels from onstage and/or offstage? How reinforced are the levels? How many performers can dance on a level at one time?

4 *Stairs*: With stairs, especially ones that will be used for dance, it is critical for safety that each stair has the same rise and tread. Discuss with the set designer any choreography that will be happening on the stairs to help determine size.

5 *Additions to the space*: Adaptations to the space may include a raked stage, a passerelle (walkway on the outside of the orchestra pit), a runway over the audience, or a turntable. The Actors' Equity Association has rules regarding several of these elements for performer safety. These additions can offer some exciting pictures and interactions with the audience, but might also require modifications in movement.

6 *Surfaces*: What material will be used for floor construction? What treatment will be used on the floor? Is the floor sprung to absorb the impact of leaps and jumps? If tapping, is the floor sound alive or dead? If the floor becomes too slick, is a treatment such as liquid rosin a possibility? What if the floor is not slick enough? Many of these issues can be resolved by examining the paint treatment and how it is applied. A choreographer can request a small sample of the flooring with the planned paint treatment to try out in rehearsal with dance shoes. This will allow time to solve any issues that arise before the performers start rehearsals onstage.

7 *Safety concerns*: Are there any planned elements that may potentially cause challenges for dance such as tracks in the floor or trap doors? Costume designers should be consulted with regard to shoes and heel sizes. The choreographer can adjust choreography, spacing, and movement patterns to minimize safety issues. Safety measures might also be requested or put into place such as glow tape, orchestra netting, railings, and toe kicks.

8 *Orchestra/band*: Where will the orchestra or band be placed (onstage, in the pit, under the floor)? How is the conductor visible to the performers?

9 *Number line*: The choreographer should deliberate with the director, set designer, and stage manager about the necessity, placement, and style of a number line (see Chapter 11).

10 *Technology*: Will there be additional technology incorporated into the design such as projections? Where on the stage will the images be projected? How might the choreography interact with or hinder that technology?

The choreographer wants to make sure that the movement and formations are appropriate to the size of the stage. If possible, the choreographer should visit the theatre space before beginning pre-production and again once the skeleton of the set has been assembled. The set designer will also provide several visual aids that will assist in deciphering the scenic design as well as visualizing the space for conception of choreography.

1 *Research images, sketches, and storyboards*: Designers provide research images and sketches to express ideas and provide inspiration. A storyboard is useful for shows that require a large number of scenic changes.

2 *Ground plan* (Figure 10.1): A ground plan displays the set design from a bird's-eye view and is drawn to scale. The choreographer can analyze entrances and exits, the amount of floor and playing space, the size of set units and furniture pieces, and the placement of flying elements such as the main curtain, drops, and cycs.

3 *Front elevation or perspective drawing/rendering* (Figure 10.2): A front elevation or a perspective drawing (or rendering if it is in color) is an image of the set from the audience's perspective. The choreographer can use this to visualize stage pictures and levels.

4 *Section*: A section is drawn as if the theatre has been cut in half down the center line of the stage and is viewed from either stage left or stage right. This drawing reflects the height of platforms, scenic units, masking, and lighting fixtures, and usually includes a human figure to give the viewer a sense of scale.

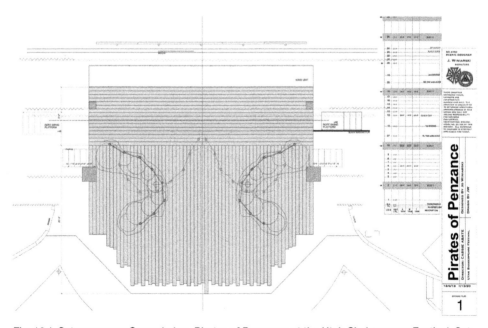

Fig. 10.1 Set resources: Ground plan. *Pirates of Penzance* at the Utah Shakespeare Festival. Set design by Jo Winiarski.

Fig. 10.2 Set resources: Rendering. *Pirates of Penzance* at the Utah Shakespeare Festival. Set design by Jo Winiarski.

5 *Three-dimensional model* (Figure 10.3): A set designer might build a miniature three-dimensional white model or a full color model of the set. It typically includes proportionally sized human representations to give the viewer a sense of scale. The choreographer can use this model in pre-production and rehearsals to determine stage pictures and transitions. As the industry is transitioning technologically, more designers are also producing digital models.

Properties, or props, are an integral part of a production and can not only interact with choreography but become a centerpiece of an entire dance number. A stage full of walkers with taps on the bottom turned the traditional tap number on its head and became one of the most iconic dance moments in musical theatre in the original Broadway production of *The Producers*, directed and choreographed by Susan Stroman with associate choreographer Warren Carlyle and assistant choreographer Lisa Shriver. When requesting props, the choreographer must be as accurate as possible in terms of number needed (15 wedding bouquets that match the color of each sister's dress) and dimensions (a flag that is 4 feet by 6 feet). Deciding how the prop will be utilized will impact the design, weight, and material of the prop. A box that a performer carries while skipping will be constructed differently than a box that needs to hold three dancers. It is important to inquire about what furniture and scenic elements (tables, chairs, desks, couches, benches) are sturdy enough for standing and dancing. Do any pieces roll on casters or slide on furniture pads? Specify which furniture or set pieces will be utilized during a dance sequence so they can be properly modified or reinforced.

Rehearsal props are often provided. They are representative in the size and function of the final props. It should be decided in advance what components are imperative to have in the rehearsal room (either a stand-in rehearsal prop or the final prop) versus pieces that will

Fig. 10.3 Set resources: Three-dimensional model. *Pirates of Penzance* at the Utah Shakespeare Festival. Set design by Jo Winiarski.

not be available until technical rehearsals. The choreographer can use stand-ins to work out choreography in the rehearsal room and predict any issues that might arise. Sometimes, like when weapons are involved, it is essential to receive the actual performance item early on in the process as it will take performers time and practice to become comfortable and nimble with the prop. It is also important to note that occasionally items are crossover pieces that could be considered either a prop or a costume piece (parasols, scarves, gloves). The responsible department may vary from theatre to theatre as well as production to production and might require a collaboration of multiple departments.

The Costume Designer

The costume designer is responsible for designing and overseeing construction and assembly of the costumes for every character including clothing, hair, makeup, and accessories. Many theatres have separate hair, makeup, and/or crafts designers and supervisors who coordinate with the costume designer on the complete vision for each character. Depending on the time frame, budget, and number of personnel, costumes may be built from scratch, bought, pulled from existing stock, rented, or a combination of these options. Costume designers utilize shape, silhouette, fabric, color, texture, pattern, hairstyle, and makeup to convey character, setting, time period, and style.

The choreographer and the costume designer work together to uphold the integrity of the costume design while also encouraging physical movement. Some important discussion topics include:

1 *Shoes*: This is the most important choice for the choreographer and costume designer. A balance must be achieved to match the costume design while meeting the practical needs of the choreography. Vintage shoes can complete an ensemble but may not be sturdy enough for more intensive dancing. With regards to dance shoes, the production team must decide whether to purchase new shoes, pull from stock, or rent the performer's personal shoes. If new shoes are ordered, it is essential that they arrive in enough time for the dancers to have them in rehearsal and "break them in" for performance.

2 *Mic pack placement*: Choreography can impact where on the body the performers will place their mic packs. For example, often mic packs rest in the small of the back, but this might not be possible if the dancer rolls on the floor or is held on the small of the back for a lift. Alternative mic pack placements, such as attached to the leg, underneath the wig, and attached to undergarments, should be decided as needed.

3 *Wigs*: The right hair and makeup can complete a design and help the performer fully embody the character. As the choreographer articulates the intensity of movement for each character or each song, the costume and wig designers can choose the proper durability of wig and style.

4 *Undergarments*: Proper undergarments are essential for the comfort and safety of the performer. The necessity of certain undergarments might affect the shape or dimensions of a design. The choreographer should express the need for items such as knee pads. Conversely, if the costume designer has decided to use corsets, the choreographer must take this into account when determining the range of movement available to the dancers.

5 *Movement abilities*: With heavy dance sequences, the costumes must embody maneuverability and durability. Sometimes this means slightly altering the authentic period shape to allow for extra movement, especially in a skirt or sleeve. The flow of the costumes can also become an essential part of the choreography. The costume designer will also need to know about choreographic elements that will impact the costumes such as floor slides and split leaps.

6 *Ensemble*: Together, the director, choreographer, and costume designer consider the feel of the ensemble and whether they all become part of a uniform group or are portrayed as individuals (see Chapter 3).

7 *Specialized costume needs*: Specialized costume needs would include items (such as scarves, hats, canes, parasols, gloves, blazers, dance skirts, tap shoes) or functionality (such as rip away pants, skirts that can be rolled out of, magic quick change, trick top hat). The choreographer relays any specialized costume ideas to the costume designer. Start discussions with the dream and whittle down to what is realistic. An initial idea that is not feasible could evolve into something fresh and interesting.

The choreographer works with the director, costume designer, and stage manager to compile a list of rehearsal costume pieces. These are not the actual costumes, but they operate in a similar fashion to the final pieces. Common rehearsal costume requests include jackets, skirts, corsets, and hats. Encourage performers to demonstrate large dance movements in costume fittings to identify any issues before dress rehearsals begin. Tools provided by the costume designer include costume renderings, fitting photos, and a costume plot that describes every character's costume for each scene or number. This document tracks each character's costume journey and identifies needs and quick changes that must be worked into transitions.

The Lighting Designer

The lighting designer is responsible for creating all lighting aspects of a production. These duties include deciding what types of lighting instruments will be used, designating where the instruments will be placed, determining when light cues will occur, and designing the look of the light cues. While on a fundamental level the lights enable the audience to see the action onstage, lighting is a complex and powerful art form that uses highlight and shadow to model shapes and depth. Lighting can also indicate mood and style, create location and time of day, evoke emotion, reinforce accents in music and movement, and manipulate focus.

A large portion of the collaboration between the lighting designer and choreographer happens during paper tech and technical rehearsals when the lighting design comes to fruition. It is beneficial for a choreographer to understand some basic lighting terminology to facilitate communication. Some concepts to become familiar with include:

1 *Directional lighting*: top light, side light, back light, front light, cross light
2 *Lighting instruments and equipment*: spotlight, moving light, footlights, birdie, boom, gobo, color gels, cyc, scrim, ground row, practical, hazer, fog machine
3 *Lighting effects*: fade, bump, chase, crossfade, build, iris, strobe, pinspot, shutter.

During the design process, the choreographer should articulate to the lighting designer what visual detail is most important during moments in a dance sequence. Should the audience be watching the dancers' faces (when the story or character is the priority) or the movement of the body? Dance lighting highlights the form of the body, usually utilizing side light. Are there specific lighting effects critical to the choreography such as dancers appearing in silhouette? Are there accents that the lighting can punctuate? Should the energy during the button of the number get larger or smaller? Paper tech is a rehearsal without performers where the stage manager sits down with the creative team to discuss the placement of cues. In this meeting, the choreographer can point out specific moments where a lighting cue would enhance a number's build.

Once technical rehearsals begin, the creative team has the opportunity to see the full lighting design. It is not the job of the choreographer to dictate directions to designers. More inventive avenues open up when moments are discussed in descriptive terms and the designer is entrusted to interpret. Some examples include, "This moment feels very warm," "During the partner section, the feel should be very romantic and intimate," or "This number

"Kiss Me Kate"

Petruchio #1

Fig. 10.4 Costume rendering. Petruchio in *Kiss Me, Kate* at Texas State University. Costume design by Michael Raiford.

should feel like a rock concert!" In technical rehearsals, the choreographer should express any issues and trust the lighting designer's expertise to solve it. For instance, a choreographer should simply state, "I need to see the performers' faces more," instead of saying "turn on more front light," as that might not actually be the best solution. During certain transitions, the team decides if there should be a blackout, where lights completely go out, or a blueout, where lights turn blue and the onstage performers are in silhouette. As learning never ends, it can be an enlightening experience to sit in earshot of the lighting designer during technical rehearsals to listen and absorb the dialogue between stage manager, director, and lighting designer.

The Sound Designer

The sound designer supervises all facets of the production related to sound including but not limited to designing sound effects, creating soundscapes and compositions, augmentation of the performers and musicians, and finding a balance of sound both for the audience and the performers. Choreographic sound needs may arise such as a special sound effect or boosting a particular orchestra member in the performers' monitor during a specific moment in a dance break. When a show requires tap dancing or percussive sounds made by the dancers, the choreographer and sound designer collaborate on finding the best solution for amplification. This may include floor mics or personal tap mics that are worn on the performers' feet.

The Stage Manager

The stage manager is an indispensable member of the production team who serves as liaison between all departments. The stage manager's duties are vast and include the following:

1 Prepare and update show-related paperwork

2 Schedule, coordinate, and communicate rehearsals, meetings, fittings, and appointments

3 Generate and distribute daily reports, daily calls, and production meeting notes

4 Tape out the outline of the set and performance space in the rehearsal room

5 Run all rehearsals and performances including start, stop, and break times

6 Create and maintain the prompt book with all blocking and technical cues

7 Organize and distribute rehearsal prop, set, and costume pieces

8 Create rehearsal reports which inform the production team about what happened in rehearsals and any changes, questions, or concerns that arose

9 Communicate with all departments about production developments

10 Accurately call the show in tech and performances

11 Supervise the stage crew

12 Once the show opens, uphold the artistic vision of the director and creative team including accuracy in blocking and performance intentions

13 Represent the performers when issues arise regarding safety and professionalism.

The stage manager works closely with all members of the creative team during the entire production process. It is the stage manager's responsibility to run rehearsals including making sure they start and end on time, stay on schedule, and that breaks are provided at the mandated intervals. The choreographer may request that the stage manager give them warning when a break time is approaching in order to gauge how much choreography can effectively be staged. At the end of each rehearsal, the choreographer communicates with the stage manager about any changes, needs, or issues that should be mentioned in the daily rehearsal report dispensed to all departments. Notes in the rehearsal report should be as detailed as possible and include a description of the problem so the responsible team member can be part of the discussion in finding a solution. During technical rehearsals, the choreographer will stay in communication with the stage manager to establish the proper timing of light and set cues with relationship to the dance sequences.

The Director/Choreographer

As the leader of the team, a strong director enlists colleagues who they trust, are highly skilled, bring unique diverse perspectives, and share in the director's vision—and then listens to them. This is never more important than when a person takes on the challenge of both directing and choreographing a musical. It is often difficult in this position to maintain a system of checks and balances, so the director/choreographer wants to surround themselves with a music director, musicians, designers, stage managers, and associates who can be a sounding board while also offering critical feedback.

The biggest challenge of directing and choreographing is time management. Commonly the director/choreographer will be able to stage a scene or dance but cannot run the cleaning or spacing rehearsals because their attention is needed elsewhere. Strong associates are vital in giving the director/choreographer time to focus on big picture items while they take care of the refinement.

ACTIVITY INQUIRIES AND MUSINGS

1 Go through your movement arc (see page 33) and compile any questions, ideas, or discussion topics to address with other members of the creative team. Divide these thoughts up by department.

2 For each creative team member, separate your list into items for a preliminary creative meeting versus items for a more detailed design meeting or a break out solo meeting with that team member.

11 Rehearsals

Before rehearsals begin, the choreographer will need to estimate how much rehearsal time will be required to set each dance number. The director and stage manager use this information to create a preliminary rehearsal calendar and breakdown. This timeline is an approximation and rehearsal goals will constantly shift as rehearsals proceed. However, the more accurate everyone can be in these time predictions, the more successful the production will be at staying on time and budget. A rule of thumb is to schedule one hour of staging rehearsal for every minute of choreography. It is better to overestimate rehearsal time for numbers and have time left over for cleaning than to underestimate and try to make up time somewhere else in the schedule.

Types of Rehearsals

After months of hard work and preparation, the day finally arrives when rehearsals begin and the choreographer is able to witness their imagined movement come to life. Rehearsals are a dichotomy of established procedures and yet a unique ephemeral experience with each show. The length of the rehearsal process and the experience of the performers will dictate how rehearsals are structured and utilized, but most productions follow the same basic rehearsal progression.

Staging Rehearsals

During a staging rehearsal, the choreographer sets the movement and creates the build, formation, and movement patterns of a dance with the performers. For large dances, the choreographer usually stages independent of the director, who observes and gives notes once it has been learned. The choreographer will either collaborate during the rehearsal with the music director and/or rehearsal pianist, or stage to tracks. Preparation is crucial to the productivity and energy of rehearsals. Choreographers earn the trust of people in the room by entering prepared with a clear vision. The level of pre-planning varies. A choreographer might have a number completely staged ahead of time including formations and movement patterns. In this scenario, the choreographer comes in with a plan, but must also be willing to change and adapt as needed in the room. Other times, a choreographer might have a beginning and an ending or an outline of the story and develop the actual movement during rehearsal alongside the dancers. Some choreographers build several movement phrases and then play with order, theme, and variation. Either way, the choreographer enters rehearsals with a sense of direction and purpose. Pre-planning creates a foundation that liberates both the choreographer and the performers to try new things and take risks. No matter the amount of pre-production, it is a choreographer's responsibility to create a culture of collaboration and respect by valuing and empowering the performers as creative artists who bring their own views and unique movement qualities to the process.

Consider the best way to start dance staging rehearsals. By staging the biggest, most difficult dance number first, the performers will have the most time to practice it and to build stamina. Within a number, it can be beneficial to start staging with a section where all performers onstage are dancing, or a group exploration exercise. This gets everyone invested at the top of rehearsal and gives people choreography to practice when they are not being utilized elsewhere. The choreographer can then return to the beginning and start building the number piece by piece. Choreographers structure rehearsals in a variety of ways. Some prefer to work slow and steady through a number, focusing on details as they methodically stage. This tactic usually works best when a production has a long rehearsal period. Other choreographers paint in fast broad strokes getting an initial draft up quickly. After allowing the number time to marinate, they go back in to refine and add nuance. This method can be a good option when in a quick rehearsal process such as a summer stock contract.

The more certain a choreographer is in the material, the more assuredly people will follow the choreographer's lead. Clearly communicate the story and purpose of the number. Have a definite idea of how to count the dance sequences, or a plan to decide as a company. Collaborate with the stage manager and the creative team to decide what rehearsal items will be needed in staging rehearsals including costume pieces, show shoes, props, and set pieces. Know the parameters of your rehearsal space and how to mine its potential. The stage management team will tape out the dimensions of the stage and scenery. Ask how much distance, if any, exists between the tape and the actual framework of the theatre stage including width to the wings and depth to the front of the stage. If there are no mirrors, take time to check lines and positions of the dancers and use terms that describe the feel of the movement when teaching.

Discuss with the stage manager the best place to store personal items and where people who are not being utilized can gather to maximize space efficiency. Request that a number line is available the first day of staging rehearsals. A number line is a large ruler that performers use to hit the correct marks onstage every time. In rehearsals, it can be placed on the floor at the front of the room or taped to the mirrors or wall facing the dancers. On the number line, center stage is labeled 0. Then distance is measured starting at center and heading both stage right and stage left, typically labeling even intervals incrementally for every 2 feet as wide as the stage allows:

| 12 | 10 | 8 | 6 | 4 | 2 | 0 | 2 | 4 | 6 | 8 | 10 | 12 |

Avoid teaching large amounts of new material at the end of a rehearsal when performers are mentally fatigued. Rather, use this time to clarify and solidify. As the director and choreographer stage through the show, they should occasionally go back and review the work already done so performers can retain information. Most importantly, embrace the collaborative nature of the art form. If a choreographer can stay in a positive and constructive frame of mind, they open up their imagination and creative capabilities. Some helpful perspectives:

1 *Milestones, not masterpieces*: I learned this phrase from late director and educator Jeremy Torres. Keep in mind that every number, and indeed every show, is simply a milestone on an artist's journey. By insisting that every number be their masterpiece, a choreographer is placing undue pressure that hinders inventiveness.

2 *Set it and forget it*: It is common for a choreographer to demonstrate a step or set an entire number and then not be able to recall any of it. Often when a choreographer is creating, they are not actively storing that work to memory. This is why strong associates are important. They watch attentively and are able to repeat the movement of the choreographer. They also work in tandem with the stage manager to record the choreography and spacing into a Show Bible (see page 124).

3 *Fail forward*: Great art lies in a willingness to fail. Rehearsals are a time of experimentation—a time to try several ideas and to make big mistakes as well as big discoveries. Better to make choices that are strong and wrong than only making safe, predictable choices. If a movement fails, one can return to the research for inspiration. However, one can also tap into a choreographer's greatest resource—the dancers. Collaborate with the performers on movement notions and solutions.

4 *Get it on its feet*: Just try it. Then you can go back and see if it works. Do these steps communicate the right story? Does this dance break need to be longer or shorter? Does the button of the number have enough impact? Should this number be moved to a different part of the show? You will not have answers to any of these questions unless you see it realized.

5 *Prescribe process, not product*: Dancers bring to the table individualistic movement affinities that add depth to the choreography. Movement is interpreted differently by everyone's unique body. Dancers are chameleons, adapting to a wide range of styles, and yet should be given the opportunity to bring themselves to the piece without distorting the choreography.

Cleaning Rehearsals

Cleaning rehearsals are the time to define and refine. They encompass both the larger goals of finding the world, energy, and style of a dance sequence as well as the detail work such as the placement of a hand and the tilt of a head. Cleaning rehearsals can be some of the most fulfilling and invigorating parts of the process when the choreographer and the performers are all invested in exploring the meaning and complexity of a number. Sometimes cleaning rehearsals are run by the dance captain, assistant choreographer, and/or the associate choreographer when the choreographer is needed elsewhere. This is especially common in a fast rehearsal process.

To find precision in group movement, first discuss with the dancers the intention behind the movement. Why is the movement occurring? What is the playable action verb behind the movement (to punish, to seduce, to elicit joy)? This is true with dance numbers that forward the action as well as presentational entertainment sequences. Equally important is the relationship of the movement to the music. Does the movement *cause* or is it in *response* to the musical and percussive accents? How does the groove and musical motif reflect the character's inner thoughts, emotions, or desires?

Next, break down the initiation point of the movement (see page 100). A kick that initiates from the ankle will look much different than one that initiates from the hip. Make certain that dancers have a stop to their movement and are not using too much force to push past the desired picture of the body. What are the eyes doing? Where should the dancer's focus be? Below are some effective tools to consider when cleaning:

1 *Hit and hold*: To achieve polished and dynamic movement, have the dancers arrive at the picture at the top of the beat and then lock it into place.

2 *Shrink wrap*: This is a useful tool to focus energy if dancers' movements are too loose or "thrown." When something is shrink wrapped, it has the same amount of energy in a tighter space. The energy is bound but pushing outward. This is also helpful when dealing with a smaller performance space or a large number of dancers.

3 *Blade or splayed*: Specificity of the shape of the hand will finish the line and make dancers appear uniform.

4 *Seam the pants*: When needing a hand placement during travel steps or executing intricate footwork, like a kickline, choose a position with a clear directive. Examples include "middle finger on the seam of the pants," "hands cupped at the small of the back," and "hands on hips."

5 *How to handle*: When objects are involved in the choreography, including costume pieces and props, every detail must be analyzed and specified. How is the hand positioned on the object? Where on the body does the object rest?

During rehearsals, set clear expectations with regards to marking. In a strong mark, dancers perform full out with regards to energy and shape of the body but mark large elements such as a battement or a power jump. Even when marking a kick, the dancer can still utilize extension and line at a lower angle. However, sometimes marking devolves into an under-energized walk through of a dance. This does not allow the choreographer to see the movement actualized or help the performer to build stamina, physical specificity, and performance values. A choreographer can set expectations by requesting at the beginning of a rehearsal process that dancers perform full out at all times unless instructed to mark or if there is an issue, such as an injury. Limit the use of marking to run throughs where the goal is sequencing or spacing, if the dancers have been active for an extended period of time to reduce the risk of injury, or if a performer has indicated ahead of time a personal need to mark. Dancers should have the agency to communicate such needs without being required to state the reason or without fear of retribution. The creative team should trust each performer's knowledge of their physical capabilities, boundaries, and limitations.

If dancers are experiencing trouble in sequencing, finding the correct shape of body, or executing difficult steps quickly, the choreographer can have the dancers perform in slow motion while maintaining physical resistance. This assists the performer in finding the full extent of the movement as well as analyzing the change of weight in transitions. Another strategy is to ask dancers to sing or vocalize their changes of weight (any time they shift the weight distribution on their feet). This verbalizes the movement and reinforces rhythmic qualities of the dance. Take note of the requirements of simultaneous dancing and singing. Work with the music director to build group breath moments into the choreography. If appropriate to the piece, continue to embolden the performers to vocalize while dancing, which adds to the energy, investment, and sense of community.

When cleaning tap dance sequences, focus on the dancers' dual role of performers and musicians. Articulate whether a rhythm is even (all beats have the same value) or swung (long beat followed by a short beat). Encourage dancers to respect the moments of silence in the rhythm, sit back on the beat, and not anticipate the next step. In rehearsals, ask the tappers to take 20 percent off the volume of their taps and tune into each other while attempting to sound as one. If a rhythm is muddled, have the performers sing the rhythm together without tapping. Once they are able to sing in perfect unison, encourage them to sing and tap at the same time before finally eliminating the singing.

While defining detail and discovering precision is valuable, it is also crucial that dancers find a unified sense of style and intensity. All performers must be living in the same world. Depending on the nature of the piece, a balance must be achieved between the uniformity of the movement and the individuality of the characters. Performers can bring diverse points of view while maintaining the integrity of the choreography. In musicals, dancing is already a heightened state of being. Bolster dancers to discover this heightened state with confidence and truth. Especially with presentational numbers, the dancers should begin from a place of true emotion (joy, excitement, etc.) and then allow those feelings to grow and expand. If a dancer simply puts on a meaningless large smile, the performance will appear false and self-aware.

One of the most critical aspects of rehearsals is repetition. Repetition is needed to establish muscle memory. The more the movement is ingrained, the more freedom performers have to make strong character and narrative choices in the interpretation of the movement. Also, dancers must build stamina to perform the show eight times a week (or more in certain contracts). If time permits, run the most complicated or strenuous dance sequence at least once every rehearsal.

Run Throughs

During a run through, the performers execute a number, an act, or the entire show without stopping. This is the time for the creative team to assess the effectiveness and clarity of the narrative and for performers to understand the arc, pace, and demand of the show. It is important at this point in the process for all members of the creative team to observe with an objective eye. Editing is critical to the success of a musical. Anything that stops the storytelling or forward motion should be changed or cut. Even moments of exuberant emotion and spectacle must continue the energetic and narrative build. Everyone on the team has to be willing to "kill dreams"—let go of things that are personally meaningful but that are not working. This takes strength and humility. Sometimes a choreographer needs to step away from a number for a few days before coming back to it with fresh eyes and a renewed perspective.

Give the performers an intention before running the number such as "make sure you are hitting your numbers and maintaining the proper distance from each other," or "for this run, really connect with each other, making eye contact and feeling the energy as an ensemble." Prior to the run through, decide who on the choreographic team is taking and distributing notes. The choreographer may be watching for bigger picture items such as intention, narrative, momentum, and energy of a number while the associate might be taking notes on specific details such as body shape and timing. Alternatively, the choreographer might prefer to dictate notes to an assistant while keeping their focus on the action. When this occurs, it is helpful for the choreographer to discuss the desired note format (handwritten or typed) and template (name of the performer/group in the margin, notes separated by department).

Spacing Onstage

No matter how diligent the production team is at recreating the stage space in the rehearsal room, there will always be tweaks and adjustments to the realities of the theatre when the show is transferred to the stage. Depending on the practices of the producing institution, the beginning rehearsals onstage may have a full set, a skeleton of the major set pieces, or an empty stage floor with the set pieces taped out on the deck. When entering the theatre; the cast, crew, and production team usually complete a safety walk through of the space including the backstage pathways. This is the time to identify any potential hazards and to begin to figure out the best backstage traffic patterns. Choreographers and dancers should take note of any equipment that might impact movement or that needs to be avoided such as footlights, microphones, and monitors at the front of the stage; a ground row of lights at the back of the stage; and booms, monitors, and cables in the wings. The director and choreographer should also perform a walk through of the house, making note of sightline issues and opportunities for utilizing performers in the house when appropriate.

As spacing rehearsals begin, the first priority is to space the entire show, including the dance numbers, on the stage. It can be especially constructive to divide the show into scenes or sections and execute a "paint by numbers" of a sequence, walking through formations in order to establish spacing, before running in real time. By spacing and then running smaller sections, the performers have repetition that facilitates retention of spacing information. If a performer at any time feels in danger, they should call "Hold!" Remind all performers that if they hear the word "hold," they must freeze in their current location.

The choreographer collaborates with the director, stage manager, and set designer to determine whether or not there will be a number line onstage. The number line can take on many forms, including but not limited to: painted on the front of the stage, placed on the inside wall of the orchestra pit, or different colored lights hung on the back wall of the house or the booth for performers to reference. Landmarks must be established for performers, especially once mirrors are not available, to gauge stage pictures. Assigning numbers supports performers in achieving the proper width. Unless otherwise instructed (e.g., put your right foot on number 6), the dancer should stand so that an assigned number is dissecting the center line of their body. Numbers that were given in the rehearsal room might be adjusted or changed once onstage. It is critical that the associate/assistant choreographer and/or dance captain record the most up-to-date number assignments.

It is equally necessary that performers maintain proper depth, although finding successful guideposts can be trickier. Points of reference include the wings (in line with the curtain/leg or centering in between two curtains/legs), the proscenium, or lines and grooves on the stage deck. When attempting to execute a straight horizontal line, establish a point onstage and instruct the performers to "toe the line" or "heel the line." While choreographers should be judicious, spike marks may be requested to help dancers hit a significant point onstage, especially as it relates to technical elements like a lighting cue or a special effect.

Choreographers can use landmarks to not only establish the physical location of performers but also the focus and shape of the body. In moments of group attention, a choreographer might set a universal focal point to create unison (an exit sign, an architectural detail of the theatre, a point on the set). The dancers might be instructed to reach their arms to the rail of the balcony in order to match angle and line. When a dancer is performing in a spotlight, it can become quite difficult to see, especially when judging which direction they are facing. A *spotting light* is a small red light placed in line with center stage either at the back of the house or in the booth. A dancer can utilize this light to orient themselves to the front as well as when spotting turns.

Once the scenic elements are added, the choreographer examines how the movement looks in relation to the set. Is the flow of the architecture in harmony or discord with the movement? If the set utilizes a large number of curves, then formations with angular lines such as a wedge might not be as effective (Sunderland and Pickering 1989: 63). Does the stage look cluttered or open? Monitor the performer's interaction with the set and how it reads to an audience. While performers use the set to ground themselves in the world of the show, often performers cling uncomfortably close to set pieces causing the visual pictures to become muddied. Distance and negative space need to exist between the performers and the set.

The choreographer can gauge the audience's experience by moving throughout the house to watch from every angle. Are there sightline issues of the main action from certain seats? Is a formation impactful from all parts of the house? Are the performers including the balcony in their performance? If the performers go into the audience, does energy leave the stage? After these assessments, the choreographer must again be willing to make changes when necessary. If the stage is too crowded for the movement to register, the choreographer might cut dancers from certain sections. Performers should be reminded of the big picture and that decisions such as these are not a reflection on their individual ability or performance.

In most productions, unforeseen issues arise that require the choreographer to problem-solve. The set needs to move 2 feet downstage limiting the available floor space. The lighting boom is shifted to the second wing instead of the third causing respacing to assure that the dancers are in their light. The performer sound monitors cannot be heard on the apron of the stage so the choreographer must add physical cues to guarantee that the ensemble starts dancing together. These types of modifications challenge the choreographer to think quickly on their feet and collaborate with the entire production team to find the best solution. The ingenuity of tweaking and refining makes live theatre a thrilling and satisfying process for artists.

Sitzprobe and Wandelprobe

The first time the orchestra and the performers come together to bring the score to life is always an exhilarating experience. During this rehearsal, the entire score is played and sung through without any of the dialogue, unless essential to the musical underscoring. Some productions hold a sitzprobe, where the performers sit as a group and stand in place or at a stand mic when they sing. Other times a wandelprobe is deemed more appropriate, where the performers "wander" around the stage in the general vicinity of their spacing for musical numbers and mark through dance sequences with the orchestra. This enables the performers to test how the orchestra sounds live or through monitors on various parts of the stage. No matter which format is chosen, this is one of the music director's main times (and sometimes only time) to rehearse the orchestra and cast together focusing solely on the music. It is also the first time the performers get to hear all of the complexities encompassed in the orchestrations. Music can communicate the thoughts and feelings of the characters' subconscious as well as create mood, energy, and environment. Choreographers can use this rehearsal to assess which parts of the movement match the tone and feel of the music and whether or not any modifications are necessary.

Technical Rehearsals

Technical (tech) rehearsals are where the entire team comes together to compile all components of the production. The show, as it will be seen by audiences, is assembled and revised. Costumes, set, props, lighting, and sound are added. The director, choreographer, music director, and cast have had weeks (or at least days) of rehearsal to craft and develop the performance aspect. Technical rehearsals are the designers' and stage managers' time to hone their work. As such, the focus and priority of technical rehearsals should be driven by the needs of the designers and stage management. Tech processes usually include dress runs (costumes might be added at the top of tech rehearsals or not until the dress runs). This will differ depending on the practices of the producing entity. Sometimes at the start of tech rehearsals there will be a costume parade, where performers stand onstage in their various costume looks. The director, choreographer, and costume designer see all the costumes side by side and discuss any ideas or concerns regarding the aesthetic or function of the design.

A choreographer uses tech rehearsals to observe how the movement interacts with all the design and technical elements and address any issues that might arise. The structure of a tech rehearsal can vary. Sometimes a run through with stops and starts as cues are built or adjusted is ideal, while other times a "cue to cue" is more constructive. During a "cue to cue," performers walk through their positions onstage focusing only on moments when a cue, or technical moment (a light cue, a costume quick change, a sound effect, a scene change), occurs. The show is then run in real time either in sections or in its entirety. If there are long pauses during tech rehearsal, a choreographer can confabulate with individual departments regarding needs and ideas. Otherwise, the choreographer should take notes divided by department to discuss at the end of the night during tech notes.

In cases where performers must stand onstage for long periods of time, the director or choreographer may choose to put in understudies and swings to mitigate the physical demand on the performers as long as it does not impact the work of the designers, stage managers, and technicians. Occasionally, there are long periods of time during tech when work is being done that does not include the performers onstage. During this time, a choreographer can request additional cleaning time, with the understanding that all work must cease once the production team is ready to move on.

Previews

Theatre does not fully exist without witnesses. The audience is the last significant ingredient added to a production. Previews are a series of run throughs with a paid audience where the entire creative team continues to make revisions based on viewer reception. During the preview period, performances typically take place in the evening with rehearsals during the day to implement any changes based on the previous night's show. Musicals have built in moments of audience response. Jokes are written for a laugh. Dance numbers are structured to receive applause in specific places. A button to a number is meant to signify a clear ending. It is thrilling to watch an audience sit on the edge of their seats, fully invested in the action onstage, or burst into a standing ovation at the end of the performance. It is also critical to observe the moments when the audience does not respond in the manner intended. This is valuable information for the creative team and signifies that an adjustment must be made. Sometimes this takes trial and error to find the solution. When a moment is not working, examine the clarity of the narrative as well as the length of a section and the physical prompts meant to elicit a response.

Running Rehearsals: How to Lead

A choreographer is one of several leaders housed in the creative team. There are many qualities that define a strong leader including but not limited to: integrity, vision, courage, passion, innovation, ability to inspire, collaboration, solution-based decision-making, empathy, confidence, curiosity, transparency, humility, and gratitude. It is incumbent on the leader in the space to create a culture of support, equity, and empowerment in the room. Company members look to its leaders to set the tone. Through their actions, a choreographer can aim to create the world they want to live and work in.

A choreographer can effectively develop an atmosphere of mutual respect by knowing the name of every single person in the room and greeting everyone individually before the rehearsal begins. State your pronouns during the first rehearsal and make sure to respect and adhere to the pronouns established by everyone. People are human beings who enter the space with a set of emotions based on the events of their lives leading up to rehearsal. Acknowledge where you are that day and take stock of the energy and needs of the people in the room. One way is to take a poll: "On a scale of 1 to 5, where are we at today?"

Finding a beginning ritual for rehearsal can help focus energy as well as create a sense of community within the company. This can be unique to each production and decided on in collaboration with the cast. Beginning rituals can include many options depending on allotted time such as a group breath, setting an intention, an improvisational game, or an entire company warm up.

A balance can be achieved between nurturing and uplifting the team while still expecting the utmost in work ethic, effort, and professionalism. When conducting rehearsals, project in a clear, confident tone. When it becomes necessary to hold during staging, place a hand up as well as announcing "hold." This gives the music director or rehearsal pianist, who often cannot hear verbal cues due to the volume of the piano, a visual cue to stop playing. Be respectful of people's time by managing rehearsal time efficiently and work to utilize all the performers who have been called for rehearsal.

Art is a pendulum. It must swing fully to both sides before it finds stasis. For this balance to be achieved, a choreographer should be willing and able to try new things. The goal is to create the best possible production. A choreographer should set ego aside and encourage the collaboration process. Many choreographers believe that the best idea wins no matter whether it was their own or not. That being said, the choreographer has to lead the process and ultimately make final decisions to avoid a multitude of opinions halting the forward motion of rehearsals.

Musical theatre is a fluid art form and choreographers should be afforded the opportunity to mold and shape their work. "No choreographer should be expected to set his work in the first rehearsal and then not to change it" (Sunderland and Pickering 1989: 117). Sometimes a dance staged as version "A" ends up as version "L" before ever reaching performance. Choreographers must be nimble and adaptable in the rehearsal room and performers must equally be willing to evolve and experiment. Having solid ideas for back up plans is beneficial as major changes may occur all the way up to opening night.

A choreographer has a moral obligation to consider the dancer's experience when creating movement. Take care of your dancers physically and emotionally. Dancers often execute the performance eight times a week, sometimes for extended periods of time. Performers want to be inspired by the movement, enjoy the performance, and avoid injury. Make sure that all choreographic elements can be safely executed for the entire length of the run. Dancers should never be asked to put their bodies and careers in jeopardy for a production. As a position of power, choreographers have a responsibility to advocate for the dancers. Movement is also a very vulnerable method of expression. The goal is not to show off as a choreographer but rather to utilize the performers' strengths to make *them* look their absolute best. Ultimately, it is the performer who implements the choreography. It should appear that the character spontaneously created the movement. Any hindrance will take the audience out of the storytelling.

Working with Performers

There are several different modes of learning. As a choreographer gets to know each member of the company, they will assess the best way to impart information to every individual. Counts, steps, and rhythm (or some combination of these) are the main methods of learning movement information. Training and skill level also impact a choreographer's approach. Dancers with experience in the genre are usually more familiar with terminology as well as the system of counting music and correlating movement. Performers with limited training may be less comfortable exploring how the body moves and could be overwhelmed by unfamiliar terminology. In these cases, a choreographer may have more success introducing movement through story, objective, tactics, and movement patterns rather than steps and counts.

The brain cannot execute more than one high level function at a time. Teaching dance steps without addressing the story causes more difficulty for the dancers when it is time to add the performance aspect. If a choreographer can integrate the motivation and the movement into one idea as it is taught, the performers can more quickly explore narrative through the choreography. This is achieved by articulating the intention behind each step. One can also give performers mental images to attach to the movements for inspiration.

Create the movement for the performers in the room. Even with choreography that is prescribed, choreographers can empower the performers to be collaborative in the interpretation. While the style and physical architecture of pictures needs to be cohesive, it can be incredibly fruitful to allow dancers to translate the movement through the lens of their own bodies and movement qualities rather than by trying to simply mimic the choreographer. By asking questions rather than imposing their own opinions, choreographers can help dancers personalize the movement.

There are many exercises a choreographer can use to help dancers delve into the meaning of the movement and how to convey that to an audience. A few are described below:

1 *Dynamics*: Dynamics are the tools used by the body for storytelling. A choreographer should articulate the desired dynamics of a movement. In less structured moments, encourage dancers to experiment with opposite dynamics (high vs. low, smooth vs. sharp, bound vs. free) within a sequence or during back-to-back runs to see what the dancers discover. In a final performance, a dancer should not just play one dynamic the entire time, but rather offer a range of dynamics to give the movement ebb and flow.

2 *Emotional connection*: In moments of high emotion, a choreographer may aid performers in finding a connection. This is sometimes described as working "inside out." An internal emotional response impacts the physical manifestation of the movement. Ask each dancer what they perceive to be the primary feeling of a sequence. Then have dancers close their eyes and locate where in the body that feeling lives. Have them dance from that location in the body.

3 *Action verbs*: Action verbs are a main tenet in many acting methodologies and give performers a motivation to accomplish (see page 99). They can change throughout the dance sequence as a character's tactics evolve. For example, the main objective of a dance might be *to win over* their scene partner. Over the course of the sequence, the character might employ several tactics such as *to seduce, to impress, to intimidate, to soothe, to sass*, and *to challenge.* This gives the performer something active to play and adds dimension and depth to the narrative. There is always a scene partner, either real or imaginary, and all verbs are an action the performer is doing *to* the other person. If imagined, the dancer should pick someone specific and place them in a spot in the room. Even if the scene partner is themselves (the objective is to convince myself), the dancer should imagine playing to an externalized version of themselves.

4 *Dance as an animal*: This exercise is extremely beneficial for performers who have a tendency of being overly analytical or "in their heads." Each dancer or group selects an animal. Rather than a literal re-enactment of that creature, ask the dancers to interpret the movement using the essence of the animal. This causes the dancer to be "in the moment" as they translate every movement into the language of that animal and are not afforded time to judge or plan ahead.

5 *Embodying character*: Sometimes performers become self-conscious when they feel exposed or personally vulnerable. In these instances, it can be liberating for the performers to work on embodying a character. This can be a character in the script or someone unrelated such as a favorite evil villain. Beware with this exercise of generalized caricatures. Instead, a performer must truly understand the qualities of the character and examine their point of view during each moment throughout the dance.

6 *Full body storytelling*: With many of these exercises, performers internalize the feelings and character losing track of the physical engagement and interpretation. Remind

dancers that the body is the vessel for the storytelling. Choreographers should encourage dancers to find the full extent of the movement within the body. An exercise that helps achieve this is to instruct dancers to tell the story using the tips of the toes and fingers. This promotes line and extension within the body. When dancers begin reaching past where they thought they could go, it is common to have a real emotional response. This is what is referred to as working "outside in." An external physical exercise causes an internal emotional experience.

7 *Tackling difficult subject matter*: Performers should be given tools to approach difficult, sensitive, or charged material in a way that is healthy and sustainable. For example, a choreographer can use movement prompts and Laban efforts to build the movement in a way that does not require re-living trauma.

In rehearsals, shift the dancers' focus "out of the mirror" as soon as possible. Mirrors are a wonderful tool that can be utilized to correct alignment, match line, and practice spacing. However, when a person looks into a mirror, they are focusing on themselves rather than what they are communicating with the movement to someone else. Because people will perform the way they practice, a dancer who spends too much time observing through a mirror will have greater difficulty activating their eyes in performance. Also, dancers tend to become overly reliant on watching other people through the mirror for timing, sequencing, and spacing. It is vital to either take away the mirrors or instruct dancers to pick a focal point through the mirror *past* themselves. This allows dancers to discover how the movement *feels* rather than how it *looks* and eases the transition of the movement onto the stage. Motivate performers to remain in character even if mistakes happen. If a step is forgotten, a dancer should continue with the story, feel, and groove until they are able to get back on track. A choreographer can assist performers in establishing "guideposts" in the choreography — clear moments where a dancer can pick up the movement if the train gets derailed.

When working with soloists, it is important to play to their strengths and perceptions on the character and story. Preparing several options or building choreography with the dancer in the room ensures the dancer's comfort and success in execution. Ask if they prefer extensions and turns on the right or the left. Inquire about any special skills or particular strengths of the performer that you can build into the choreography if appropriate to the moment.

Giving Notes

Before beginning a note session, a choreographer can gauge the energy of the room by taking a poll of the performers: "Thumbs up, thumbs middle, thumbs down, how did that feel?" Be judicious when giving notes. Try not to overwhelm the performers. Giving dancers too many corrections to think about can be counterproductive. A choreographer should determine when and how to give certain notes. A performer might not be far enough along in their process to be able to execute more complicated notes properly. If someone is still unclear on the steps, they most likely are not ready for corrections on performance value. Conversely, the performer could still be investigating the character and intention of the movement and therefore the choreographer might want to encourage that exploration before bogging the performer down in detailed notes about timing and placement.

While a choreographer makes corrections to the movement, they also want to bolster the performers' confidence. Beginning notes with something positive can offer encouragement to the cast. Issues should be addressed constructively. Also, if a dancer succeeds in a moment where they had previously been struggling, acknowledge it verbally. Allowing people to make mistakes as well as discoveries can yield thrilling and serendipitous results. By not over-dictating every moment, dancers are afforded room to lend their artistry to the performance. Sometimes this means waiting to give specific notes until the dancer has repeatedly made the same mistake without self-correcting. However, it is a problem if a choreographer has to give the same note to a dancer multiple times without improvement. The choreographer should check in with the performer and examine the phrasing of the note to see if there is a different way to articulate the concept. A person cannot implement a negative note. If someone is told not to think about a pink elephant, all they are going to do is think about a pink elephant. A more effective note is to tell someone what to do instead. For example, instead of saying "Don't look down!" say "Make sure to play to the balcony."

ACTIVITY REHEARSAL TIMELINE

1 Consult your movement arc (see page 33) for a list of all numbers and movement moments in the show.
2 Approximate how much time will be needed to stage each sequence.
3 Within that time frame, break down what characters will be needed at which intervals.
4 EXAMPLE:
    1) Number: Song Title (4 minutes long)
    2) Staging: 4 hours
    3) Breakdown:
        a) 2 hours—Soloist
        b) 2 hours—Add full ensemble

12 All the Other Things

The choreographer is an integral part of the creative team that helps to mold an entire production. There are several responsibilities that a choreographer will either execute or collaborate on depending on the production, such as building transitions, staging the curtain call, and overseeing understudy and swing rehearsals. Some shows also necessitate unique, specialized demands that warrant a discussion.

Transitions

Transitions are the silent star of a musical. They determine the pace, flow, and energy of a production. Effective transitions can create environment, set a mood, and continue storytelling. Conversely, poor transitions can bring a show's momentum to a halt. The director, choreographer, and music director work closely with the design team to decide what parameters and conventions will be used for transitions. The style and feel of transitions should remain consistent throughout the production to help create the world of the piece. Any deviations should be intentional to make a specific point or to elicit a response from the audience. When looking at each transition, questions to ask include:

1 What transition purpose is built into the script (change of location, passage of time, mood shift)?

2 Will transitions be "a vista," or in view of the audience, or covered with drops, curtains, or visual diversions to isolated parts of the stage?

3 Is there an "in one," or a scene meant to be performed in front of the main curtain while a set change is occurring, built into the script?

4 Based on the design, what changes to the stage need to occur?

5 Will set changes be performed by cast, crew, or automation? (Keep in mind that there are union rules that dictate how Equity performers can be utilized in set changes.)

6 If the performers are executing the transition, are they moving as characters or as performers?

7 What other backstage business needs to occur that will affect the length and timing of the transition (costume change, prop handoff)?

8 Is there music underscoring the transition?

9 What story is being told through the transition?

The creative team uses this information to build the look, timing, sequence, and action of each transition. Often this includes choreographing not only the performers, but the technical elements as well. The order, timing, and design of each move must be determined for safety, efficiency, visual appeal, and narrative meaning to the audience. In the 2016 Broadway revival of the musical *Falsettos*, designed by David Rockwell, the set largely consisted of oversized building blocks that were constantly rearranged by the performers to demonstrate the characters' attempts to rearrange their lives and relationships. The transitions of the set aided in the visual storytelling.

First determine the order and movement pattern of all the performers and technical elements involved in the transition. Do all parts of the transition happen at once or does order impact function and story? It is imperative to track the offstage traffic patterns along with the onstage traffic patterns. Are all stage entrances and exits viable or are specific wings blocked with set pieces? Does a performer need to exit on a specific side of the stage due to a quick change or re-entrance? Then the choreographer works with the director to decide where the audience's focus should be placed. Does the transition itself advance the story or should the audience's eye be diverted using lighting, choreography, or blocking in a different part of the stage? Once these questions have been resolved and conventions established, the choreographer can begin developing specific movement for each transitional moment. Keep in mind the energy of the scene or song right before and right after the transition. Determine what energy shift is needed to continue the momentum of the musical.

Some musicals have transitions built into the musical numbers themselves. In the musical *Legally Blonde*, characters change location many times over the course of a production number. The musical *Gypsy* contains a vaudeville sequence that demonstrates the passage of time. In the original production directed and choreographed by Jerome Robbins, the younger performers executed trenches with a strobe light flashing as the older performers replaced them onstage repeating the same trenches. This transition made its way permanently into the script. These transitions have the added element of very prescribed timing based on the music. The choreographer must seamlessly weave the transition into the build and movement of the production number. Transitions are created in the rehearsal room and re-addressed in technical rehearsals to ensure that all components work together smoothly in the correct rhythm and timing.

Contact and Intimacy

Most musicals require some form of contact between performers ranging from a kiss to physical contact while dancing, to intense moments of physical intimacy or violence. Physical contact must be closely monitored to ensure the comfort and safety of all performers. Moments of intimacy and violence should be meticulously choreographed and repeated in practice to create trust and consistency. Most importantly, consent must be established. Performers need to be given an avenue to set boundaries and express discomfort or remove consent without fear of retribution in order to truly create a safe and ethical work environment. Organizations such as the SAFD (Society of American Fight Directors) and IDC (Intimacy Directors and Coordinators) offer training and resources for producers, directors, choreographers, performers, and educators as well as certification programs for fight directors and intimacy directors/choreographers/coordinators. The book *Staging Sex: Best Practices,*

Tools, and Techniques for Theatrical Intimacy (2020) by Chelsea Pace and Laura Rikard establishes guidelines and exercises that can be applied to any type of physical contact, including partnering and lifts. Take time at the start of a rehearsal process for performers to outline their physical boundaries. Boundaries can shift daily or based on who is present in the room, so a check in with partners before each rehearsal or show is recommended. If a production has violence or intimacy, it is recommended that producers hire specialized or certified directors/coordinators/choreographers to stage and oversee these moments.

The founders of Intimacy Directors International, Tonia Sina, Alicia Rodis, and Siobhan Richardson, developed five pillars related to stage intimacy that choreographers can apply to *all* moments of physical contact in a production, including lifts and partner dancing (Percy 2020). The first pillar is *context.* Conversations take place about the characters and why the moment is necessary for the story dictated by the script. Performers should recognize what in the show has led up to this moment and why the characters act the way they do. Questions to examine include: How do these characters feel about each other? Who initiates the contact? How does it affect their relationship? What needs for the characters as well the script does the contact fulfill? Moments of contact should be broken down beat by beat identifying objectives and obstacles and analyzing the build. Once performers understand the necessity and role of the contact or intimacy, staging can begin.

The second pillar is *consent.* No matter what a script, choreographer, or director dictate, the only person who can give consent is the performer involved in the contact. A choreographer must acknowledge the power that they hold and actively work to create a space where performers are able to freely give or deny consent without coercion. Permission is not the same as consent. Performers have the right to withdraw their consent or change their boundaries at any time, even after the show has opened. This is necessary to ensure performer safety and well-being.

The third pillar is *communication.* The first conversation should center around people's boundaries. Encourage performers to be as specific as possible when outlining their boundaries. Together establish a word that can be used in rehearsal and performance any time a performer's boundary is crossed. When discussing and staging moments of contact or intimacy, there should always be a third party present in the room such as a stage manager. Stay in constant communication about moments of contact. Make sure they continue to serve their narrative purpose and find solutions to any issues that arise. Directors, choreographers, and stage managers should check in with performers. Look for signs that someone is uncomfortable, recognizing that some people might not be as confident to voice their concerns.

The fourth pillar is *choreography.* Contact, intimacy, and violence must all be choreographed as precisely and clearly as dance steps. Break down contact step-by-step and build up to the more intense moments slowly. Give alternatives for contact that is outside of a performer's established boundaries. Be specific and detailed down to every hand placement. Create a common language for the choreography and stress the importance of eye contact and breath. Continue to connect the choreography to the story told in the script. All contact, including intimacy, violence, partnering, and lifts should be rehearsed initially in slow motion and then increased to three-quarter speed once performers are confident and proficient in the choreography. Repetition creates trust and comfort. Once contact choreography is set, it must never change unless approved by the performers and the creative team.

The final pillar is *closure*. Closure allows the performers and creatives in the room to separate character from performer and fiction from reality. It is not uncommon for lines to become blurred when working in an intimate setting. Extremely intense moments can become emotionally taxing. Creating a ritual that is performed at the end of a contact moment or the finish of a rehearsal or performance allows participants to release tension or emotions of the characters without carrying it into their personal lives.

At times, choreography will call for intricate lifts. Hand placement, timing, positions, and weight distribution should all be addressed before attempting to run a lift sequence at full speed. Spotters must always be present as the performers are learning the mechanics of a lift. Dancers should always make eye contact before a lift occurs or have a signal of readiness if eye contact is not possible. Lift, fight, and intimacy calls are established with a list of moments that should be practiced before every run through or performance. If requested by the dancers, spotters are present for lift calls. Moments of intimacy usually only require a check in before performances unless something needs to change. Most times the

Fig. 12.1 Lifts. Photo by Bret Brookshire.

stage manager is responsible for maintaining the consistency and safety of fights and intimacy.

Some musicals require a large amount of partner dancing in the choreography. Each genre of dance has its own technique and style. If these are not an area of expertise, the choreographer should consider bringing someone familiar with the dance style onto the choreographic team or hire a consultant for the production. Look at the rehearsal period allotted to evaluate if there is time to train performers or if casting emphasis should be placed on dancers who are already skilled in that specific genre.

Partner dancing relies on the idea of leading and following. It is a non-verbal conversation between two people using the body and a personal connection to communicate. When choreographing partner moments, take time to discuss the story and what is being communicated between the two characters while they dance. How does dancing change the relationship of the characters? Who is leading and who is following? Use rehearsals to solidify trust and connection between partners. Even in structured choreography, it should appear as if it is happening for the first time. The person choreographed to follow must actually respond to the cues the leader is indicating, even when they know what moves come next in the choreography. An audience can deduce if a dancer is anticipating the next movement rather than connecting and sharing resistance with their partner.

If dancers are being trained during the rehearsal period, everyone in the room should be taught to lead and to follow. This creates mutual trust and opens up the possibilities for the choreographer. Is there a dance sequence where the person leading constantly shifts back and forth? Are there opportunities to break free of heteronormative structures traditionally placed on partnering? How can partner dancing most effectively be used to advance the story? The possibilities are endless as choreographers tap into the narrative and character development potential encompassed in partnering.

Improvisation

Improvisation can be used to arrive at structured movement (see Chapter 7), but it can also be woven into the fabric of a performance. In rehearsal, a choreographer might have dancers improvise until a desired mix of movement has been achieved. The moment is then frozen, and must be repeated the same way each night. However, it is also common for a choreographer to allot a specified amount of time for performers to improvise as characters or within the mood, emotion, and environment of the moment for the length of the production. For example, a choreographer working on a production of The Wiz might introduce moments of guided improv when the characters enter the Emerald City. During improvised moments, encourage performers to be specific in their choices. For example, a choreographer attempting to create a group celebration in a number might ask the performers to improvise celebratory movement. While the choreographer is trying to achieve a general celebration, if the performers all execute "generalized" celebration movements, the end result will appear under-energized and flat. Each performer should decide how their specific character would celebrate and commit fully to that movement. One character might leap across the stage. Another might grab a partner and spin them around. Someone else might find a more internalized boogie. The combination of committed, distinct, individualized improvisational dancing will result in an energized feel of celebration for the audience.

Moments of improvisation invite the performers into the creative process and keep each performance fresh and new. These moments will evolve and grow as the dancers delve deeper into the meaning and emotion. It is important that a member of the choreographic team continues to observe and monitor improvisational points during the run of the show to ensure that the integrity of the story remains intact.

Child Performers

Musicals such as *Billy Elliot*, *Oliver*, *Annie*, *Matilda*, and *School of Rock* rely on their young protagonists to bring a story to life. When choreographing for younger performers, treat them as equals to the rest of the cast, expecting the same level of work ethic and showing respect and compassion. Young minds are sponges eager to absorb information. At the same time, understand that it may be a longer learning process and build that into the rehearsal timeline.

Any time there is a child in a production, there will be a guardian whose responsibility it is to watch the child when backstage as well as make sure the child enters and exits from the set location at the proper time. This guardian should also learn any choreography that the young performer dances so they can rehearse with the child during down time. For most productions, child parts are cast with multiple young performers who rotate rehearsals and performances due to the intense time commitment. There are also specific rules and guidelines dictating rehearsal length, proper conditions, and the necessity for tutors.

For choreography, there are some strategies to ensure a consistent performance. Keep personnel that interact with young performers as regular as possible. For very young performers, it can be beneficial to assign an adult performer who is always with the child onstage and can help them hit their marks in the proper timing and stay safe. For older children, markers can be created in sequence and even made into a game. For example, "We run and sit on the circle. Then we follow the leader and end up standing next to the staircase." These games give context, help memorization, and make it fun and repeatable. For structured steps, a choreographer can either have an adult onstage dance the same movement so the child can watch, or it can be turned into a call and response where an adult dances the step first and the child repeats it back. When helping a child performer find the appropriate emotion for a scene or song, directors and choreographers often work with the child to develop an individual story. For example, if a child needs to be scared in a dance number, the choreographer might create a story where the child is running away from a large monster. This story can be different for each child playing the part.

Special Skills

Special skills may be intrinsically or extrinsically necessary for a production. Intrinsic needs are dictated by the script. *Xanadu* requires performers to roller-skate. A strong knowledge of ballroom dance is required for *Dirty Dancing*. Extrinsic needs are based on the directorial and choreographic concept as well as special desires of the creative team. The 2013 Broadway revival of *Pippin* was told through the lens of a circus, requiring cast members who had specific circus skills.

When choosing a musical or a concept that requires special skills, a choreographer looks at the talent pool to ascertain if there are enough skilled performers available or enough rehearsal time to train performers. A choreographer should consider the safety and long-term impact on the performer. Ensure that the conditions are safe and sustainable eight shows a week for the duration of the run. Finally, examine whether the special skill enhances or detracts from the story being told.

When training dancers in a new skill, it is ideal to begin the training early in the rehearsal process. This affords the performers time to learn the skill with proficiency and confidence. For a production of *Mary Poppins*, the performers should have training on the flying rigging before technical rehearsals. When necessary, an expert should be consulted or brought in for the training period. In Texas State University's production of *The Hunchback of Notre Dame*, aerial specialist Joshua Dean was hired to train performers representing "the bells" on Spanish web and cloud swing. Training started as soon as the theatre space was available and several weeks before technical rehearsals began. Time was built into the rehearsal calendar every day for instruction and practice.

If a show or concept calls for puppetry, the choreographer should collaborate with the entire creative team to determine what conventions would most benefit the production. How will the puppeteer and the puppet interact with each other as well as the audience? Is the puppeteer visible to the audience? Are they masked behind props and scenery? Are black lights or other lighting effects used to hide the performer? Are they visible but treated as if they are not there? Are the puppeteer and puppet treated as one entity? Are they two separate characters that interact? Musicals such as *Avenue Q*, *The Lion King*, and *Beauty and the Beast* handled this interaction differently, but with equal success because the parameters were clear.

Once work with the puppets begins, the choreographer can experiment with the movement quality of each puppet. This impacts how the puppet is crafted and ways in which the puppeteer manipulates the puppet. Distinct movement qualities bring the puppet to life as a unique and fully developed character. Consider the focus of the other people onstage. Make sure they look at the puppet when the puppet is singing or speaking. A unified focus of the ensemble will direct the audience's attention and help track the movement and story of the puppetry.

Any specialties desired for a production should be addressed during early budgetary discussions and rehearsal planning. The production team must also ensure the special skill can be executed safely and proficiently within the allotted time frame.

Curtain Call

Curtain call is a ritualistic moment during theatre productions. For the length of the event, performers are put on a figurative (or literal) pedestal as they act out stories. The curtain call is a time for performers to humble themselves before the audience and ask to be accepted back into society. The audience is afforded the opportunity to show their gratitude and enthusiasm (or lack thereof) for the show. The bows serve as a bridge from the theatrical illusion back to reality.

Directors and choreographers all have differing opinions about the function and the form of a curtain call. Artistically, the bows can be used to continue the narrative, reinforce the main theme, or evoke an emotional response. The famous curtain call at the end of *A Chorus Line* transforms into a large unison kickline that accentuates the central idea. Even though the audience has spent two hours getting to know these individual characters, at the end of the day the performers all become another cog in the machine. As the curtain comes down on the dancers kicking, it gives the illusion that the kickline continues forever. No matter the performer, the cycle is unending.

Commercially, the bows can create uplifting energy and offer the audience a tune to hum as they walk away. At the end of *Moulin Rouge*, rather than leave the audience with the sorrow of Satine's death, the curtain call includes a megamix of reprises from the show as well as additional tunes. "These post-curtain moments have less to do with telling the story and more with telling the audience how to feel about the story they have just seen and what they should tell their friends" (Soloski 2019). In his article "On Bow and Exit Music," Derek Miller stated, "Bow and exit music announce with particular poignancy the musical's struggle for both cultural significance and financial success" (2017). No matter how it is constructed, curtain calls for musicals have become an extension of the performance and are almost always a fully staged and choreographed production number.

The order of the curtain call is particularly meaningful and impacts the audience's perception of the story. Directors and choreographers make decisions depending on the production, but usually, the ensemble bows first followed by characters in ascending order of prominence. This solidifies the audience's understanding of the message of the piece. Some musicals, especially ones that leave the audience on a heavy, dramatic note or are extremely ensemble-based, will forgo individual bows for a unison company bow. Pre-existing bow music might also have an impact on order as well as length of bows if musical motifs are attached to specific characters.

The choreographer often times the bows to the music to keep the pace flowing. Entrances should overlap with the peak of the previous bow. In group bows, determining whether or not to hold hands will create unity and consistency. A leader can be assigned to ensure unison timing to the bow. The choreographer might offer tricks or internal phrases to help the ensemble breathe and move together. Vincent Cardinal, Professor in the Department of Musical Theatre at the University of Michigan, recommends that performers repeat the following phrase in their minds while bowing: "Thank you very much. We certainly do appreciate it." Personal bows can have a range of prescribed movement from simply a set number of counts per bow to full sections of choreography. A curtain call wants to feel clean and fast paced without the bows themselves feeling rushed. Encourage performers to not start bowing until everyone in their group has fully landed in their position.

After a group or individual has bowed, they typically move to a designated point onstage, slowly building a tableau of the entire company as more performers join. Look at all available entrances for bows including voms, wings, stairs, and upstage center. A choreographer can keep forward momentum by alternating entrances between stage right and stage left. As performers complete their bow and head toward their assigned position, they should "throw focus" or "pass the food" to the next performers entering to bow. This can be accomplished with eye focus or a gesture.

For a pair, couple, or trio bowing together, it is tradition to bow as a group and then step forward one at a time for an individual bow. As the characters that carry the emotional connection of the piece, the leading characters, or protagonists, bow last. After everyone has bowed, the full company comes forward, often in multiple lines with the principals in the front line. The company bows all together, taking the cue from the lead or the performer standing downstage center. Then the full company presents to the orchestra. Unifying this gesture adds polish and precision. Some creative teams will also present to the booth to indicate stage management and technical crews. Bows typically end with one additional company bow. The cast either remains onstage while the curtain drops or exits the stage.

Bows can be a time to use special effects, gimmicks, tricks, or costume changes for dramatic effect or audience appeal. The 2019 Broadway production of *A Christmas Carol* ended the curtain call with a collection for charity and the cast playing "Silent Night" with handbells (Soloski 2019). The 1966 Broadway production of *Mame* saw the title character enter in a completely new gown created solely for the final bow. The 2009 Broadway revival of *HAIR* ended with a dance party as performers went into the house and invited audience members up on stage. The 2016 Broadway production of *SpongeBob SquarePants: The Broadway Musical* went all out ending with bubble blasters, streamers, beach balls, and confetti cannons. No matter how a creative team chooses to approach the curtain call, it must be carefully planned with thorough consideration of meaning, energy, and audience engagement.

Photo Call

Photo call is an opportunity once the show has opened for the production team to take planned photographs that demonstrate specific moments in the show to highlight design elements as well as powerful stage pictures. Usually, the creative team will be asked to submit a list of requested shots. A shot list is created based on the requests made and the time allotted for the photo call. Often in regional productions, the director and choreographer leave after opening and are not present at the photo call. In these instances, an assistant or dance captain is placed in charge of staging pictures and facilitating the arrangement of performers.

When making photo requests, consider moments of strong pictures or visual impact. It is difficult in a staged photograph to replicate the energy, force, and flow of a movement. Oftentimes, a running photo call, or pictures taken during an actual performance, are more useful for a choreographer to accurately demonstrate the choreography. However, especially in large group numbers or full stage pictures, there might be moments that are better captured in a staged photo call. Choose moments that work as a still pose. This can include a tableau, the final pose, or shapes within the choreography that can be held for a period of time while creating interesting lines with a high amount of negative space.

To aid in capturing the essence and vivacity of the movement, a choreographer might ask the performers to run a few counts of 8 leading up to the picture moment. The performers can also execute movement in slow motion with resistance to maintain the intensity of the choreography while allowing time for the photography. A choreographer must keep in mind the physical strain on the performers, especially if the photo call is after a performance.

Dancers should not be expected to execute an entire second performance and risk injury late at night for the sake of photographs.

The choreographer or a member of the choreographic team might also be tasked with facilitating set ups of various shots housed within a musical number. If a set designer requests a photograph of a specific production number, the choreographer might be asked to pick a pose from that sequence. The choreographer should understand the goal of the photograph when selecting a look.

Rehearsing Understudies and Swings

Occasionally, an understudy or swing rehearsal might occur during the regular rehearsal process, but they most often take place once the show has opened. They are usually run by the stage manager in collaboration with a member of the choreographic team. These rehearsals rely on the accuracy of the Show Bible (see page 124) to make sure understudies and swings are confident in the various tracks they cover. These rehearsals are typically only with the other understudies and swings, so performers must imagine the rest of the cast as they practice.

For an understudy or swing, one of the most valuable tools is having the opportunity to be in the rehearsal room when scenes and numbers are initially staged. This allows them to witness the original intention and motivation behind the movement and to observe how the relationships between characters evolve organically. For replacements who are hired once a production is open, the members of the production team leading rehearsals should convey these details to the performer.

In rehearsal, performers are walked through a dance number finding spacing and numbers. Any questions are clarified before the performers run the number with full performance value. It is difficult to replicate show energy without a complete cast, so performers might need encouragement to find a full-out movement and performance quality. For swings who cover multiple tracks, it is more productive for them to pick one track to rehearse for each run through rather than attempting to practice all of them at once. This enables the swing to follow one track through the entire show and compartmentalize the separate responsibilities. Understudies and swings must understand the boundaries needed to have a consistent performance for the rest of the cast onstage that remains true to the original intent of the creative team, but should also have a chance to bring their individuality to the role.

When an understudy or swing is slated to go on, a put-in rehearsal will happen before the performance. This utilizes the entire cast, but only the performer going on for a new track is in costume and microphone. That performer's entire onstage and offstage track is executed, including difficult lift sequences and quick changes. In addition to put-in rehearsals, particularly tricky or potentially dangerous elements might be run with understudies and swings during a fight or lift call. This includes specialized moments such as aerial work or jumping off tall platforms, or a complicated partnering sequence that cannot be run in swing rehearsals because it requires multiple cast members. A choreographer can consult with the stage manager to schedule out these practices to ensure that performers feel safe and confident when performance time arrives.

ACTIVITY TRACKING TRANSITIONS

Transitions are essential to the flow and energy of a production. Tracking transitions serves many purposes for a choreographer:

1 Isolates the story and practical needs of each transitional moment
2 Helps determine where the audience's focus should be during a transition
3 Allows the choreographer to map out transitions during pre-production
4 Becomes a reference that can be added to the Show Bible.

First, answer the following questions:

1 *Transition name*: This may be assigned in the script or generated by the creative team.
2 *Page number*: Where does it appear in the script?
3 *Length of music*: If there is orchestrated transition music, this can be listed as a length of time, number of measures, or number of counts.
4 *Story needs*: What narration occurs during this transition? Is it dictated by the script or developed by the creative team?
5 *Practical needs:* What needs to happen during this transition for the performance to be able to continue? This includes scenic changes, costume changes, prop handoffs, and lighting shifts.
6 *Focus*: What is the audience's focus during the transition? Are they watching the characters move the scenery? Is there a dance or staging moment occurring on an isolated part of the stage?

As the choreographer builds the transition, they can fill in the following table:

Table 12.1 Transition tracking sheet

Character	Activity	Start position	End position	Cue	Notes

Transition tracking sheets might additionally be accompanied by stage diagrams that illustrate formations and traffic patterns.

Table 12.2 Example transition questionnaire

Transition name	Love Finds a Way
Page	47
Length of music	6 counts of 8
Story needs	Transition from evening to the following day. See Joseph and Mauricio finally come together.
Practical needs	Set transitions from bar to office.
Focus	Joseph and Mauricio entering from opposite sides of the stage in spotlight and meeting DSC to embrace.

Table 12.3 Example transition tracking sheet

Character	Activity	Start position	End position	Cue	Notes
Joseph	Enters DR—meets Mauricio DC and embraces	DR	DC	Blackout	In spotlight— at same time as Mauricio
Mauricio	Enters DL—meets Joseph DC and embraces	DL	DC	Blackout	In spotlight— at same time as Joseph
Ensemble 1	Enters UL—takes off bar	UL Wing 3— get bar located UC	SR Wing 2	Joseph and Mauricio land DC	Cross DS of office desks
Ensemble 2 & 3	Brings on office desks	UR Wing 3	Desks CL at 6 and 8	Bar begins to move	Exits SL Wing 2 after placing desks

13 Nice Work If You Can Get It

Every choreographer finds their way to musical theatre through a different path. Some people are drawn to choreography from a young age and actively pursue a career as a musical theatre choreographer. Others find a seamless transition from onstage to behind the table as a member of the creative team. Sometimes people are thrust into the role of choreographer out of necessity and discover an affinity and passion for the art form. No matter what the impetus, there are many avenues and opportunities available to people with the vision and drive necessary to make it as a choreographer.

Opportunities for a choreographer range from local to international as well as across several mediums. Within a community, choreographic needs can be found in schools, camps, dance studios, and local community and professional theatre. Nationally and internationally, musical theatre choreographers are employed in regional theatre, Broadway and Off-Broadway productions, national tours, workshops, theme parks, cruise ships, industrial conventions, music videos, television, film, commercials, opera, circus, and theatres throughout the world. Each venue, medium, and genre has its own methodology of producing and collaborating. One of the most important traits for a choreographer is the ability to be flexible and adapt. Because there is no clear-cut path to a career and continued employment, choreographers must also be resilient, persistent, self-motivated, and innovative in finding and creating work.

Musical theatre choreography is an art form that requires exposure and experience in order to learn. It is key for an aspiring choreographer to be in the room and watch other choreographers work. Take note of what is successful. Analyze why approaches did or didn't work. If you are a performer in a production, ask if you can sit in during rehearsals when you are not called. When possible, sit in the house during tech rehearsals and watch the show come to life. Constantly test yourself as you observe the addition of all the technical elements. What needs to change or shift in the choreography? What questions would you ask each individual department? Become a sponge and soak up as much information as possible.

When working on a show or socializing with a choreographer you admire, ask for an opportunity to pick their brain. Never go into these conversations with the goal of requesting something from them. Rather, inquire about their path to becoming a choreographer. Ask questions about their personal creative process. Offer to be available if they ever need dancers for pre-production work. When starting out, choreographers should take every opportunity to develop their skills. No matter how much a person trains, studies, or theorizes, ultimately a choreographer will only improve and grow as an artist by doing the work and learning from the moments of failure as much as the successes. Accepting smaller scale jobs early on enables aspiring choreographers to build their craft and start to create a network.

Assistant/associate positions and apprenticeships, such as the Observership Program through the Stage Directors and Choreographers Foundation (SDCF), can also offer invaluable mentorship, insight, and guidance. The Society is "the theatrical union that unites, empowers, and protects professional stage directors and choreographers throughout the United States" (SDCF 2020). Along with negotiating and enforcing employment agreements, the union offers benefits, resources, and education for its members.

Although formal degrees in musical theatre choreography are scarce, some universities are beginning to offer a musical theatre degree with an emphasis or concentration on musical theatre choreography. In addition, universities offering degrees in musical theatre performance, musical theatre direction, and dance can provide young choreographers with skills, training, and creative outlets. All of these options require the student wanting training and experience in musical theatre choreography to seek out mentors and to curate their own college enterprise based on the courses and opportunities available at each university.

Finding Work

Musical theatre choreography is still largely a business about networking and connections. Somewhere in the backstory of almost every prominent choreographer is a moment where a personal connection or contact fortuitously led to a stepping-stone or a job. A choreographer who is unavailable for a project might recommend their assistant. The writers of a new musical bring on their friend to choreograph the workshop. Two castmates on a bus and truck tour reconnect a decade later as an agent and client. Because of the significance of associations, an aspiring choreographer should cultivate relationships with other artists that inspire and push them.

A conventional road to choreographer involves apprenticeship. A performer can climb the ladder from ensemble member to dance captain, assistant choreographer, associate choreographer, and finally branch out on their own. On this trajectory, connections are made along the way, building a resume filled with collaborations and assistantships with reputable choreographers and directors that encourage a producer to take a chance on a new, up-and-coming choreographer. For high stakes productions, such as Broadway, producers might request a young choreographer to "audition" for the position by choreographing one or two numbers.

The wide and easy access of the internet has created additional pathways for enterprising choreographers. One can search for choreography jobs on countless job search websites that are geared toward various avenues such as studio work, professional theatre, and educational jobs both locally and nationally. Choreographers can also research theatres that are creating the type of work that interests them and submit materials to the artistic director or organization for consideration. While this can be a laborious process, a submission might arrive on the day a theatre is looking for a choreographer with that specialty.

Finding work as a choreographer is often an exercise in patience, determination, and preparedness when opportunity comes knocking. There are agents, especially in New York and Los Angeles, that represent theatrical and commercial choreographers. Making a connection with an agent is a different experience for every artist. Sometimes a connection is made through a personal recommendation of a colleague or mentor. Or an agent will see a choreographer's work and contact them. Other times a choreographer who has been offered a prominent contract can approach an agent to negotiate for them. This could potentially lead to a long-term collaboration. Many times, an artist will begin with an agency as a performer and gradually transition into representation from other departments within the agency. An agent is able to submit choreographers for major projects, advise choreographers on materials that best represent them, and negotiate contracts on behalf of the choreographer.

Greg Uliasz, a creative and talent agent with McDonald/Selznick Associates commented, "If the world is excited about your work, it is time for an agency." When discussing what an agent looks for, he stressed that the art is first and foremost with an emphasis on storytelling followed by a look at the choreographer's trajectory. What experience and connections does the choreographer have? Have they worked as an assistant or associate? Do theatres rehire them? All of these factors weigh into the decision of an agent to take on a choreographer as a client.

Showcases and festivals aimed at fostering young choreographers allow a choreographer to present their work for leading industry producers, agents, directors, and other professionals. Samples include DanceBreak and BC Beat for theatrical dance and Choreographer's Carnival and Club Jeté for commercial dance. While showcases can be a wonderful chance for choreographers to develop and display their work, they can also be costly or house strict parameters. Investigate the effectiveness of showcases. Who will be present? What avenues have opened up for previous participants? Will this format showcase the work to its fullest potential? Choreographers can then make an informed decision on how to utilize a showcase to maximize exposure.

Outside of stage work, the job opportunities for choreographers continue to grow. Musical theatre is experiencing a new renaissance in film and television through live televised musical theatre events, live action reimagining of animated classics, film versions of shows from the musical theatre canon, and the incorporation of musical numbers in scripted television series and movies. Live capture technology allows the work of a choreographer to be transferred to an animated medium. Commercials, music videos, and recording artists employ choreographers in a diversity of styles. Major corporations hire choreographers to create entertainment for large industrial conferences. Theme parks and cruise ships are constantly creating new content. Collaborations with artists from different artistic mediums including opera, visual arts, magicians, and the circus allow for interdisciplinary crossovers such as installation pieces and entertainment experiences. Choreographers who enter the education market are afforded the opportunity to try out and showcase their choreography as well as gain a following and notoriety.

Creating Your Own Work

Musical theatre is increasingly becoming an artist-initiated industry where ground-breaking work is being developed and self-produced by artists. Digital and technological advancements have created an environment where high-quality work can become widely accessible.

Creators no longer have to rely on major theatres or producers to commission their work in order to make an impact.

Finding true collaborators who uphold a similar artistic vision is a lifelong journey. When people find their artistic soulmates, they look for any possible avenues to continue creating together. New work is being developed constantly and showcased through a wide range of mediums. Once a choreographer becomes connected with a new project, many options are available to present the work. Workshops both in New York and throughout the country are an industry standard. Many regional theatres and universities have established a foothold in development by commissioning and premiering new work. There has been a rise in virtually produced musical workshops, which expands the audience reach and scope.

Many theatres and organizations have also instituted artist residencies, fellowships, and grants that give artists time and/or funds to develop their artistic ideas. Additionally, a choreographer can create their own dance company for the freedom to make art about the topics and stories that speak to them and as a means to have their work seen.

Choreographers have begun producing their own dance films. Once they have a vision for a piece, they hire dancers, rent a space, and put together a production team to film and edit the video. With the improvement and affordability of equipment and the development of user-friendly software, a tech-savvy choreographer with a high-quality device and good lighting can stage, shoot, and edit the dance film independently. Social media and streaming platforms allow these videos to have massive distribution for little cost in a short time and create a name for young choreographers. Additionally, a choreographer with an idea for a large-scale piece can develop a high-quality concept video that transforms the imagination into a product that aids producers and investors in visualizing a fully formed production.

Social media has aided in a dance revolution. Never has dance been more prevalent and widely accessible. Choreographers can utilize social media to build a career. Dance films, blogs, podcasts, action photographs, demonstrations, and instructional videos can turn a choreographer into a household name. A well-curated social media presence displays a choreographer's art while also offering an insight into their lives. Many producers, agents, and creative teams follow the handles of popular viral choreographic artists. Theatres and producers seek choreographers with an established fan base. Social media has aided in creating more equity in the visibility of artists. It breaks down the traditional gatekeeper hierarchy and makes space for the voices of artists traditionally excluded from or under-represented in the professional industry.

Displaying Your Work

A choreographer's portfolio is the most comprehensive and powerful tool in the search for fulfilling and lucrative employment. All of the materials a choreographer displays should be cohesive and tell a unifying narrative to an objective observer. A strong portfolio demonstrates a choreographer's body of work while also presenting the essence of the choreographer as an artist and a human with a vision for the type of work they are interested in creating.

A vast amount of work in the industry today is being acquired digitally. People can display work, audition, and interview without ever being in the same room as the interviewers. Potential employers search for information about prospective employees online and on social media. While these platforms can be extremely useful at distributing work, anyone in the industry must also be vigilant about monitoring their online presence. Social media accounts should appear professional, relevant, and up-to-date, and choreographers should remove any content that is no longer representative of their artistic evolution.

An effective and efficient place for a choreographer to house their portfolio is on a personal website. Many web hosting sites have templates that are user-friendly and allow anyone to build a website, but one might also consider hiring a professional for the initial development. A website can display information about the choreographer's background and artistic or activism mission as well as provide news updates, resumes, upcoming events and productions, reviews, photographs, video examples, and contact information. The material should be well organized and attention-grabbing. People typically will not sift through hundreds of photographs, but a dozen carefully selected images can leave a lasting impression. Rather than posting an entire review, extract the key phrases addressing the choreographer's work. For video examples, individual clips can be just as helpful as an edited reel. If an artist creates in several capacities (performer, choreographer, director, educator, activist), each should have its own clear page.

A choreography resume gives producers and directors all the pertinent information at a quick glance. Credits should include the show, the choreographer's position (assistant, associate, co-choreographer, choreographer, director/choreographer), the theatre or producing entity, and the director; and can be listed in order of significance and renown rather than in chronological order. Order can also highlight a specialty in certain types of shows or styles. A choreographer who specializes in tap might list all the tap shows first, regardless of when they occurred. Individual categories may include Broadway/National Tour, Regional, Educational/University, Commercials, TV/Film, and Special Events/Industrial. Awards and training, including earned degrees, are also relevant information. References may be included or requested separately.

A choreographic reel is one of the most powerful marketing tools. Within three minutes, a choreographer can present a plethora of information to producers and potential employers about their previous work, strengths, and personal aesthetic. When compiling a choreography reel, the first question to ask is: "What do I want this reel to say about me?" The goal of a reel is not to show every production a person has ever choreographed but rather to give viewers a taste of their style, unique voice, and potential. It is great to demonstrate range as a choreographer, but one doesn't want to send a confused message about the type of work they aim to create.

The first step for a choreographer is to choose three to four elements or qualities of their work that they want to highlight such as extensive partner work, humor in movement, staging of large groups, or expertise in specific dance genres. Mine through the body of work to select clips that are most impressive and convey vision. These moments can be anywhere from 2 to 30 seconds long. There is a balance between so short that there isn't time to register the images and too long where interest is lost. The quality of the video clips is important and is ideally consistent. Grainy, low-quality video that is filmed from a distance makes it difficult for viewers to truly assess the work. If a high-quality clip that displays a critical aspect of the choreographer's work doesn't exist, they can film clips with dancers in a studio independent of a production.

Once all the video has been amassed, the editing process begins. An editor offers an objective, outside view. Express the key qualities to exhibit along with the catalog of video clips and then grant the editor freedom to assemble a draft. An open dialogue about revisions will enable the choreographer and editor to arrive at an ideal final product. If the choreographer decides to edit the reel themselves, outside eyes should be brought in for feedback.

An effective reel is typically 2–4 minutes in length. Do not make a reel too long—short and sweet leaves viewers with piqued interest. When editing, extra flairs such as flashy transitions should be used sparingly to allow the work to speak for itself. It is critical that all rules and regulations around the length of video clip permissible and the use of images of union performers are researched and observed. Include relevant and noteworthy captions pertaining to show title, theatre, and performers. Display the choreographer's contact information, including website and social media handles, at the end of the reel.

Music used to underscore a reel can set the tone and give additional clues to a choreographer's aesthetic. Occasionally, it may be preferable to use the original sound of the footage, but typically one to two songs are selected as the undercurrent of the reel. When choosing music, copyright and royalty laws must be followed. Once the reel is completed, it can be displayed on social media, a choreographer's website, and distributed to industry professionals.

ACTIVITY CHOREOGRAPHY REEL

1   Decide on three to four elements or qualities of your work to highlight.
2   Choose a piece of music that matches your vision and style.
3   Review video footage and select clips that tell your story as well as are impressive or flashy.
4   Secure any permissions and rights necessary for footage and music.
5   Shoot any additional footage needed.
6   Give the materials to an editor or begin the editing process.
7   Use accents in the music when deciding on clip placement.
8   Review drafts and make revisions until every moment of the reel tells a unified story and holds the viewer's attention without lagging or moving too quickly.
9   Go back to the list made in step 1 and guarantee that all the elements and qualities are addressed.
10 Share with a few trusted colleagues for an objective outside perspective and make adjustments.
11 Publish the reel.

Bibliography

"Access." The National Theatre. Accessed January 5, 2022. https://www.nationaltheatre.org.uk/your-visit/access.

Asian American Performers Action Coalition (AAPAC). "The Visibility Report: Racial Representation on NYC Stages 2018–2019." June, 2021. http://www.aapacnyc.org/2018-2019.html.

Atkins, Irvin J. "Directing for the Open Stage." *The Director in a Changing Theatre*. Ed. J. Robert Willis. Palo Alto, CA: Mayfield, 1976: 231–234.

Baldwin, Chris. *Stage Directing: A Practical Guide*. Ramsbury: Crowood, 2003.

Benedetti, Robert. *The Actor at Work*. 8th ed. Boston, MA: Allyn & Bacon, 2001.

"Blindness." Accessed January 5, 2022. https://www.blindnessevent.com/&obreve;ut.

Bogart, Anne and Tina Landau. *The Viewpoints Book: A Practical Guide to Viewpoints and Composition*. New York: Theatre Communications Group, 2005.

Broadway World. "Pie Shop Closed! SWEENEY TODD Concludes Off-Broadway Run Today." *Broadway World*. August 26, 2018. https://www.broadwayworld.com/article/Pie-Shop-Closed-SWEENEY-TODD-Concludes-Off-Broadway-Run-Today-20180826.

Brown, Jason Robert. "A Songwriting Masterclass with Jason Robert Brown." February 22, 2013. The Dramatists Guild of America. *YouTube*, 1:31:00. https://www.youtube.com/watch?v=oXyyhKHyEzo.

Caldarone, Marina and Maggie Lloyd-Williams. *Actions: The Actor's Thesaurus*. London: Nick Hern Books, 2004.

Chase, David and Ian Weinberger. "Gimme a Crash on 7: An Introduction to Dance Arranging (Part I)." American Society of Music Arrangers and Composers, Webinar, April 17, 2021.

Chekhov, Michael. *To the Actor: On the Technique of Acting*. New York: Routledge, 2002.

Citron, Stephen. *Jerry Herman: Poet of the Showtune*. New Haven, CT: Yale University Press, 2004.

Clement, Olivia. "Why You Shouldn't Call These Actors 'Differently-Abled.'" *Playbill*. June 13, 2017. https://www.playbill.com/article/the-double-edged-sword-that-is-being-a-disabled-actor.

Cooper, Susan. *Staging Dance*. New York: Routledge, 2016.

Cousin, Tomé. "Lack of Diversity in Theatre's Directors and Choreographers. *Live & In Color*. June 18, 2019. https://liveandincolor.org/blog/2019/6/18/lack-of-diversity-in-theatres-directors-and-choreographers.

Cowan, Suzanne. "Accessibility and Dance." *Danz Magazine*. December 10, 2018. https://danz.org.nz/accessibility-and-dance.

Cramer, Lyn. *Creating Musical Theatre: Conversations with Broadway Directors and Choreographers*. New York: Bloomsbury, 2013.

Dean, Alexander and Lawrence Carra. *Fundamentals of Play Directing*. 5th ed. Long Grove, IL: Waveland Press, 2009.

Deer, Joe. *Directing in Musical Theatre: An Essential Guide*. New York: Routledge, 2014.

Diakhaté, Ousmane and Hansel Ndumbe Eyoh. "The Roots of African Theatre Ritual and Orality in the Pre-Colonial Period." *Critical Stages*, June, 2017, issue 15. Accessed February 20, 2021. http://www.critical-stages.org/15/the-roots-of-african-theatre-ritual-and-orality-in-the-pre-colonial-period/.

"Disability Impacts Us All." Centers for Disease Control and Prevention. Last reviewed September 16, 2020. https://www.cdc.gov/ncbddd/disabilityandhealth/infographic-disability-impacts-all. html#:~:text=61%20million%20adults%20in%20the,is%20highest%20in%20the%20South.

Ewan, Vanessa and Kate Sagovsky. *Laban's Efforts in Action: A Movement Handbook for Actors with Online Video Resources.* London: Methuen Drama, 2019.

"Expressionism." *Encyclopaedia Britannica*. Accessed March 5, 2021. https://www.britannica. com/art/Expressionism.

Eyer, J. Austin and Lyndy Franklin Smith. *Broadway Swings: Covering the Ensemble in Musical Theatre.* London: Bloomsbury, 2015.

Fierberg, Ruthie. "After Endless Hours, Spencer Liff Formed a New Language—The Choreography of *Spring Awakening.*" *Playbill*. December 29, 2015. https://www.playbill.com/article/after-endless-hours-spencer-liff-formed-a-new-language-u2014-the-choreography-of-spring-awakening-com-376781.

Fierberg, Ruthie. "Theatre Jobs: Do You Have What It Takes to be an Associate Director on Broadway?" *Playbill*. October 21, 2017. https://www.playbill.com/article/theatre-jobs-do-you-have-what-it-takes-to-be-an-associate-director-on-broadway.

Fierberg, Ruthie. "Theatre Jobs: What Exactly Does a Dance Arranger Do?" *Playbill*. January 15, 2018. https://www.playbill.com/article/theatre-jobs-what-exactly-does-a-dance-arranger-do.

Gelb, Arthur. "Thornton Wilder, 63, Sums Up Life and Art in New Play Cycle." *The New York Times*. November 6, 1961.

Gladstone, Emma. "Disabled Leaders in Dance." British Arts Council. July 1, 2016. *YouTube*, 0:7:46. https://www.youtube.com/watch?v=2A7AjmfpNY4.

Green, Adam. "Tap-Dancing Legend Savion Glover Reanimates the Game-Changing Broadway Musical *Shuffle Along.*" *Vogue Magazine*. April 28, 2016. https://www.vogue.com/article/tap-dance-legend-savion-glover-broadway-musical-shuffle-along.

Guarino, Lindsay and Wendy Oliver. *Jazz Dance: A History of the Roots and Branches.* Gainesville, FL: University Press of Florida, 2015.

Haas, Jacqui Greene. *Dance Anatomy.* 2nd ed. Champaign, IL: Human Kinetics, 2010.

Haskins, Jane. "How to Copyright a Dance." *Legal Zoom*. November 19, 2020. https://www. legalzoom.com/articles/how-to-copyright-a-dance.

Hayes, Janys. "Gesture in Actor Training: Embodied Partial Narratives." *Southern Semiotic Review* (2013). Accessed February 21, 2021. http://www.southernsemioticreview.net/gesture-in-actor-training-by-janys-hayes/.

Hodge, Francis and Michael McLain. *Play Directing: Analysis, Communication, and Style.* 7th ed. New York: Routledge, 2016.

Humphrey, Doris. *The Art of Making Dances.* Princeton, NJ: Dance Horizons, 1987.

Isherwood, Charles. "Review: 'Falsettos,' a Perfect Musical, and Imperfect Family." *The New York Times*. October 27, 2016. https://www.nytimes.com/2016/10/28/theater/falsettos-review.html.

Japan Arts Council (JAC). "Distinctive Expressions: Mie." Invitation to Kabuki. 2019. https://www2. ntj.jac.go.jp/unesco/kabuki/en/production/performance5.html.

Jones, John Bush. *Our Musicals, Ourselves: A Social History of the American Musical Theatre.* Waltham, MA: Brandeis University Press, 2003.

Jones, Margo. *Theatre-in-the-Round.* New York: Rinehart, 1951.

Joseph, Stephen. *Theatre in the Round.* New York: Taplinger, 1967.

Kendrick, John. "Elements of a Musical: The Score." *Musicals101.com*. The Cyber Encyclopedia of Musical Theatre, Film & Television. Revised 2020. February 17, 2021. http://www. musicals101.com/score.htm.

Kim, Christine Sun. "The Enchanting Music of Sign Language." August, 2015. TED Conference. *YouTube*, 0:15:17. https://www.youtube.com/watch?v=2Euof4PnjDk.

Kirk, John W., Ralph A. Bellas, and Christina M. Kirk. *The Art of Directing*. 2nd ed. Xlibris Corporation, 2004.

Kranking, Emily. "Physical Disabilities Take the Rare Spotlight on Broadway." *RespectAbility*. April 19, 2019. https://www.respectability.org/2019/04/physical-disabilities-broadway/.

Laban, Rudolf and Lisa Ullman. *The Mastery of Movement*. 4th ed. Alton: Dance Books, 2011.

Lerman, Liz. *Hiking the Horizontal: Field Notes from a Choreographer*. Middletown, CT: Wesleyan University Press, 2011. Kindle.–

Loney, Glenn. *Unsung Genius: The Passion of Dancer-Choreographer Jack Cole*. New York: Franklin Watts, 1984.

Mazzeo, Esme. "*Oklahoma!*'s Ali Stroker Knows That Wheelchair Choreography Can Be Sexy, and Wants You to Know It Too." *Vulture*. March 19, 2019. https://www.vulture.com/2019/03/oklahoma-s-ali-stroker-on-wheelchair-dancing-and-sexiness.html#comments.

McCarthy-Brown, Nyama. *Dance Pedagogy for a Diverse World: Culturally Relevant Teaching in Theory, Research and Practice*. Jefferson, NC: McFarland, 2017. Kindle.

McWaters, Debra. *The Fosse Style*. Gainesville, FL: University Press of Florida, 2008.

Merriam-Webster.com Dictionary, s.v. "anachronism." Accessed March 14, 2021. https://www.merriam-webster.com/dictionary/anachronism.

Miller, Derek. "On Bow and Exit Music." *The Journal of American Drama and Theatre,* Fall 2017, vol. 30, no. 1.

Minton, Sandra Cerny. *Choreography: A Basic Approach Using Improvisation*. 3rd ed. Champaign, IL: Human Kinetics, 2007.

Miranda, Lin-Manuel (@Lin_Manuel). "BUTTON—a musical theater term for the bump at the end of a song that lets you know it's okay to applaud. Usually a light cue, linked to an instrumental bump." *Twitter*, January 10, 2018. https://twitter.com/lin_manuel/status/951215051633037312?lang=en.

Newlove, Jean. *Laban for Actors and Dancers*. New York: Routledge, 2001.

Noble, Adam. "Sex and Violence: Practical Approaches for Dealing with Extreme Stage Physicality." *The Fight Master*, Spring 2011, vol. 33, no. 1, 14–18.

Novak, Elaine A. and Deborah Novak. *Staging Musical Theatre: A Complete Guide for Directors, Choreographers, and Producers*. Cincinnati, OH: Betterway Books, 1996.

O'Brien, Nick. *Stanislavski in Practice: Exercises for Students*. New York: Routledge, 2011.

Østern, Tone Pernille. "Developing Inclusive Dance Pedagogy: Dialogue, Activism and Aesthetic Transformative Learning." In *Dance, Access and Inclusion: Perspectives on Dance, Young People and Change*, edited by Stephanie Burridge and Charlotte Svendler Nielsen, 12–19. New York: Routledge, 2018.

Pace, Chelsea and Laura Rikard. *Staging Sex: Best Practices, Tools, and Techniques for Theatrical Intimacy*. New York: Routledge, 2020.

Paulson, Michael. "Lights, Gestures, Action! How to Stage a Broadway Musical with Deaf Actors." *The New York Times*. October 2, 2015. https://www.nytimes.com/2015/10/04/theater/lights-gestures-action-how-to-stage-a-broadway-musical-with-deaf-actors.html.

Percy, Marie C. "The Pillars." *The IDC Resource Guide*. 1st ed. Intimacy Directors and Coordinators, July 2020. https://static1.squarespace.com/static/5e1c12f49383f8245b857d01/t/5f2470bdc8a09c2a6c405251/1596223729318/IDC+Resource+Guide.pdf.

"Repeats and Codas." Step by Step Music. 2018. https://stepbystepmusic.com/repeats_and_codas.html.

Rosenberg, Lynne Marie. "How (Not) to Write a Casting Breakdown." *HowlRound*. August 24, 2015. https://howlround.com/how-not-write-casting-breakdown.

Sandwell, Ian. "Hamilton's Most Significant Character is Someone You Won't Have Noticed." *Digital Spy*. March 7, 2020. http://www.digitalspy.com/movies/a33022157/hamilton-disney-plus-the-bullet-explained/.

Saucier, Adelaide. "Dance and Copyright: Legal 'Steps' for Performers." Center for Art Law. October 30, 2018. https://itsartlaw.org/2018/10/30/dance-and-copyright-legal-steps-for-performers/.

Shawn, Ted. *Every Little Movement: A Book About François Delsarte.* 2nd ed. New York: Dance Horizons, 1963.

Simas, Rick Anthony. *From John Durang to George Balanchine: The Development of Dance in the American Musical Theatre 1796–1936.* Berkeley, CA: The University of California Press, 1992.

Sina, Tonia. "Safe Sex: A Look at the Intimacy Choreographer." *The Fight Master,* Spring 2014, vol. 36, no. 1, 12–15.

Smith-Autard, Jacqueline M. *Dance Composition.* 6th ed. London: Methuen Drama, 2010.

Soloski, Alexis. "The Show Must Go On, And On, And On." *The New York Times*. December 18, 2019. https://www.nytimes.com/2019/12/18/theater/musical-finales-curtain-calls.html.

Sondheim, Stephen. *Finishing the Hat: Collected Lyrics (1954–1981) with Attendant Comments, Principles, Heresies, Grudges, Whines and Anecdotes.* New York: Alfred A. Knopf, 2010.

Stage Directors and Choreographers Foundation (SDCF). "One on One with Steven Hoggett." *Masters of the Stage.* Podcast audio, 1:19:22. April 4, 2014a. https://sdcfmastersofthestage.libsyn.com/website/one-on-one-with-steven-hoggett.

Stage Directors and Choreographers Foundation (SDCF). "Staging Revivals: Marcia Milgrom Dodge and Chet Walker." *Masters of the Stage.* Podcast audio, 1:8:42. April 4, 2014b. https://sdcfmastersofthestage.libsyn.com/website/staging-revivals-marcia-milgrom-dodge-and-chet-walker.

Stage Directors and Choreographers Society (SDCF). Accessed April 7, 2020. https://sdcweb.org/.

Stearns, Marshall and Jean Stearns. *Jazz Dance: The Story of American Vernacular Dance.* Boston, MA: Da Capo Press, 1994.

Stempel, Larry. *Showtime: A History of the Broadway Musical Theater.* New York: W.W. Norton, 2010.

Sunderland, Margot and Ken Pickering. *Choreographing the Stage Musical.* New York: Theatre Arts/Routledge, 1989.

Tharp, Twyla. *The Creative Habit: Learn It and Use It for Life.* New York: Simon & Schuster Paperbacks, 2003.

Thelen, Lawrence. *The Show Makers: Great Directors of the American Musical Theatre.* New York: Routledge, 2000.

U.S. Copyright Office (USCO). "Circular 52: Copyright Registration of Choreography and Pantomime." Accessed December 14, 2020. https://www.copyright.gov/circs/circ52.pdf.

Whatley, Sarah and Kate Marsh. "Making No Difference: Inclusive Dance Pedagogy." In *Dance, Access and Inclusion: Perspectives on Dance, Young People and Change*, edited by Stephanie Burridge and Charlotte Svendler Nielsen, 3–11. New York: Routledge, 2018.

Whitfield, Sarah (Ed.). *Reframing the Musical: Race, Culture and Identity*. London: Red Globe Press, 2019.

Wilson, Lindsey. "ASK PLAYBILL.COM: Dance Captains." *Playbill*. July 24, 2008. https://www.playbill.com/article/ask-playbillcom-dance-captains-com-151911.

Wolf, Stacy. *Changed for Good: A Feminist History of the Broadway Musical.* New York: Oxford University Press, 2011.

Wong, Khadifa, dir. *Uprooted: The Journey of Jazz Dance.* LDR Creative. July 19, 2020. https://uprootedfilm.com/.

"Working in the Theatre: Sign Language Theatre." January 20, 2016. American Theatre Wing. *YouTube*, 0:30:55. https://www.youtube.com/watch?v=IlX4Zt4sPtE.

Index

canon
    musical theatre canon 10, 177
    physical canon 70, 79–80, 84, 89–90, 94
    of work 4, 22
Cardinal, Vincent 170
cast recording 45, 48, 127, 137
cheat out 55, 60, 113
Chekhov, Michael 100
choreographic team *see* assistant
circle
    formation 71, 82–83, 111, 113
    moving circle 17, 86–88, 115–117
cleaning rehearsal 124–125, 147, 149,
        151–153, 156
cliché 57, 62, 92, 96, 127
climax or climactic 25–26, 51, 65, 67, 69, 73,
        102
clump 70, 76, 79, 82, 86, 88
color
    complexity and definition 59, 63, 93–94, 98,
        131
    in design 75, 83, 140–142, 144, 154
    in images 12, 15, 23, 33, 89, 95
combination (dance) 128–132
comedy
    comedy, comedic, or comical 6, 27, 30,
        53–54, 104
    comedy song 26–27
    musical comedy 5, 63
    physical comedy 64, 110, 118, 136
Commedia dell'Arte 61, 64
composer *see* writer
composition
    artwork and music 15, 95, 137, 145
    compositional qualities 68, 83, 108
    compositional variety and emphasis 74–75,
        77, 113, 116
    compositions in arena configuration
        110–112, 117–118
    stage composition 52, 61, 64, 78, 85, 88
concept musical 5, 26
conductor 36, 40–41, 44, 136, 39
conflict 69, 73, 82, 84, 95, 100
consent 56, 129, 164–165
contact (physical) 19, 56–57, 68, 101, 153,
        164–166
contagion 70, 79, 88, 119
contrast
    juxtaposition 58, 64, 91
    physical 59, 61, 68, 75–76, 83, 102
consultant 7, 11, 15, 126, 167, 169
copyright 22, 180
costume *see* design or designer

counting 46, 124, 130, 137, 150, 158
Cousin, Tomé 7
creator *see* writer
cross
    the body 73, 105, 130, 167
    formation and movement pattern 71, 82,
        86, 88, 90, 115
    individual cross 59–61, 71, 115, 174
    notation 66
cue
    audience cue 31, 43
    music cue 36, 43–44, 53–54, 73, 157
    physical cue 11, 73, 79, 89, 155, 167, 171
    technical cue 73, 133, 144, 146, 154, 156
Cunningham, Merce 79
curtain call or bow 44, 121, 163, 169–171
curve
    architectural curve 16, 113, 155
    curved formation and pathway 60, 66,
        82–84, 86, 115
    curved physical shape 59, 92, 101
cut
    audition cut 128–129, 131–132
    edit 40, 45–48, 94, 126, 137, 153, 155

Dabbon, David 138
dance arranger 35, 44–45, 127, 136–138
dance break
    lack of a major dance break 6, 66
    music in a dance break 35, 46, 48, 127,
        134, 137–138
    staging a dance break 40, 136, 145, 151
    structuring a dance break 67, 69, 103
dance captain 123–125, 151, 154, 171, 176
dance journaling 18, 94, 96–97, 106
Deaf West Theatre 9–11
Delsarte, François 61, 99
depth
    crossing 60, 86
    meaning 94, 104, 151, 159
    stage picture 68, 80–81, 83, 85, 154
    stage space 107, 144, 150
design
    costume design 134–135, 142–145, 156, 172
        interaction with 7, 28, 104, 143, 152
        costume pieces 9, 12, 104, 142, 144,
        146, 150
        costume change 28, 32, 118, 143–144,
        156, 163, 171–173
        for focus or highlight 75, 88, 116
    elements 88, 133–135, 138–139, 147, 171
        advancement and spectacle 7, 67
        focus and emphasis 52, 55

expressive movement 59, 61–63, 68, 95, 98, 111

Fagan, Garth 7
failure 8, 92, 94, 99, 123, 151, 176
farce 63
figurative choreography 27–30, 32
figure 8 71, 86
flow
    dynamic 32, 159
    fabric flow 16, 104, 143
    of individual movement 58, 82, 92, 100, 103, 155, 171
    Laban theory of flow 97, 99
    of music 44, 48, 61
    of a sequence, number or show 65, 69, 73, 86, 163, 170, 173
focus
    audience
        different stage configurations 31, 107, 111, 113, 116–119
        divert, redirect, or change focus 27, 73, 79, 118–119, 164
        ensemble directing focus 31, 68, 75, 116, 169
        highlighting or framing 76–77, 82, 102
        manipulate audience focus 4, 75–76, 89, 102, 104, 164, 173
        movement pulling focus 56, 58, 60, 75–76, 132
        stage composition creating focus 53–55, 72, 75–76, 80–82, 113
        technical elements creating focus 75–76, 104, 116, 144
    performer
        body direction impacting focus 75–76
        changes in focus 58, 63–65, 101, 117, 160
        focal point 72, 74, 160, 101, 152, 155, 169
        passing focus 75, 80, 86, 119, 170
force (physical) 9, 16, 74, 100, 102, 152, 171
formation
    circle see circle
    line see line
    semicircle 75–76, 82, 88
    stage formation 72, 78–84, 89, 93, 111–115, 118–119
        building formations 68, 126, 131, 149
        framing formations 75–76, 116
        ideas for formations 35, 127
        movement and transition 78–79, 85–90, 115, 119

notating formations 88–90, 105, 119, 125, 173
in relation to stage and set 140, 154–155
"V" formation 76, 81–82, 113, 115
wedge 79, 82, 88, 111, 113–114, 155
fourth wall 64, 88
Fosse, Bob 4, 22, 30, 101
framing or frame 75, 78, 82, 107, 132
freeze 71, 102, 119, 154

generalized 22, 30, 96, 129, 159, 167
gesture
    abstraction of gesture 63–64, 95–96
    behavioral gesture 16, 19, 33
    in dance 71, 73, 77, 100
    prompting gesture 11, 73, 170–171
    while singing 58–59, 61–63, 76, 117
gimmick 32, 171
Glover, Savion 4, 95
groove
    in body 131, 160
    inspiration for choreography 46, 69, 138, 151
    in music 36, 38, 42, 101, 138
ground plan 88–89, 133, 140

heightened
    energy 18, 51, 57, 67
    movement 28, 58–59, 63, 85, 91, 95–96
    realism 25, 61, 64, 96, 153
Herman, Jerry 27
Hoggett, Steven 6
house
    audience section 52, 60, 107, 118, 124, 154–155, 175
    performers in the house 74, 83–84, 154, 171
    personnel and equipment 12, 133
Humphrey, Doris 92

"I Am" song 26
"I Want" song 26
imaginary center 94, 100, 106
improvisation
    in auditions 128–129, 132
    for choreographic ideas 18, 91, 96–97, 127
    exercises 11, 97, 157
    in performance 57, 71, 90, 126, 167–168
indicative movement 61–62, 94–95, 167
initiation
    creative initiation 17, 177
    music initiation 40

objective
   character analysis 19–20, 26, 51–52, 66, 68
   motivating movement 57, 60, 158–159, 165
   as movement inspiration 11, 58, 94, 97, 99,
       101, 106
obstacle
   character obstacle 11, 19, 55, 78, 99, 165
   dancers embodying obstacle 31, 96, 103
   obstacle exercises 11, 97
original
   choreographer 17, 20, 22, 97
   choreography 21–22, 105
   intention 3, 13, 20, 44, 124, 172
   new 7, 20, 22, 94–95, 97, 180
   originality 3, 14
   originally developed and produced 4, 6
   production 5, 20–22, 30, 44–45, 141, 164
   source or inspiration 20–21, 59, 95
orchestra
   playing 44, 47, 73–74, 102, 145, 155–156
   rehearsals, performance, and space 36, 45,
       137, 139, 154–156, 171
orchestra rehearsal 45, 137
orchestrations
   movement to match orchestration 61, 102
   orchestral passages 13, 35, 45–46, 127,
       137, 156, 173
operetta 26, 137
opposition 78, 100, 111
overture 43, 47

Pace, Chelsea 56, 165
Parker, Janice 9
partner
   dancing 144, 165, 167, 179
   scene partner 35, 52, 54–57, 101, 119,
       159, 164–166
   space between partners 55–56, 72, 117
partnering 70, 90, 129, 132
   teaching or creating partnering 124, 126,
       165, 167, 172
pastiche 5, 51, 63
pattern see movement pattern
peel-off 71, 85
physical comedy see comedy
physical glottal 102
physicality 11, 19, 56–57, 63–64
physical representation 94, 96, 106
Pickering, Ken 72, 80, 96, 102, 104, 155, 158
pinwheel 86
plane 55, 60, 97, 99, 111
pose 61, 71, 73–74, 83, 100, 102, 171–172
pragmatic choreography 27, 32

precision
   dance 6, 115
   precise formation 72, 93
   synchronization and specificity 101,
       124–125, 151, 153, 165, 171
pre-production
   adapting after pre-production 66, 126, 150
   assistants in pre-production 123–124, 126,
       175
   documentation in pre-production 89, 127,
       173
   music and design in pre-production 138,
       140–141
   process 18, 21, 91, 121, 125–127
presentational 81, 86, 93, 118, 151, 153
preview 27, 31, 73, 125–126, 156–157
producer 7–8, 14, 21, 47, 164–165,
       176–179
   as collaborators 4, 23, 128, 132–133
properties or prop
   interaction with props 11–12, 28, 32–33,
       71, 86, 104, 152
   prop comedy 64
   prop design 133, 135, 138, 141–142, 156
   prop handoff or masking 163, 169, 173
   rehearsal prop 141–142, 146, 150
proscenium
   crosses in proscenium 60, 115
   formations in proscenium 17, 52, 78–80,
       82, 113, 154
   movement patterns in proscenium 85, 88,
       115–116, 132
   proscenium versus arena 107–111, 113,
       115–119
public domain 22, 137
pulse 36–38
puppetry 7, 169
put-in rehearsal 124, 172

quick change 28, 88, 143–144, 156, 164, 172

raked 60, 83, 107, 116, 139
Razaf, Andy 65
realism or realistic 25, 51, 57, 63–64, 93
realistic gesture 61, 63
reel 23, 63, 134, 179–180
Reid, T. Oliver 15
relationship
   to audience 57, 64, 82, 110
   character relationship
       character analysis 19, 165
       as dance inspiration 32, 58, 79, 92, 167,
           172

variety (compositional) 74, 77–78, 107, 113, 116

vaudeville 5–6, 63–64, 118, 164

"V" formation *see* formation

vocabulary *see* movement vocabulary

vomitorium or vom 108, 110–113, 115–119, 170

wandelprobe 45, 155–156

wave 70, 85–86, 88, 116

website 23, 176, 179–180

wedge *see* formation

weight
    change of weight 59, 103, 129, 132, 152
    compositional weight 15, 75, 78
    distribution 9, 11, 166
    dramatic emphasis 55, 59, 115
    mass 19, 141
    music emphasis 40
    resistance 98

whirlpool 32, 86

wing 124, 139, 150, 154–155, 164, 170, 174

workshop 11, 27, 175–176, 178

Wolf, Stacy 26, 30, 64

writer
    composer 6, 26–27, 40, 45, 127, 136–137
    examples
        composer 26, 41–42, 44, 63, 65, 137
        composer/lyricist 25, 27, 52, 73, 138
        lyricist 26–27, 65, 137
    lyricist 25, 136
    writing team 10, 16, 22, 133, 178
        background and style 20, 63
        collaboration 3–4, 67, 176
        intention 13, 20–21, 33, 138
        script 3, 25, 27, 30, 51, 136, 138

Ziegfeld circle 86–87

zone 19, 94, 99–100, 106